AFTER VIOLENCE

Andrea Bieler / Christian Bingel
Hans-Martin Gutmann (Eds.)

AFTER VIOLENCE

RELIGION, TRAUMA AND RECONCILIATION

EVANGELISCHE VERLAGSANSTALT
Leipzig

Die Deutsche Bibliothek verzeichnet diese Publikation in der
Deutschen Nationalbibliographie; detaillierte bibliographische
Daten sind im Internet über ‹http://dnb.ddb.de› abrufbar.

© 2011 by Evangelische Verlagsanstalt GmbH · Leipzig
Printed in Germany · H 7471

Das Buch wurde auf alterungsbeständigem Papier gedruckt.

Cover: Zacharias Bähring, Leipzig → google
Satz: Steffi Glauche, Leipzig
Druck und Binden: Hubert & Co., Göttingen

ISBN 978-3-374-02919-8
www.eva-leipzig.de

Acknowledgments

This volume gathers the revised papers given at a conference at the Aby Warburg Haus at Hamburg University in December, 2010. A group of mainly Christian scholars and activists from different disciplines, countries, and viewpoints came together to discuss passionately questions of violence, trauma, and religion.

First of all we give thanks to our colleagues from different parts of the world who accepted our invitation to join in a dialogue and who expanded, challenged, and deepened the ways we think about this most important topic of religious discourse and practice: the transformation of violence in the midst of trauma. This exchange has been most meaningful to us.

We would like to express our gratitude to students and colleagues who helped prepare the conference and who worked diligently throughout the actual event to provide hospitality, food, technical support, and centering moments of prayer and singing. Marianne Pieper invited us graciously into the Aby Warburg Haus. We thank Sabine Sharma, assistant at the Institute of Practical Theology. We were so lucky to have the reliable and kind support of the following student workers: Susanne Kropf, Swantje Luthe, Franziska Seichter, and Simon Eckhardt. We thank Laura Koch and Anne Wehrmann, who listened closely to the presentations and who gave a response at the end of the conference.

We appreciate Professor Wolfgang Grünberg, who gave us a tour of the Jewish quarter in Hamburg, the Grindelviertel, as well as Pastor Groehn, who extended his hospitality to us.

We thank the University of Hamburg, who sponsored financially the conference as well as the publication of this volume.

We thank Dr. Brigitte Sion for gifting us with the captivating photograph for the cover of this book. It shows the memorial »The Deserted Room« (Der verlassene Raum), which can be visited in Berlin at the Koppenplatz.

Andrea Bieler is grateful to Pacific School of Religion for granting a sabbatical that made it possible for her to participate in this transatlantic project and for sponsoring a research assistant. We are most indebted to Sheri Prud'homme, doctoral student at the Graduate Theological Union in Berkeley, who has been a superb companion on the journey as a careful reader of texts and as a native speaker. Without her help, we would have been lost. Beth

Ritter-Conn supported us graciously with the final proofreading of the manuscript.

We thank Dr. Annette Weidhas, chief editor at the Evangelische Verlagsanstalt in Leipzig (Germany), as well as Anne Grabmann for their professional and kind cooperation as we were working towards the publication of the papers.

Berkeley and Hamburg, August 2011

Andrea Bieler,
Christian Bingel,
and Hans-Martin Gutmann

Contents

INTRODUCTION

Andrea Bieler, Christian Bingel, Hans-Martin Gutmann

After Violence: The title of this volume provokes controversy.

There have been significant moments in history which have marked the official end of atrocities such as the Shoah, the end of the genocide in Rwanda, or the end of systemic, state-sponsored racism, represented in Apartheid in South Africa. These particular moments in history mark significant turning points. And yet, many historians, sociologists, psychoanalysts, and theologians who study the effects of collective trauma in the aftermath of atrocities doubt that there has ever been a clear-cut »after violence situation« in the sense that the impact of the past has been overcome. Rather, the violence unleashed in various forms of warfare and systemic injustice does not simply disappear once a war or a dictatorship is officially ended. The effects of violence continue to live on powerfully in both psychic processes and in communal and personal relationships. Living in the aftermath of violence thus often means the emergence of further or new forms of violence as collective trauma unfolds.

This volume explores religious, cultural, and political resources geared towards addressing the complex aftermath situations of collective atrocities. Major practices are critically analyzed, such as public witnessing and truth telling, as well as ritual and aesthetic practices of remembrance. The authors consider religious practices, theological reflections, and cultural resources which hold the potential to address the aftermath of violence in constructive ways. Biblical narratives, symbols, and rituals that address the experience of trauma come into play. Grounded in their particular contexts, the authors investigate and analyze liturgical as well as theological traditions that grapple with the task of reconciliation, political and cultural initiatives that seek to work through conflicts, and the ambivalences of memorials dedicated to the victims of collective atrocities. The essays are mindful of the ambiguous roles that churches have played in many of these conflicts, either by partially promoting acts of violence or by tolerating them. Many reflections take into account that theological reflections and religious practices have failed to address the issues at hand in constructive and life-giving ways.

The authors ask what it means to open up spaces of remembrance and mourning which interrupt the mimetic reproduction of violence. If the realities of trauma are taken into account, practices of remembrance and reconciliation appear as a particular challenge. Yet, from a Christian perspective, theological insights on the transformation of violence and the necessity of remembrance are at the heart of the Gospel. Jewish thinkers emphasize the role of memory on the path towards redemption. For Buddhist practice, it is pivotal to perform particular rites for the dead so that their souls may be released. Christian theologians ponder what it means to reflect on divine reconciliation and the restitution of human relationships in the light of collective atrocities.

The inquiries in this field have to be grounded in theoretical and theological reflections as well as in attentiveness with regard to concrete contexts and lived experience. Consequently, an array of situations in the aftermath of violence are explored, including post-Apartheid South Africa, Rwanda after the Genocide, postcolonial New Guinea, Ireland and Northern Ireland since the ›Good Friday Agreement‹, Argentina after militarist rule, Western Africa after civil wars, and Germany after the Shoah.

We have invited colleagues from various disciplines to address the questions raised. They represent fields such as performance studies, francophone literature and literary theory, history, systematic theology, liturgical studies, practical theology, religious studies, ecumenical theology, and missiology. The writers come from a wide range of Christian traditions, including Roman Catholic, Mennonite, Lutheran, and Reformed. Brigitte Sion is a Jewish scholar who also reflects on a Buddhist context. Theodor Ahrens draws on indigenous practices in Papua New Guinea.

Tinyiko Sam Maluleke frames the conversation by posing the fundamental question: Is it ever possible to declare a state of »after« violence? The author grew up in times of severe repression and comprehensive structural violence in South Africa under the Apartheid regime. From this perspective, he critically assesses the notion of »after violence«. Even after the end of Apartheid, Maluleke deems a perspective »after violence« to be both romanticizing and cynical in light of the massive physical, sexual, and psychological violence permeating South African society today. In his view, »after violence« is just the beginning of a new »pre-violence«. Maluleke disputes the analytical value of a linear time-structure which differentiates between a *before, during,* and *after* with respect to violence. Only in eschatological perspective is it viable to maintain the concept of »after violence«. From this perspective, Maluleke retraces the steps of social change after the peaceful revolution of 1994. He evaluates the ambiguities and shortcomings in the work of truth commissions, their importance to the public appearance of today's South Africa notwithstanding.

The second part of the book maps the complicated terrain of theologies and practices of remembrance that seek to address the aftermath of collective atrocities.

Andrea Bieler reflects on remembering violence as a practice by taking into account psychoanalytical and theological insights from trauma studies. If processes of forgetting are a means of survival, what does it mean to remember atrocities at all? Bieler explores what it takes to return to wounds that are actually inaccessible in an immediate sense and what it means to shape practices of remembrance that are respectful of the dead and life-giving to the survivors, and that make visible the misdeeds of the perpetrators and of those who lived lives in between. In light of current research on collective trauma, Bieler revisits Christian traditions, such as the Eucharist, the time-space of Holy Saturday, and the invocation of the Holy Spirit as Paraclete. She claims that these traditions imply the potential to hold experiences of trauma as a space between death and life.

Brigitte Sion invites the reader to explore three memorial sites erected to the victims of state-sponsored violence: the Memorial to the Murdered Jews of Europe in Berlin, the Monument to the Victims of State Terrorism within the Park of Memory in Buenos Aires, and the Choeung Ek killing fields in Phnom-Penh. These three sites, located in Germany, Argentina, and Cambodia, reflect very divergent historical and political circumstances as well as cultural and religious environments. Yet, they share in common the absence or the destruction of the bodies of the people who have been murdered and who could not be buried. Sion explores the social drama that unfolds at these sites, seeking to honor and remember the dead whose absent or destroyed bodies hint at unimaginable collective atrocities. As a scholar who focuses on performance practices, Sion is especially interested in the interaction of visitors with these sites.

Jean-Pierre Karegeye, who is the co-founder of the Genocide Research Center in Kigali (Rwanda), concentrates his research on the question of how this enormous outburst of massive collective violence could occur in a country that consists mainly of a Christian population. In his essay, he focuses on a series of letters that were issued by Roman Catholic bishops during the war. In a close intertextual reading, Karegeye demonstrates the influence of the political rhetoric, especially of the former President Habyarimana, that prepared the stage for genocide. In disturbing ways, this political rhetoric undergirded the messages of the bishops as they were speaking of unity, peace, and reconciliation. This intricate convolution of political and religious speech turned into an uncanny support of governmental perspectives by the church. In light of this intertextual analysis, Karegeye emphasizes that it is pivotal for the future of African theologies to address issues of complacency of the church in thorough ways. This necessary critique challenges basic assumptions about ecclesiology and about reconciliation. It implies a kind of memory work that calls for a radical paradigm shift in doing theology in countries such as Rwanda as the genocide is put at the center of contextualizing theology.

Liberia continues to be traumatized by the fourteen-year-long war that ended in 2003; everyone feels victimized in some way. Sabine Förster uses portraits to depict different groups affected by the war. She writes of the men recruited by warlords and the use of ›jungle names‹ to separate their sense of themselves from the unspeakable atrocities they committed in the war. She writes of the female fighters, often left destitute and isolated after the war, with no way to reintegrate into their communities, either because their breach of the taboo against women doing battle was too great for others to accept or because the defined female roles in their communities were solely the traditional ones they had escaped by joining the fighters. She writes of women forced to flee their villages and of the Women in White, who protested for peace and eventually insisted the men reach a peace agreement in 2003.

Alongside the shocking narratives of the trauma and devastation of the war and its aftermath, Förster presents evidence of healing: cathartic worship services where people share their stories, women's groups helping each other overcome feelings of isolation and shame, church-sponsored training programs, and men serving as change agents in their communities. She underscores the need for improvement in justice and equality among men and between men and women in order for true change to occur in the country. She also suggests the importance of a deepening theological reflection on the image of God in Liberia and its effect on men and women. She insists churches, as community-based organizations, can have a vital role in creating spaces of safety.

In Australia, the tradition of celebrating Anzac Day has changed since the last soldiers of First World War died and took their personal histories with them, shifting the commemoration from an occasion to mourn violence and war to a triumphal and celebratory one. In a thoughtful discourse on the ethical dimensions of history and the construction of narrative memories and national identity, Phillip Tolliday explores the development of Anzac Day from its earliest years until the present in the context of social forces, such as the rise of nationalism and the glorification of militarization. He illuminates how the re-construction of Anzac Day not only is untrue to history but also dangerously elides competing interpretations of Australia's Aboriginal history and the white supremacy of the early Australian leaders. He suggests that rather than elevating the Anzacs to a god-like status, remembering that they fought for male, white, imperial freedoms could shed light on contemporary immigration issues as well as lead the nation to a critical consciousness of such commemorative practices.

Hans-Martin Gutmann is a practical theologian of Lutheran persuasion who is deeply invested in the question of how the mimetic power of reciprocity can work to evoke the gift of grace instead of reciprocal violence. He is especially interested in exploring practices that embody the communication of the Gospel in which grace is poured out as abundant life offered to all by God. Such practices are geared to inspire a religiously grounded sense of mutual commitment. He engages pastoral counseling as a practice in which traumatization might be addressed. Drawing on insights of Luise Reddermann, a specialist in trauma therapy, he sketches out a process in which the imaginative engagement with biblical narratives along with body energy work might serve as transformative impulses. This process might aim at a protected re-framing of the self *in* the violent situation without being drawn back into the vulnerable place of trauma.

Werner Kahl's essay concludes the section on trauma and memory as he shares insights from his experiences with worship services and biblical interpretations in West African Migrant Churches in Germany. Migrants coming from West Africa to Germany have oftentimes left situations of violence in their home countries with the hope of finding a better life in Europe. Most often, they were escaping from civil war, poverty, and a sense of spiritual violence in which poverty is understood as a curse. Coming to Germany, the majority is confronted with new forms of racism and various forms of exclusion. Kahl describes how in worship services the desire for spiritual killings emerges as the congregants are invited to pray to Jesus for saving them from spiritual missiles sent by family members from Ghana and by returning these missiles to the senders, potentially causing their death. Kahl explores the reasons for such a ritual practice by engaging sub-Saharan worldviews

concerning the impact of evil spirits on the community and biblical interpretations arising in that context. From there, he moves on to present some
insights on dealing with violence from his reading of New Testament texts, as
he seeks to engage a dialogue about the abovementioned practices.

The third part of the book explores the fragile path towards reconciliation
and healing in the aftermath of violence. At times, people are led astray and
return to old patterns of exclusivist views; at times, small steps towards the
mending of broken relationships are taken. In these ambiguous situations, the
question about the meaning of divine reconciliation emerges.

The 1998 Good Friday Agreement in Northern Ireland brokered a political peace for an ethno-nationalist conflict, but it did not address religion, an
arena of life that harbors the most pernicious old habits of division and ani-
mosity as well as the most hopeful opportunities for genuine reconciliation
in Northern Ireland. Presenting findings from her seven-year study of Protestant and Catholic churches in the Republic and Northern Ireland, Siobhán
Garrigan observes that while church communities often prayed for nations
and peoples in other parts of the world, any mention of Ireland or Northern
Ireland was strikingly absent in the prayers, rituals and community celebrations of the church year. Moreover, language in worship in both Catholic and
Protestant churches often subtly or strongly created *otherness* in mentioning
the *opposite* religion. Garrigan maintains that the adage taught school children in England and Ireland, »forgive and forget«, is inadequate until true forgiveness and reconciliation has occurred. She suggests a thoughtful interro-
gation and reframing of language used in worship could illuminate what has
been prematurely »forgotten«, name new realities and truths, and help bring
about forgiveness. She also calls upon the strength of the practice of honoring anniversaries in Irish culture as she proposes that honoring significant
anniversaries in recent Irish history needs to be added to the liturgical year.
Garrigan concludes that this kind of memory work needs to happen in
worship also, so that a culture of casual forgetting can be challenged.

Theodor Ahrens presents a case study from the Western Highlands in
Papua New Guinea, in which he focuses on a group of Melpa-speaking clans
who live under the conditions of a post-colonial state. Ahrens explores how
modified traditional ritualized forms of conflict management are in competition with the legal system of the nation state, and actually at times deterio-
rate the legal jurisdiction of the state. Simultaneously, these rituals carve out
a space of experimentation in which the Melpa Lutheran Church offers models for the restriction of violence by drawing on biblical resources as well as
traditional spiritual practices. Ahrens interprets interventions of Bishop

Sanangke Dole and his mediation teams as constructive examples of how potentially violent reciprocity between members of different clans can be constrained and transformed into a situation of non-violent coexistence.

Fernando Enns looks back upon the Decade to Overcome Violence, which had been proclaimed by the WCC in 2001 and which concluded in the international ecumenical peace convocation in Kingston, Jamaica, in May 2011. True to its name, its vision was to begin processes to actually overcome violence and to achieve peace here and now. Among the efforts made was the project »Peace to the City«, in which seven cities were chosen to form a laboratory of »best practice-initiatives« to respond to challenges of violence: Belfast (Northern Ireland), Boston (USA), Colombo (Sri Lanka), Durban (South Africa), Kingston (Jamaica), Rio de Janeiro (Brazil), und Suva (Fiji). For an array of reasons, each of these cities is exceptionally engaged in the vicious circles of violence and retaliation. Enns theologically interprets the very efforts to overcome violence as illustrated by the »Peace to the City« initiative, stating that its efforts are no mere ethical consequence of the reconciliation of God with its creation. Rather, they are its very manifestation. The gift of reconciliation is realized wherever churches take part in the sanctification of life, in building positive relationships among people, and in confronting violence, enmity, and injustice.

Ulrike Link-Wieczorek revisits Anselm of Canterbury's theory of satisfaction as she teases out the connection between divine reconciliation and human restitution in light of experiences of massive structural violence. She emphasizes that, in this context, the meaning of the coming of Christ as bringing about once-and-for-all salvation and forgiveness of sins for all humankind needs to be spelled out anew. The Christ event has at its center the gift of reconciliation. What this means, however, needs to be an open question. Link-Wieczorek turns to Anselm's contested satisfaction theory. This is a surprising move since Anselm's theory has been interpreted as implying a rather rigid and retributive sense of divine righteousness which might even promote the idea that the killing of the Son was necessary for the damaged honor of the Father to be restored. Link-Wieczorek argues against this interpretation by situating Anselm's theory within a theology of creation which seeks to reflect the damages done to creation and creatures, touching upon God's own vulnerability.

The volume concludes with a brief response by Anne Wehrmann and Laura Koch, who served as student observers at the conference.

I
AFTER VIOLENCE:
FRAMING THE PERSPECTIVE

After Violence, (No) More Violence? A South African Perspective

Tinyiko Sam Maluleke

A Violent Century

The year of my birth was also the year in which the ANC (African National Congress), currently the ruling political party in South Africa, formed its armed wing, the *Umkhonto we Sizwe*.[1] This was the year (1961) in which the ANC finally decided to add armed struggle to its multifaceted struggle tactics and strategies attempted ever since the ANC was formed in 1912. The ANC was ostensibly forced onto the path of an armed struggle by the increasingly violent methods used by the Apartheid government to suppress peaceful demonstrations. The massacre of demonstrators protesting against the oppressive pass-laws in the township of Sharpeville east of Johannesburg in 1960, known ever since as the ›Sharpeville Massacre‹,[2] was the proverbial last straw. Indeed, the years 1950–1960, following the 1948 whites-only elections in which the Afrikaners had emerged victorious, ushering in a legalized form of Apartheid, had seen more violent and more ruthless forms of repression of black resistance. My teen years, 1960s to late 70s, were some of the most repressive years in the history of the country. During this period, political leaders like Nelson Mandela were thrown into jail. The banning of persons and organizations became the order of the day. The state spread a veritable blanket of terror across the land as many political activists were killed. Most resistance was driven underground. Repressed black anger was, in some instances, turning inwards and consuming the black community itself, as the condemned, despairing and self-hating black community seemed to surren-

---

[1] Zulu words meaning »Spear of the Nation«.

[2] See http://africanhistory.about.com/od/apartheid/a/SharpevilleMassacrePt1.htm (accessed March 21, 2011).

der to nihilism. Yet, out of the artificially created desert of political activism of the 60s and the 70s emerged the Black Consciousness Movement.[3]

In 1976, I joined thousands of other high school students in Soweto to protest, initially against the introduction of the Afrikaans language as a medium of instruction. Ultimately, the Soweto student uprising was a protest against the inhumane and repressive system of Apartheid. Many of my fellow students were killed or exiled. These protests became the crucial turning point, triggering a renewed wave of resistance against the Apartheid system. In the fifteen-year period between 1976 and 1991, the idea of a democratic South Africa became more and more attainable, thanks to the sacrifices of those who were prepared to resist the terror and violent tactics of the Apartheid state. In 1994, the historic elections that propelled Nelson Mandela into the presidency of the country were held. But the cost – in human lives – of the three hundred years of struggle against colonial conquest and Apartheid is neither calculable nor fathomable. The South African story of violence was neither unique nor isolated.

I was born into a violent century, the 20th century. In this one century, two horrific world wars were fought,[4] dozens of liberation wars were waged, and several genocides committed.[5] Indeed, one of the »gifts« of this century to humanity is the very notion of genocide. Genocide had occurred before this century, but such was the scale and frequency of wholesale attempts to exterminate groups or nations in the 20th century that Raphael Lemkin, a Polish Jewish jurist who fled to Sweden after the Nazi occupation of Poland in 1939, coined the term ›genocide‹.[6] He did so at the height of the Holocaust in 1944.[7] My own personal biography, stretching back three generations of my family, is deeply marked by the violence and conflicts of the 20th century. But mine is not a unique biography. The lives of many, if not all, of us born in the 20th

---

[3]   See http://science.jrank.org/pages/7530/Black-Consciousness.html (accessed March 21, 2011).

[4]   My own grandfather, Mnene Nwa-swihaleni Huhlwani Maluleke, was a South African black conscript in the First World War. He served in North Africa.

[5]   A comprehensive list would exceed the scope of this paper. Just let me remind you of the following: Namibia 1904–1907, Armenia 1915, Ukraine 1932, The Holocaust 1939–1945, Cambodia 1975, Guatemala 1982, Rwanda 1994, Bosnia 1995.

[6]   See David Olusoga and Casper W. Erichsen, *The Kaiser's Holocaust: Germany's Forgotten Genocide and the Colonial Roots of Nazism* (London: Faber and Faber, 2010).

[7]   See http://www.hawaii.edu/powerkills/GENOCIDE.ENCY.HTM (accessed March 21, 2011).

century have been touched and even shaped by its violent conflicts. This is to say who we (think we) are, what we (think we) have or do not have, the countries we (think we) belong to, and what we hope for has been influenced by our experiences in the 20th century.

THE AFRICAN STORY OF VIOLENCE

For Africa, the 20th century was announced by wars of genocidal proportions. From the Great Lakes region, a brutal reign of terror was inflicted upon the inhabitants of the Congo Free State by King Leopold II of Belgium between 1885 and 1908, which led to the loss of millions of lives.[8] The lives were deemed so unimportant that records of the dead were either not kept or deliberately destroyed. In the South, there was the Namibian Herero and Namaqua genocide of 1904 until 1907, now generally regarded as the 20th century's first unequivocal genocide. Once again, the records of the numbers of the exterminated were handled callously and mischievously, so that they remain contested to date. For independence to be gained in the majority of African countries, wars of liberation had to be fought. The shift to ›armed struggle‹ often came after many years during which peaceful protests were needlessly crushed violently. This was certainly the case in South Africa.

As if this was not enough, in many African countries, there have been violent conflicts after independence and liberation – post-independence conflicts in which many former colonial powers are deeply interested and deeply implicated. For sixteen years after independence, Mozambique was mired in a war as costly, if not more costly, in terms of loss of human lives as the war of independence. The same happened in Angola. Some of the notable post-liberation wars include Uganda, the Democratic Republic of Congo, Liberia, and Ivory Coast, to mention but a few.[9] But we must not make the mistake of limiting the violence of our century to the obvious full-scale and »celebrated« wars. These were themselves violent explosions in situations where politically sanctioned and politically induced violence had been reigning for a long time. The Rwandan Genocide was one horrific illustration of this reality.[10]

---

[8]   See Adam Hochschild, *King Leopold's Ghost* (New York: Pan Macmillan, 1998).
[9]   See Martin Meredith, *The State of Africa: A History of Fifty Years of Independence* (London: Simon and Schuster, 2005).
[10]   See Mahmood Mamdani, *When Victims Become Killers: Colonialism, Nativism, and the Genocide in Rwanda* (Princeton: University Press, 2001).

AFTER VIOLENCE: AN ESCHATOLOGICAL METAPHOR?

The notion of ›after violence‹ is captivating. It suggests that violence exists in a continuum that has a ›before‹, a ›during‹, and an ›after‹. Behind this theorization of violence may lie an understanding of violence as something that is not inherent to human living and human social arrangements. This way of conceptualising violence does not subscribe to the idea that considers violence as an inherent aspect of human life since Adam and Eve were expelled from the Garden of Eden. Since it is not inherent, its advent, its genesis, and its insertion into human socio-economic arrangements can be tracked, traced and unpacked. Seen in this way, then, violence is not natural, not original, not preordained, and not necessarily permanent. Only from this standpoint can we meaningfully and seriously speak of an ›after violence‹ moment.

If, however, we subscribe to the notion that violence is intrinsic and inherent to human life and human coexistence with fellow humans and with other creatures, then we cannot seriously speak of ›after violence‹, except in a temporary or a metaphorical sense. If violence is a chronic human condition, it can only be managed, not prevented, mitigated, not eliminated, controlled, not healed. What we mean by ›after violence‹ is therefore important. Do we mean by ›after violence‹ a moment of management, mitigation, or control of violence, or do we truly believe that it is possible, in this world and in this life, to move from ›during violence‹ to ›after violence‹? Is the difference between the two stages essential or is it a difference of degrees of violence so that ›during violence‹ means ›most violence‹ and ›after violence‹ means ›less violence‹? The view we take on this matter may affect not only our philosophical and theological understandings of the place of violence in human life but also the tenor, tempo and trajectory of our prevention strategies. We can tackle the scourge of violence with minimalist strategies or we can be more robust, depending on our philosophical position. We can act as if violence can be overcome or we can act as if violence can only be assuaged. There is of course a more familiar and, dare I say, more popular option, namely one based on the maxim that says ›violence can only be overcome by more violence‹. In terms of this understanding, only a superior violent regime can end all violence.

We can therefore not afford to become too romantic about the concept of ›after violence‹. For millions of people in this world, ›after violence‹ is a faraway dream. Try speaking to the people of Darfur about ›after violence‹, and they will tell you to dream on. Attempt persuading Palestinians and Israelis of an ›after violence‹ phase, and they will ask which planet you come from.

Paint an ›after violence‹ scenario to women trapped in violent relationships, and they might accuse you of insensitivity and even complicity in their plight. Describe the meaning of ›after violence‹ to the children of Uganda trapped in the rogue militia named »Lord's Resistance Army«, and they will look at you with utter disbelief. The women who are rape victims in the Democratic Republic of Congo[11] might consider it a sick joke to speak of ›after violence‹ in a context where their bodies have become a battleground. ›After violence‹ is a condition that is difficult to imagine in a world in which several violent wars are ongoing and others are threatening to break out.

If the previous century has been violent, the young 21st century was ushered in by the 9/11 terror attack, the sounds of bombs in Iraq and Afghanistan, the increasing threats of war against Iran, threats of war between North and South Korea, as well continuing rattle of guns and bombs in the Middle East. Therefore, the cynical might argue that the very phraseology of ›after violence‹ is deceptive, if not delusional – an opium phrase coined by the secure in order to delude the victims of violence? The experience of many who live in violent contexts is that after violence comes even more violence. The violence may change its face. Its victims might change face. But violence continues. The divide between ›before‹, ›during‹, and ›after‹ violence must not be artificially exaggerated.

Much violence occurs before obvious violence. The ›before violence‹ moment is often deceptive. What looks like a violence-free situation may already be a situation riddled with violence – violent power relations, structural violence, economic violence, psychological violence, and the violence of terror. Just because there is no blood on the floor, it does not mean that there is no violence! Years before blood is drawn, many months before the soldiers march down the streets, before prisoners are rounded up and before the torturing begins, violence is already there.

Violence is at its deadliest when it does not speak in its own name; the time when it hides in apparently benign policies, in culture, structures, in traditions, in ›the rule of law‹ and in ›law and order‹. The so-called ›before violence‹ phase is actually the most dangerous phase, because that is when the seeds of violence are planted and watered. We make a mistake if we think bloodshed is the only and ultimate phase of violence. There is violence before the outbreak, violence during the outbreak and violence after the outbreak. Violence is often smart and devious enough never to break out into the open.

---

[11]   http://www.reformedelapnc.org/documents/Rape-in-DRC_Final-Report.pdf (accessed March 21, 2011).

It stays ›behind doors‹, deeply embedded in closely-knit families, passed on in secret codes, rituals, religions, and secret oaths, from generation to generation, for as long as possible.

All the while, violence ensures that it never speaks in its own name. It masquerades as justice, as fair play, as the free markets, as the voice of society, as culture, as history, as reason, as common sense, and even as wisdom. In South Africa, we spoke of separate development and not of a violent system that condemned blacks to poverty and elevated whites to wealth. While we wax lyrical about equality and human rights, women are being victimized, non-nationals are being treated like sub-humans, and the rich are getting richer while the poor are getting poorer. These developments have nothing to do with violence, right? Wrong! We have to recognize that violence has many names and many faces. Some of its names reveal, others conceal, and yet others do both at the same time.

If the ›before violence‹ phase can be violent without letting on, so can the ›after violence‹ phase. After violence, there is the violence of damaged memories, traumatized persons, brutalized psyches and terrorized souls. After violence there is the legacy of violence that lives on in the structures, social hierarchies and economic arrangements of society – ensuring the reproduction of the same discrepancies that brought us to open violence in the first place.

The physical destruction that is observable in a city or a village after the war bombs have rained on it is a fair estimation of the social and psychological damage caused to a person and a society after violence. Whereas the restoration of physical facilities and infrastructure may be swift and almost perfect, the rebuilding of persons and people takes longer – much longer. The rebuilding of persons and communities should be done even more meticulously and even more rigorously. Superficial and palliative measures to deal with the legacies of violence may not only fail to take us forward, but might send us back into the abyss of violence and alienation.

The continuum ›before violence‹, ›during violence‹, and ›after violence‹ is not a straight and perfect line. It's a crooked continuum of high tension with lots of zig-zag. The notions of ›before violence‹ and ›after violence‹ are metaphorical ideals to be embraced and to be doggedly worked for. They are not realities that exist automatically and innocently. Nor are they moments that will break into our world mysteriously. Ultimately, therefore, the notions of ›before violence‹, and ›after violence‹ can only be eschatological metaphors and futuristic dreams – metaphors worth embracing and dreams worth cherishing. We have to believe without any trace of romanticization, not only that violence can be overcome, but that it will be overcome. Indeed, such belief is the ultimate basis for our struggle against violence.

THE ECUMENICAL DREAM OF OVERCOMING VIOLENCE

It was in late 1999 when I joined a small group of theologians requested by the World Council of Churches (WCC) to help flesh out an idea that was mooted during and shortly after the Harare Assembly, namely to conceptualize an intensive programme of churches working for the promotion of peace. Our first meeting took place in Colombo, Sri Lanka. We were a diverse group. There were North Americans, Asians, Europeans, and at least one African in the group. At that time, conflict between the Tamil Tigers and the Sri Lankan authorities was raging in the North of that country. During one of the days, we travelled to the North to the town of Jaffna, where conflict was ongoing. The long trip from Colombo up North was itself quite stressful, and nothing had prepared us for our experiences as we travelled. The security check-points reminded me of Apartheid-era road blocks. When we arrived in Jaffna, we found the town deserted and desolate – residents having been advised then of an imminent Tamil Tigers attack. The residents were in refugee-like makeshift shelters outside the city, huddled together like animals; men, women and children carrying the possessions they could salvage. Terror was written in the faces of the people. The ultimate result of our Sri Lankan consultation was what was to become known as the ›Decade to Overcome Violence‹ (DOV), a ten-year programme launched in the year 2001. For seven years, I remained a member of the reference group advising the WCC on the Decade to Overcome Violence programme[12].

A lot has been achieved through the programme, especially in terms of the mobilization of churches to work together for the promotion of peace in some key regions of the world. This programme has mobilised the WCC and the churches to take unpopular and prophetic stances regarding some of the conflicts going on in the world today, notably the Iraq war and the Israeli-Palestinian conflict. The DOV was first and foremost a programme of the churches, for the churches, to mobilize the churches for the promotion of peace. Advocacy outside of the family of churches was important, but it was

---

[12]   See Tinyiko S. Maluleke, »The DOV and the Challenges Before Us: Ten Concluding Reflections.«, in *Come Holy Spirit, Heal and Reconcile,* ed. Jacques Matthey (Geneva: WCC, 2005), 195–201.

not central to the work of the DOV. Understandably, the DOV did not have a huge impact on such entities as NATO and the states that comprise it. It was during the duration of the decade in question when new wars broke out – notably following 9/11 – and the subsequent war on terrorism.

The problem with violence is that it remains a seductive and powerful notion almost always preferred by those with and those without power. Fascination with violence can be intoxicating. Imagine the ideological and theological shift that could have followed if the WCC programme had not been called the ›Decade to Overcome Violence‹ but rather the ›Decade to Wage/Promote Peace‹. The cameras might have moved from manifestations of violence to manifestations of peace-building and peacemaking. We can never know for sure. But it has been my view that perhaps the decade process was too focused on violence at a time when those working against violence all over the world were focusing on peace. Since World War II, the instruments used for dealing with post-violence situations have included trials (the Nurnberg trials being one of the most famous examples), commissions of inquiry, and, more recently, truth commissions. The opportunities for peace-building opened up by Truth Commissions are an avenue that could have been exploited more by the WCC Decade to Overcome Violence.

THE SOUTH AFRICAN TRUTH AND RECONCILIATION COMMISSION

BASIC MANDATE AND CHARACTERISTICS

The South African Truth and Reconciliation Commission (TRC) was a judicial commission. The very fact that it took an act of parliament to establish it illustrates its unusual authority and mandate. It was no ordinary presidential commission like the dozens of commissions that may be appointed by any sitting President as permitted by the South African constitution. The implication is that this commission was not merely answerable to the President of the country but to the *people* of the country through parliament – parliament being the body to which both the executive and the President are answerable.

Also unusual was the fact that the commission was not headed by a judge – a fact which has led some to criticize the commission. Instead, a person of great moral stature widely respected nationally and internationally was deliberately chosen to head the commission. From this alone, it was clear that this was a commission intended not merely to satisfy the legal requirements for amnesty and compensation, but a commission to propel the country into a higher moral plane, and hopefully lay the foundations for a society based on human rights and a culture of democracy. Indeed, the act of parliament which gave birth to the TRC was called the ›Promotion of National Unity Act‹, revealing the wider mandate of the commission.

But the journey from national disunity to national unity was strewn with thorns and human corpses. Between national disunity and national unity stood hundreds of years of brutal conquest and violent conflict. Between the two realities stood the years of brutal Apartheid repression, which saw thousands killed and millions impoverished. What was the commission to do with the messy history of repression? What were they to do with the rivers of blood, tears, and pain that had flowed for centuries? How can a small commission rehabilitate victims and perpetrators? What about the beneficiaries? What about the future? The commission could not skip these important issues in the quest for national unity. Without reference to these issues there would indeed be no national unity to speak of.

A clue to the basic blueprint and methodology of the commission is to be found in its basic mandate and competencies:

- It had investigative as well as judicial power: It could investigate allegations and grant amnesty to individuals in exchange for the truth.
- It had powers of subpoena as well as ›search and seizure‹.
- Its hearings were public and open.
- It entertained various types of hearings: individual, institutional and so-called special hearings.
- It created a witness protection programme.
- It was a rather large commission in terms of personnel and resources.

Naturally the mandate of the commission was proscribed and limited in the detail of the act. It had four major tasks[13]:

- Analysing and describing the ›causes, nature and extent‹ of gross violations of human rights that occurred between 1 March 1960 and 10 May 1994.
- Recommending to the President measures to prevent future violations of human rights.

---

[13]   See *Truth and Reconciliation Commission Report, vol. 1*. South African Truth and Reconciliation Commission together with the Department of Justice (Cape Town: Juta & Co, 1998), 57. In the following abbreviated as TRC Report.

- The restoration of the human and civil dignity of victims of gross violations through testimony and recommendations to the President concerning reparations.
- Granting amnesty to persons who made full disclosure of relevant facts relating to acts associated with a political objective.

ASSESSMENT

The question to ask is whether the TRC facilitated or ushered in an ›after violence‹ dispensation in the country. Without the end of Apartheid, without the compromise brokered by Nelson Mandela between the ANC and the Apartheid government, without the cessation of hostilities, however imperfect and precarious at the time, there could never have been a TRC. In this sense, the TRC is itself a product of and not the cause of an ›after violence‹ situation.

One of the unspoken tasks of the South African TRC was to suggest what South Africans should be and do ›after violence‹, in other words, to suggest what to do with that space in national life and in the national psyche that used to be occupied by violence. More importantly, the commission had the task of making recommendations that would ensure that after violence there would be no more violence.

The TRC was the recipient of as much praise as criticism. In the report itself, Desmond Tutu in his foreword, admits to several criticisms levelled against the commission. He notes that the commission has been accused, among others, of the following:

- Being a witch-hunt (mainly by those claiming the TRC was biased in favour of the ANC).
- Being in danger of encouraging impunity through the amnesty process.
- Being loaded predominantly of a membership that came from the struggle against Apartheid.
- Being conciliatory and accommodating to Apartheid leaders, e.g. PW Botha.
- Allowing the likes of Wouter Basson[14] (Apartheid's biological warfare expert), PW Botha (former President) and Winnie Madikizela-Mandela to ›get away with murder‹.

---

[14]   See http://en.wikipedia.org/wiki/Wouter_Basson (accessed March 21, 2011).

But there were many other criticisms:

- The constraining and rigid model and format of testimony-giving, which was not friendly to women[15], children, or those who cannot read or write.[16]
- The fact that while perpetrators had immediate amnesty as carrot, victims had no tangible personal carrot, and the commission had neither authority nor power to offer the victims anything except the promise that they would make recommendations to the President and parliament. Indeed, by the time the commission presented its final report to the sitting President Mbeki, he was watering down, if not flatly refusing, most, if not all, its recommendations for reparations.
- The ›real‹ TRC was, in fact, its subcommittee for amnesty, which, unlike the rest of the commission, was chaired by a judge and not by Tutu.
- The very notion of »gross violations of human rights«, which was central to the mandate of the commission, was problematic: Which violations are gross and which ones are not, and who is to decide?[17]
- The arbitrariness and shortness of the period under consideration, 1 March 1960 to 10 May 1994. Why not start in 1913, when the notorious Land Act was introduced? Why not 1948, when Apartheid became official policy?
- The division of society into victims and perpetrators. How many real victims of Apartheid could go and physically testify before the commission? What was so special about those called to testify? And what about the beneficiaries who were neither victims nor perpetrators?[18]
- Can national reconciliation be stage-managed by a commission?
- Tutu himself stated that »the greatest sadness that we have encountered in the commission« has been the reluctance of white leaders to urge their followers to respond to the remarkable generosity of spirit shown by the vic-

---

[15]   For a brilliant illustration for this shortcoming of the TRC see Antjie Krog, Nosis Mpolweni and Kopano Ratele, *There Was This Goat: Investigating the Truth Commission Testimony of Notrose Nobomvu Konile* (Pietermaritzburg: UKZN Press, 2009).

[16]   See Antjie Krog, et al. *There Was This Goat.* See also Tinyiko S. Maluleke, »The Truth and Reconciliation Discourse: A Black Theological Evaluation.«, in *Facing the Truth: South African Faith Communities and the Truth and Reconciliation Commission,* eds. James Cochrane, John de Gruchy and Stephen Martin (Cape Town: David Philip, 1999), 101–113.

[17]   See Tinyiko S. Maluleke, »Truth, National Unity and Reconciliation in South Africa: Aspects of the Emerging Theological Agenda.« *Missionalia* 25, no. 1 (April 1997): 59–86.

[18]   Tinyiko S. Maluleke, »Dealing Lightly With the Wound of My People? The TRC Process in Theological Perspective.« *Missionalia* 25, no. 3 (November 1997): 324–343.

tims. This reluctance, indeed this hostility, to the commission has been like spitting in the face of the victims.«[19]

- A commission like this could only deal with the soft political issues and not the hard economic issues and, therefore, might fail to prevent future violence and conflict by not tackling the real roots of conflict and violence.

COMMENDATIONS

Despite the above criticisms and more, the South African TRC has been largely seen as a success both inside and especially outside the country. This is seen through the many attempts to reproduce the model in many countries and the various honours and decorations received by the commissioners. More substantially, the commission has been praised for making a monumental attempt to »repair the irreparable.«[20]

The commission is especially credited with having assisted in preventing the violence that usually comes ›after violence‹. Such violence can take many forms. It is the violence that comes after the collapse of an authoritarian regime, as rival forces attempt to occupy the vacated centre of state violence. But the violence that comes after violence can also take the form of revenge. Most importantly, the commission, especially the contribution of its chairperson Desmond Tutu, is credited with having assisted greatly in inspiring South Africans to imagine themselves as a ›rainbow nation‹ - one people existing in diversity. Reconciliation is therefore seen as something which the commission managed to inculcate and promote, if not achieve altogether.

Nor should we underestimate the value and amount of the ›truth‹ the TRC helped to unearth. This the commission achieved, not because the commission was perfect but because it was imperfect:

> With all its mistakes, its arrogance, its racism, its sanctimony, its incompetence, the lying, the failure to get an interim reparations policy off the ground after two years, the showing off - with all of this - it has been so brave, so naively brave in the winds of deceit, rancour and hate. Against a flood crashing with the weight of a brutalizing past on to new usurping politics, the Commission has kept alive the idea of a common humanity. Painstakingly it has chiselled a way beyond racism and made space for all of our voices. For all its failures, it carries a flame of hope that makes me proud to be from here, of here.[21]

---

[19]   TRC Report , vol. 1, 17.

[20]   Eric Doxtader and Charles Villa-Vicencio, eds., *Repairing the Irreparable: Reparation and Reconstruction in South Africa* (Cape Town: David Philip, 2004).

[21]   Antjie Krog, *Country of My Skull* (Cape Town: Random House, 1998), 278.

Yet the ›achievements‹ of the commission must not be seen in isolation from the groundwork and leadership of the likes of Desmond Tutu and Nelson Mandela. The real commission started when Mandela started secret negotiations with his jailors. All of what happened from then, the negotiations, the historic elections of 1994, and the installation of Nelson Mandela as President, the subsequent democratic elections which have seen Mbeki elected President twice and more recently Zuma – all of these events, and not merely what happened in the formal TRC, were part and parcel of the national truth and reconciliation process.

Ultimately, the ›achievements‹ of the TRC – of any TRC – can only be symbolic and suggestive. No TRC can be expected to single-handedly stage-manage and manufacture reconciliation. TRCs are catalysts that trigger and inspire attitudes, actions, and processes that may lead to the end of violence and conflict. They cannot by themselves end violence and conflict.

Conclusion and Current Challenges

The first challenge that we still face is that of violence. South African society continues to be a violent society. In 2010, the South African parliament received a damning report about the levels of violent criminality in the country. The report was one in a series of reports, commissioned by the government. While admitting that comparative statistics are hard to come by as many countries do not record criminal activity and murder rates adequately, the report ranked South Africa among the countries with the most violent crime statistics. Other such countries include El Salvador, Colombia, Jamaica, the Democratic Republic of the Congo and others. When the question is asked as to why South Africa has such a high murder rate, the answers seem to point back to the history of the country: a) a brutal past that bred a culture of violence, b) the impact of Apartheid on family and education systems, c) racism, d) a rampant gun culture, e) a culture of impunity, f) inequality, and finally g) economic factors. Especially troubling is the racial and gendered character of the violence. We have unacceptably high incidences of violence against women and children.

If one reads any of the reports of the Centre for the Study of Violence and Reconciliation commissioned by the government in an attempt to understand the causes of violence in present day South Africa, sixteen years after democracy, one may be pardoned to think that we never had a TRC. After the violence of Apartheid, there remains much violence in post-Apartheid South Africa. Notably, the great majority of victims come from largely the same sections of society that bore the brunt of Apartheid violence! Fifteen years later, after the TRC, we still do not have a perfect ›after violence‹ scenario.

Secondly, the recommendations of the TRC pertaining to the compensation of the victims it identified have not been sufficiently interrogated, let alone implemented. The President Fund, which was established to assist in the compensation of victims, lies virtually unused. The TRC Unit within the Department of Justice either has been working very slowly or has been virtually dysfunctional. Without an organization to represent them, the victims have not been able to negotiate meaningfully with the department and hence with the government. The emergence of the Khulumani Support Group,[22] an advocacy group of the victims of gross violations of human rights under the Apartheid era, has been like a ray of sunshine. In October 2010, the Khulumani Support Group launched its ›Still Expecting Campaign‹, a campaign meant to »bring into focus the failures of the country and in particular the failures of its post-apartheid government, to ensure that justice is provided for victims and survivors of the gross human rights abuses that characterized the daily experience of thousands of South Africans under apartheid.«[23] There are currently discussions between the Khulumani Support Group and the Department of Justice – thanks to, among others, the ›Still Expecting Campaign‹ aimed at addressing long-standing issues of reparations. I hope these discussions bear fruit; otherwise, the apparent achievements of the TRC will slowly but surely be eroded. Already the country runs into spasms of violent protests far too often. Indications are that the frustrations of the victims of Apartheid are becoming more unbearable by the day.

Thirdly, at a political level, the country appears to be stuck in a reconciliation rhetoric dead end. Having manufactured a lot of reconciliation symbols, gestures, monuments, events, and moments, the country now appears unable to take the next step. In the words of Njabulo Ndebele, having managed to move from Apartheid to a Post-Apartheid country, the country is now struggling to become a Post-Reconciliation society.[24] In his view, the political

---

[22]   http://www.khulumani.net (accessed March 21, 2011).

[23]   http://www.khulumani.net/khulumani/statements/item/412-launching-our-»still-expecting«-campaign-for-justice-for-victims-and-survivors-of-apartheid-atrocities.html (accessed March 21, 2011).

[24]   Njabulo Ndebele, »Arriving Home? South Africa beyond Transition and Reconciliation.«, in *In the Balance. South Africans Debate Reconciliation*, ed. Fanie Du Toit, and Erik Doxtader (Pretoria: Jacana, 2010), 54–73.

elite has become too comfortable with the terms, classifications and categories designed to help the nation cross the bridge from Apartheid to democracy. The same political elite stands to benefit the most from a prolongation of transitional arrangements. The growing scourge of corruption in the public sector illustrates the kinds of ›benefit‹ the ruling elite can extract from a prolonged transition. Ndebele urges that we move on to a truly democratic society where notions of historical disadvantage and racial discrimination no longer become the basis of political discourse and the allocation of economic resources.

Yet even Ndebele fails to appreciate some of the reasons why the country is struggling to take the next step. In his view, it is the vested interests of the new political elite plus the bankruptcy of their political ideals that is holding the country back. But how can we »move on« without doing the things that will allow us to move on? How can we move on when we complicate the problems of Apartheid era victims by leaving them unattended and then adding to that the new challenges of the post-Apartheid poor? How shall we move on to become a ›normal‹ democracy by pretending that things are better than they actually are? Can we become a normal democracy when our real unemployment rate is around 35%? How can we move on when 50% of the population lives on 8% of the national income in South Africa? How can we move on to the next stage in our democratic revolution when the Gini coefficient, which has become worse since the dawn of democracy, is urging closer to 0.7? How can this country move on when nearly 4 million young people between 18 and 24 are said to be neither employed nor receiving any form of education[25]?

Lastly, South Africa is a perfect laboratory for our assertion that there is no straight line from ›before violence‹ to ›during violence‹ to ›after violence‹. A country steeped in a divided and violent past, South Africa has struggled to install a culture of no violence after the end of Apartheid. We have argued and tried to demonstrate that the high levels of violence in South Africa have a basis in various social and economic factors from both the past and the pres-

---

[25] These figures are taken from a speech given by the General Secretary of the Congress of South African Trade Unions, Mr Zwelinzima Vavi, on the 26th of February 2011. For the speech of Vavi, see http://www.polity.org.za/article/cosatu-vavi-address-by-the-general-secretary-to-the-sacbc-justice-and-peace-agm-26022011-2011-02-26 (accessed March 21, 2011).

For my speech on the same occasion, titled »Lazarus and the Dogs« see http://www.unisa.ac.za/contents/research/docs/Lazarus_Dogs.pdf (accessed on March 21, 2011).

ent. Both South Africa's ›negotiated revolution‹[26] and the TRC are in and of
themselves great achievements. Without these two achievements, the country
of South Africa, as we have come to know it, would not exist. The challenge
that lies before the country is one of building peace on top of the foundations
of a ›negotiated revolution‹ and the work of the TRC. For peace to sprout and
spread, we need just and equitable socio-economic arrangements and structures. But we need more. We need to build a culture of peace. This is where
faith-based communities have a huge role to play. South African churches in
particular and South African people in general have mounted one of the
longest non-violent campaigns in the world. It is no accident that Mahatma
Ghandi discovered his non-violent resistance methodology in South Africa.
Here is a people who for nearly three hundred year resisted oppression mostly
in non-violent ways. An often unspoken reason why the victims of Apartheid
occupied the so-called moral high-ground is the fact that for years they and
their predecessors refused to sink to the low of violence. The role of South
African churches, under the leadership of the likes of Albert Luthuli,[27]
Desmond Tutu,[28] and Allan Boesak,[29] is quite special in the inculcation of the
spirit of non-violence. The churches have to return to the fountains and
sources of their traditions of non-violence and in that way assist the people
of South Africa to usher in a true ›after violence‹ scenario.

On the WCC front, I am encouraged by the fact that what started out in
2001 as the ›Decade to Overcome Violence‹ will end with a focus *not* on violence but on peace, at an event billed as the ›International Ecumenical Peace
Convocation‹, to take place in Jamaica during May 2011. Clearly, the focus has
switched from violence to peace. There, the churches of the world will be invited to use the lessons learnt during the ›Decade to Overcome Violence‹ in
building peace in different countries all over the world.

---

[26]   Allister Sparks, *Tomorrow is Another Country. The Inside Story of South Africa's Negotiated Revolution* (Sandton: Struik, 1994).

[27]   See Albert Luthuli, *Let My People Go. The Autobiography of Albert Luthuli* (Johannesburg: Tafelberg, 1962).

[28]   See Desmond Tutu, *Crying in the Wilderness. The Struggle for Justice in South Africa*
(Grand Rapids: Eerdmans, 1982).

[29]   See Allan Boesak, *Running with the Horses. Reflections of an Accidental Politician*
(Cape Town: Joho Publishers, 2009).

LITERATURE

Alec, Russel. *After Mandela: The Battle for the Soul of South Africa*. London: Random House, 2010.

Boesak, Allan. *Running with the Horses. Reflections of an Accidental Politician*. Cape Town: Joho Publishers, 2009.

Baum, Gregory. *The Reconciliation of Peoples: Challenge to the Churches*. Maryknoll: Orbis, 1997.

Cochrane, James, John De Gruchy, and Stephen Martin, eds. *Facing the Truth: South African Faith Communities and the Truth and Reconciliation Commission*. Atlanta: SBL, 1999.

Doxtader, Eric and Charles Villa-Vicencio, eds. *Repairing the Irreparable: Reparation and Reconstruction in South Africa*. Cape Town: David Philip, 2004.

Du Toit, Fanie, and Eric Doxtader, eds. *In the Balance. South Africans Debate Reconciliation*. Pretoria: Jacana, 2010.

Hochschild, Adam. *King Leopold's Ghost*. New York: Pan Macmillan, 1998.

Krog, Antjie, *Country of My Skull*. Cape Town: Random House, 2000.

Krog, Antjie, Nosis Mpolweni and Kopano Ratele. *There Was This Goat: Investigating the Truth Commission Testimony of Notrose Nobomvu Konile*. Pietermaritzburg: UKZN Press, 2009.

Levi, Neil, and Michael Rothberg, eds. *The Holocaust: Theoretical Readings*. New Brunswick: Rutgers University Press, 2003.

Luthuli, Albert. *Let My People Go. The Autobiography of Albert Luthuli*. Johannesburg: Tafelberg, 1962.

Maluleke, Tinyiko. S. »The DOV and the Challenges Before Us: Ten Concluding Reflections.« In *Come Holy Spirit, Heal and Reconcile*, edited by Jacques Matthey, 195–201. Geneva: WCC, 2005.

Maluleke, Tinyiko S. »Truth, National Unity and Reconciliation in South Africa: Aspects of the Emerging Theological Agenda,« *Missionalia* 25, no. 1 (April 1997): 59–86.

Maluleke, Tinyiko S. »Dealing Lightly With the Wound of My People? The TRC Process in Theological Perspective,« *Missionalia* 25, no. 3 (November 1997): 324–343.

Maluleke, Tinyiko S. »The Truth and Reconciliation Discourse: A Black Theological Evaluation.« In *Facing the Truth: South African Faith Communities and the Truth Commission*, edited by James Cochrane, John de Gruchy and Stephen Martin 101–113. (Cape Town: David Philip, 1999).

Mamdani, Mahmood. *When Victims Become Killers: Colonialism, Nativism, and the Genocide in Rwanda* (Princeton: University Press, 2001).

Meredith, Martin. *The State of Africa: A History of Fifty Years of Independence* (London: Simon and Schuster, 2005).

Ndebele, Njabulo S. »Arriving Home? South Africa Beyond Transition and Reconciliation.« In *In the Balance. South Africans Debate Reconciliation*, edited by Fanie Du Toit and Erik Doxtader 54–73. Pretoria: Jacana, 2010.

Olusaga, David, and Casper W. Erichsen. *The Kaiser's Holocaust: Germany's Forgotten Genocide and the Colonial Roots of Nazism* (London: Faber and Faber, 2010).

Shriver, Donald W. *An Ethic for Enemies. Forgiveness in Politics.* Oxford: University Press, 1995.

Sparks, Allister *Tomorrow is Another Country. The Inside Story of South Africa's Negotiated Revolution.* Sandton: Struik, 1994.

Truth and Reconciliation Commission of South Africa. Report. Vol. 1–5. Cape Town: South African Truth and Reconciliation Commission together with the Department of Justice. Cape Town: Juta & Co., 1998.

Tutu, Desmond. *Crying in the Wilderness. The Struggle for Justice in South Africa.* Grand Rapids: Eerdmans, 1982.

Tutu, Desmond. *The Rainbow People of God: South Africa's Victory over Apartheid.* New York: Bantam, 1994.

Volf, Miroslav. *Exclusion and Embrace.* Nashville: Abingdon, 1996.

Wink, Walter. *Unmasking the Powers. The Invisibe Forces That Determine Human Existence.* Philadelphia: Augsburg Fortress, 1986.

Wink, Walter. *When the Powers Fall: Reconciliation in the Healing of Nations.* Minneapolis: Fortress, 1996.

II
MEMORY AND TRAUMA

Remembering Violence: Practical Theological Considerations

Andrea Bieler

Remembering as Elusive Phenomenon

> »For nothing is resolved, nothing is settled,
> no remembering has become mere memory.«[1]

The following reflections on remembering violence do not intend to offer readymade concepts and advice for how to remember ›well‹. The purpose of this essay is rather to reflect on the issue in light of current studies on collective remembering and trauma. After some introductory remarks on the elusiveness of the phenomenon, I will introduce a process-relational approach to collective remembering, which offers avenues to perceive and analyze remembering as practice. I will then allude to a few lessons we can learn from trauma theory, which can help us to reframe theological resources the Christian traditions have to offer the current conversation.

As a practical theologian, I am ultimately interested in exploring acts of remembrance which are respectful to the dead and which take the uncontrollable, at times haunting, past into account, while probing how life might flourish – at least in fragmentary ways – in the aftermath of violence.[2] Within the ecclesial realm, I seek to envision practices that do not simply reify the boundaries of collective identity formation in our ways of remembering, but

---

[1]   Jean Améry, *At the Mind's Limits: Contemplations by a Survivor on Auschwitz and Its Realities* (Bloomington: Indiana University Press, 1998), 5.

[2]   See with regard to the phenomenon of haunting memories and haunting spirits from a pneumatological perspective, Mayra Rivera, »Ghostly Encounters: Spirits, Memory and the Holy Ghost.«, in *Planetary Loves: Spivak, Postcoloniality, and Theology*, ed. Stephen Moore and Mayra Rivera (New York: Fordham University Press, 2010), 118–135.

rather honor the unspeakable, that which remains unresolved and which returns in unexpected places and hits those who have survived situations of violence. At times, it might also be necessary to perform rituals which invite forgetting and release; at times the disempowerment of haunting spirits might be the task of the hour.

These acts of remembrance relate in significant ways to stories of the Jewish and Christian traditions, which are deeply steeped in remembering violence and rescue: the tortured and the resurrected body of Christ, the salvage of the slave Hagar in the desert, the survival of the people of Israel fleeing from bondage in Egypt. These stories of redemption and survival have at their very heart the transformation of violence; they are stories that call upon God to remember God's people in the aftermath of violence.

As we endeavor to explore practices of remembrance in the aftermath of violence, it seems necessary to attend to the ambiguity of sacred texts as well as current practices. We just need to call to mind, as an example, the violence that is depicted in the Exodus tradition, the liberation of God's people from slavery in Egypt: the assassination of the firstborn male Egyptians, the death of animals such as locusts and horses, and the killing of the soldiers who served the Egyptian army.[3] The book of Deuteronomy testifies that the chain of memory created in relation to the Exodus story can serve to protect slaves and aliens; yet it can also be used to support the command to punish Israel's enemies.[4]

Regarding our current practices, we also need to explore the negative effects that acts of memory can provoke. What are distorted practices of remembrance that might produce the opposite of what they claim to do? When does remembrance produce mere nostalgia, or deepen resentment between groups, or create a pitiful sense of collective guilt? How does remembrance look that hinders deeper processes of reconciliation? How do we take into account the different perspectives from which people relate to particular atrocities?[5]

The call to remember has been powerfully articulated with regards to the Shoah in Germany after decades of paralyzing silence on the side of the victims, the perpetrators, and those who have lived in places in-between. Philosopher and cultural critic Theodor W. Adorno wrote in 1966 an essay, *Erziehung*

---

[3]   See Exodus 10:19; 12:9; 14:30 and 15:19.

[4]   See Deuteronomy 24:17–18 and 25:17–19.

[5]   I list these questions in order to sketch out the vastness of the issue at hand. Concentrating on all of them is obviously beyond the scope of this paper.

nach Auschwitz (Education after Auschwitz), in which he claimed that the basis of all educational endeavors had to be grounded in the moral demand that Auschwitz must never happen again.[6] This text became a kind of manifesto which inspired a heightened sense of responsibility for myriads of educators, therapists, clergy, politicians, and artists, who tried to make sense of their work and, perhaps more fundamentally, their purpose in life in the aftermath of violence – after Auschwitz.

Elie Wiesel's work as a writer who survived the Shoah has centered on the conviction that we, »remember Auschwitz and all that it symbolizes because we believe that, in spite of the past and its horrors, the world is worthy of salvation; and salvation, like redemption can be found only in memory.«[7] For him, remembering in the aftermath of violence is a sine qua non, it is the key to the future; it leads into the mystery of salvation. He makes these huge claims although he is aware of the disastrous and painful dimensions the act of remembering can evoke. In *The Accident,* he grapples with the dilemma that holding on to the memory of the dead can keep those who have been hurt from deeply loving the living in the present.[8] The desire to erase memories that are steeped in violent events is portrayed as a means of survival in the present. Wiesel reflects on the ambiguous practice of remembering within a framework of a negative theology that cannot count on God Almighty anymore. Facing the crematories of Treblinka and Auschwitz, Elie Wiesel notes, »For the first time I felt revolt rise up in me. Why should I bless His name? The Eternal, Lord of the Universe, the All-Powerful and Terrible, was silent. What had I to thank Him for?«[9] He awoke to the idea that he was »alone – terribly alone in a world without God.«[10] The despair that this profound void and loneliness provokes is echoed in the voice of a man whom Wiesel met in the hospital of Auschwitz: »I've got more faith in Hitler than in anyone else. He's the only one who's kept his promises, all his promises to the Jewish people.«[11]

---

[6]   See Theodor W. Adorno, »Erziehung nach Auschwitz.« (1966), in *Erziehung zur Mündigkeit, Vorträge und Gespräche mit Hellmut Becker 1959-1969,* ed. Gerd Kadelbach (Frankfurt am Main: Suhrkamp, 1970), 92–109.

[7]   Elie Wiesel, *From the Kingdom of Memory: Reminiscences* (New York: Summit, 1990), 221.

[8]   Elie Wiesel, *The Accident,* trans. Anne Borchart (New York: Hill and Wang, 1962).

[9]   Elie Wiesel, *Night* (New York: Bantam Books, 1982), 31.

[10]   Wiesel, *Night,* 65.

[11]   Wiesel, *Night,* 77.

Another pioneering attempt to remember in the form of autobiographical writing and testimony culminated in an act of incredible courage which the author did not survive. Twelve years after Jean Améry wrote *Jenseits von Schuld und Sühne,* he committed suicide.[12] In Améry's writing, the haunting quality of the past events, their powerful vividness which resists closure is very much present. Accordingly, he writes in the foreword of his book: »I do not have [clarity] today, and I hope that I never will. Clarification would amount to disposal, settlement of the case, which can then be placed in the files of history. My book is meant to prevent precisely this. For nothing is resolved, nothing is settled, no remembering has become mere memory.«[13]

More than 44 years have passed since Jean Améry began writing. The situation we are facing in Germany right now is very ambivalent. The call to remember the Shoah has been taken seriously by many individuals, groups and institutions. Monuments and places to remember have been created. A huge amount of autobiographical and fictional writing, movies, and documentaries are easily available. Christians have created rituals of confession and remembrance. In 1970, we saw German Chancellor Willy Brandt kneeling in front of the memorial dedicated to the Jewish ghetto of Warsaw and its dead. This gesture gained an iconic quality in the process of its reception in Europe.

We can recognize waves of memory practices and at the same time various forms of resistance to them. Religious educators in Germany perceive a certain opposition against the call to remember so powerfully articulated by the survivors of the Shoah. Many young students graduating from high school wonder why they should mourn as they do not know the victims of the Second World War, they did not participate in the violence, and they do not want to form their sense of self in relation to a past they have not created.[14] It would be too easy to dismiss these thoughts as right-wing attitudes. Rather, they point to the fundamental challenge of what it takes to pass on memories of atrocities to generations who have not been involved in them as contemporaries. Other empirical studies point out that the majority of German high

---

[12]   Jean Améry, *Jenseits von Schuld und Sühne. Bewältigungsversuche eines Überwältigten* (Munich: Klett Cotta, 1966). In English, *At the Mind's Limits: Contemplations by a Survivor on Auschwitz and Its Realities* (Bloomington: Indiana University Press, 1998), 5.

[13]   Améry, *At the Mind's Limits,* 5.

[14]   See Michael Wermke, »Einführung.«, in *Die Gegenwart des Holocaust. ›Erinnerung‹ als religionspädagogische Herausforderung* (Münster: LitVerlag, 1997), 1.

school students experience shame, a sense of guilt, as well as feelings of being paralyzed as they think of the Shoah. The haunting past captivates the hearts and minds of the younger generation. Grasping glimpses of the unspeakable terror, it seems that many educational endeavors fail in inspiring a sense of responsibility for the present as the past is remembered.[15]

Furthermore, there have been huge controversies with regards to the aesthetic and political dimensions of commemorative monuments. The *Memorial to the Murdered Jews of Europe,* for instance, caused such a debate.[16] This memorial covers a 4.7 acre site right in front of the Berlin *Reichstag* with a field of 2,711 stelae, or concrete blocks, one for each page of the Talmud. The stelae are ordered in a crisscross pattern on a sloping ground. According to the architect Eisenman, he intended to evoke an apprehensive and perplexing atmosphere for visitors who are wandering between the stelae. The whole monument hints at the ›well-ordered‹ bureaucratic Nazi system of annihilation, which was out of touch with human reason and empathy. Eisenman refused to create a pedagogical frame which could have included further explanations or educational instructions. One of the major points of critique, however, focuses on the creation of this kind of indeterminate space.[17] Today, when you visit this memorial, you can see people having lunch on the stelae, sunbathing, or smoking a cigarette. The performative space that is shaped by the visitors' interaction with the memorial can create a sense of bewilderment for guests who seek to find a place of respectful remembrance. It might evoke Hannah Arendt's thoughts on the banality of evil, which hint at the ordinariness of lives lived day by day while the most severe atrocities are happening simultaneously.[18] Some monuments, as some critics would say, carry the danger to trivialize and to domesticate the past.

---

[15] See Konrad Brendler, »Identitätsformationen von Jugendlichen im Schatten der Schoah. Zur Wirkungsgeschichte der Schoah und den Chancen der Erinnerungsarbeit.«, in *Zugänge zur Erinnerung. Bedingungen anamnetischer Erfahrung. Studien zur subjektorientierten Erinnerungsarbeit* (Münster: LitVerlag, 2000), 31–56.

[16] The memorial was erected in 2005, designed by the architect Peter Eisenman and engineer Buro Happold. See more on this controversy in Brigitte Sion's essay in this volume.

[17] Beneath the monument, you can find a place that documents traces of the Shoah more explicitly. Many tourists, however, do not discover this place. Eisenman emphasizes that it is not part of the memorial.

[18] Hannah Arendt, *Eichmann in Jerusalem: Report on the Banality of Evil* (New York: Penguin Classics, 2006). Brigitte Sion discusses in detail the interaction of visitors with memorial sites. See her contribution in this volume.

Another individual whose voice complicates the call to remember is Miroslav Volf.[19] Volf, who was himself interrogated by the Yugoslavian Secret Service and by the members of the army in the 1980s, poses the question of how victims of wrongdoings can remember in salutary rather than destructive ways so that the well-being of those who have suffered can be served. He also explores the question of what it means for the perpetrators of violent acts to remember maturely. What are the circumstances in which memory practices can prepare the ground for reconciliation? By engaging defenders of forgetting such as Freud, Nietzsche, and Kierkegaard, he comes to the conclusion that – at least with regard to individual biographies – forgetting as the release of remembered wrongs might be beneficial under well-defined circumstances.[20]

And finally, we need to name the obvious fact that remembering violence does not automatically prevent violence from reoccurring in the future. While many people all over the globe tried not to forget the Shoah, new genocides did happen: for instance in Bosnia, in Rwanda, and in Darfur.

Remembering in the aftermath of violence is indeed an elusive and multifaceted phenomenon.

A PROCESS-RELATIONAL APPROACH TO COLLECTIVE REMEMBERING

> »Neither remnant, document, nor relic of the past,
> or floating in a present cut off from the past,
> cultural memory, for better or worse
> links the past to the present and future.«[21]

CONTESTED MEMORY

I suggest a theoretical grounding for remembering violence beyond the binary of an essentialist versus a presentist approach. An essentialist approach understands memories and images from history as straightforward representations of a past that is at the disposal of those who remember, making it a discrete unit of reality, like an object or a thing. In contrast, a presentist approach

---

[19]   See Miroslav Volf, *The End of Memory: Remembering Rightly in a Violent World* (Grand Rapids: Eerdmans, 2006).

[20]   Volf, *The End of Memory*, 232.

[21]   Mieke Bal, »Introduction,« in *Acts of Memory: Cultural Recall in the Present,* ed. Mieke Bal et al (Hanover: Dartmouth College, 1999), vii.

comprehends memories as mere constructions, which serve certain purposes for the present. In this functionalist view, acts of remembering become mainly an instrument to navigate diverging interests of various groups or individuals.[22]

Instead, I draw on the proposal of the sociologist Jeffrey K. Olick, who has put forward a *process-relational approach* for the analysis of collective remembering as practice. By choosing this approach, the following four assumptions are put into question: (1) Collective memory is understood as a *homogeneous unity,* which produces consensus and a sense of collective identity; (2) it is grounded in *mimetic directness,* which means that »collective memory in some way or another represents or mirrors a pre-representational past, rather than being from the very first embodied in representational form«;[23] (3) it is imagined as a *tangible object,* enfleshed or set in stone in aesthetic productions such as monuments, music, poetry, or sacred texts; and, finally, (4) collective memory is a distinct and separable aspect of culture.

A process-relational approach, conversely, focuses on collective remembering as a thoroughly interactive phenomenon, in which the connections between the present and the past are constantly negotiated. It can be understood as a field in which official and vernacular memory is navigated. The notion of field, as Pierre Bourdieu has introduced it, is helpful here:

> Field may be defined as a network, or a configuration, of objective relations between positions. These positions are objectively defined, in their existence and in their determinations they impose upon their occupants, agents or institutions, by their present and potential situation (situs) in the structure of the distribution of species of power (or capital) whose possession commands access to the specific profits that are at stake in the field, as well as their objective relation to other positions.[24]

Acts of collective remembering happen in different social fields, which are connected in shifting relations. Acts of remembering religious groups engage in are thus influenced by various fields, such as the political, the academic, or the educational field. Within these fields, groups and individuals relate to each other's views in their own construction of the past, and challenge each

---

[22]   See Jeffrey K. Olick, *The Politics of Regret: On Collective Memory and Historical Responsibility* (New York: Routledge, 2007), 8.

[23]   Olick, *The Politics of Regret,* 89.

[24]   Pierre Bourdieu and Loïc J. D. Wacquant, *An Invitation to Reflexive Sociology* (Chicago: Chicago University Press, 1992), 97.

other in the struggle for hegemonic positions. Collective memory thus becomes a contested terrain that produces multiple streams of remembering. It is important to recognize that the field in which collective remembering happens is, in many contexts, not a peaceful and homogenous space. It is rather highly disputed. The question of *how* stories of violent conflicts, genocide, and enduring structural violence are told and interpreted within a framework of religious interpretation is crucial. The field of collective memory is contested and fluid. Stories emerge that have been suppressed or forgotten; marginalized groups articulate their perspectives on which remnants from the past need to be foregrounded. What is supposed to be remembered becomes a locus of struggle. Reflecting on countries such as Rwanda or Chile, where massive genocide or state violence was exercised, Lorey and Beezley state,

> In the aftermath of incidents of genocide and state-sponsored violence, officials, individuals, and a broad array of social groups have attempted to shape the historical consciousness of societies. Such efforts can last for decades. Major conflicts have arisen as social groups battled for the preeminence of a certain interpretation of what happened, who is to blame, and who should be punished. One of the most troubling realities of the aftermath of genocide and collective violence was the attempt to use history in the service of forgetting; historical memory was sometimes abused in order to provide perpetrators with impunity for their earlier actions. Thus the past became key to interpreting the present and to shaping the future.[25]

MNEMONIC MEDIA AND ACTS OF MEDIATING THE PAST

Within these fields of contestation we need to pay attention to what kind of *media of memory* are engaged since the past – if you will – comes to us through some sort of representational medium, which mediates temporal distance. A process-relational approach is thus interested in the media of memory that are introduced in the field of collective remembering. These media are not just forms that could be separated from the message they carry. Form and content are rather intimately interconnected in the usage of mnemonic media. In addition, a process-relational approach focuses on memory not so much as an act of storage and retrieval, but rather as an act of mediation, as an ongoing process in which the connections between past and present are

---

[25]   David E. Lorey and William H. Beezley, ed., *Genocide, Collective Violence, and Popular Memory: The Politics of Remembrance in the Twentieth Century* (Wilmington: SR Books, 2002), xiv.

constantly modified. As we consider the act of mediation, we pay attention to the intentions as well as the effects certain acts of memory imply. These might be the production of a sense of tradition and permanence, of homogenous collectivity, or of a revolutionary time. Some practices strive for dominance through universal truth claims; others might lift up particularity.[26]

Peter Reichel distinguishes four types of mnemonic media, which he identifies as provisional and fluid categories:[27]

a) *Affective media:* These are political or religious festivals, anniversaries or high holidays of remembrance which intend to induce emotions that seek to serve a sense of collective identity and integration.

b) *Aesthetic expressive media:* These can be monuments, works of art situated in the public sphere or in museums, autobiographical and fictional writings, as well as visuals, such as pictures and images. All of these are geared toward a ›deeper‹ aesthetic truth which cannot be contained in mere facts.

c) *Instrumental cognitive media:* These encompass the creation of historical archives as practices in historiography and documentaries. Instrumental cognitive media are evaluated according to accuracy of fact collection and how they contribute to increased historical knowledge.

d) *Political moral media:* These include punishment, amnesty, reparations, or the establishment of a truth and reconciliation commission. Political moral media are judged in terms of providing justice, rehabilitation, or integration.

These media are no static means, but they change with the events they mediate: »The media of memory decisively shape not only specific memories but also memory's mediating functions.«[28] Remembering encompasses practices which can take on many forms. The media employed in the realm of religion can be mainly identified as affective and aesthetic expressive media. We remember in writing; speaking and not speaking; in ritualizing and in preaching; in building memorials; in the composition, performance and reception of music. We create specific times for remembrance. From the perspective of ritual theory, we might say that acts of memory in the public sphere function

---

[26]   See Olick, *The Politics of Regret,* 98.

[27]   Peter Reichel, *Politik mit der Erinnerung: Gedächtnisorte im Streit um die national-sozialistische Vergangenheit* (Munich: Carl Hanser Verlag, 1995), 26–27.

[28]   Olick, *The Politics of Regret,* 104.

most of the time in setting apart certain times and places. We distinguish them from the realm of the ordinary in order to create a performance space, which helps us to focus on what we otherwise seek to avoid. For instance, we gather on November 9th to remember the *Reichspogromnacht*. We gather in places which bear the marks of destruction, such as the remains of synagogues. Persons of faith do this in constant conversation with sacred texts and with the revelations and the encounters with the Divine they hold to be foundational for their lives. Acts of remembrance are grounded in aesthetic and ethical choices with regards to content and how particular media are used. We choose which testimonies to utter; we decide on the way how to evoke the name of the Holy One, how to confess our sins and the sins of our ancestors; and we settle on visual images to provoke certain responses. We develop curricula in which we teach our children and youth about the violence that has occurred in our midst and how this occurrence has shaped our sense of self and community. We seek to be mindful of the question of what it means to convey something from the past to generations who are removed from the events since they might have happened many years, even decades ago.

The Processual Character of Memory Genres

Collective memory is not a clearly bounded object that can be possessed, as I have stated before. It can be better comprehended in terms of genres, as historical constructs that are the results of an unremitting and generative process put into practice in the social-verbal exchanges of conversation partners. Each individual utterance and performance consists in a »chain of speech communion«, an accumulated succession of commemorations.[29]

Consequently, genres produce the memory of memory; they are grounded in the essential reflexivity of mnemonic practices. For instance, Abraham Lincoln has been a point of reference with regard to the chain of speech communion which has created this kind of echo, the memory of memory. John F. Kennedy's funeral was sated with references to Lincoln's funeral. Dr. Martin Luther King's appearance at the Lincoln Memorial was reminiscent of Marian Anderson's.[30]

What we can observe here is a kind of citational practice. Commemorations that went before are referenced implicitly and explicitly in order to

---

[29] See Olick, *The Politics of Regret*, 105.
[30] See Olick, *The Politics of Regret*, 105.

give the current event more weight or a particular profile. Depending on how these citations are framed, a certain sense of traditioning will emerge. According to Jan Assmann, the memory of memory is created in a shared mental space in which a particular group refers to the construction of fixed points in the past that receive a symbolic quality. Shared narratives evolve around those points of reference, which then generate new memories. Oftentimes these narratives invite a dense sense of identification.[31]

In Christian liturgical commemorations of the Shoah, we can often find texts of Jewish writers. Especially texts from Elie Wiesel, Albert H. Friedlander, and Hana Volavkova are used with the intention – I assume – to give voice to the perspectives of the victims.[32] This kind of citational practice has led to a controversial debate as to whether these good intentions inspire a space of memory in which the children and grandchildren of the perpetrator generation imagine themselves in the place of the victims, as the act of empathy dissolves in its subject-object structure. Who remembers? Who is remembered? Once these questions are not asked anymore, the challenge to find a response from the Christian side disappears.[33]

Such citational practices are embedded in the *history of commemorations,* which shows the developmental character of certain memory genres. Olick, for instance, suggests for the public commemoration of May 8th between 1949 and 1995 five distinct periods in which the commemorative rhetoric surrounding this day significantly changed.[34] Memory genres thus have

---

[31]   See Jan Assmann, *Das kulturelle Gedächtnis: Schrift, Erinnerung und politische Identität in frühen Hochkulturen* (Munich: Beck, 1992), 52.

[32]   See examples from the Christian perspective in *Liturgies on the Holocaust: An Interfaith Anthology,* eds. Marcia Sachs Littell and Sharon Weissman Gutman (Valley Forge: Trinity Press International, 1996). Elie Wiesel's autobiographic text »Night« is quoted. Hana Volavkova collected poems by children who were interned in the camps: *I Never Saw Another Butterfly* (New York: McGraw-Hill Book, 1964). Quoting from those poems is another prevailing source.

[33]   See Tania Oldenhage, »Walking the Way of the Cross: German Places, Church Traditions, and Holocaust Memories.«, in *Religion, Violence, Memory, and Place,* eds. Oren Baruch Stier and J. Shawn Landres (Bloomington & Indianapolis: Indiana University Press, 2006), 90.

[34]   Within these five periods he identifies the following themes: defeat, liberation and the German victim (1949–1969); liberation and the Pan-European future (1970–1975); normalcy and normalization (1975–1985); normalization through relativization (1985–1995), and commemoration in the new Germany (1995 – present). Olick, *The Politics of Regret,* 62.

processual character that is expressed in their historical and dialogic dimensions.

LESSONS FROM TRAUMA THEORY

Mieke Bal states: »The memorial presence of the past takes many forms and serves many purposes, ranging from conscious recall to unreflected reemergence, from nostalgic longing for what is lost to polemical use of the past to reshape the present.«[35] Oftentimes, remembering in the aftermath of collective violence takes on the form of trauma. Trauma refers to an engagement with the past in the aftermath of an event of overwhelming violence in which the actual horrific event cannot be recalled and cannot be brought into consciousness. This inaccessible event however returns and haunts the survivors in ways that causes new suffering. Formerly established skills of dealing with stress and conflict shut down; a person's ability to respond to the effects of traumatic stress is impaired. Well-known categories from the world of therapy such as ›working through‹ or ›coping‹ do not seem to be appropriate. The experience of death bleeds into the present and affects one's sense of time, sense of embodied living, as well as the capacity to use language.[36]

The distinction between knowing the (traumatic) event and the way in which that event is remembered is obscured. The traumatic event escapes accessibility – it cannot be fully known, neither by memory nor by historical reconstruction: »The shock of the mind's relation to the threat of death is not the direct experience of the threat, but precisely the *missing* of this experience, the fact that, not being experienced in time, it has not yet been fully known.«[37] The traumatic event, as it occurs in the experience of overwhelming violence, can become a missed event, a missed encounter with death. It remains inaccessible to knowledge. This missed encounter calls for the persistent repetition of the traumatic event. For persons suffering from PTSD this repetition does not entail a cognizant remembering of the trauma. Instead, the elusive return of the traumatic event is incessantly experienced as original

---

[35]   Mieke Bal, »Introduction.«, vii.

[36]   See Shelly Rambo, *Spirit and Trauma: A Theology of Remaining* (Louisville: Westminster John Knox, 2010), 18–21.

[37]   Cathy Caruth, *Unclaimed Experience: Trauma, Narrative, and History* (Baltimore: John Hopkins University Press, 1996), 62.

event, which causes the shock of survival. This shock is – as Cathy Caruth calls it – an awakening one moment too late, which carries the pounding question: Why did I survive?[38]

We can see in many societies that the passing on of trauma through various generations happens in multiple ways. The very events that produced traumatizing effects return in new shapes and are repeated in new forms of violence. We can see this happening, for instance, in the United States, in Germany, in Israel, or in South Africa. Often times the violence has also horizontal character.[39]

Trauma theory attends to a sphere of knowing that is itself continually terrorized and haunted by the violence, by the trauma of a past event. It is a knowing that remains incomplete. Or as Cathy Caruth articulates it, »Trauma ... does not simply serve as record of the past but precisely registers the force of an experience that is not yet fully owned.«[40] Trauma, in this sense, is a continual awakening to an event that was not fully understood and because of this incompleteness is being incessantly made present. Or as Dirk Lange puts it: »Repetition is not the repetition of a known event but an impossible repetition – the repetition of a missed encounter, the repetition of a missed encounter with death ...«[41]

REMEMBERING VIOLENCE:
FRAGMENTS FROM THE CHRISTIAN TRADITIONS

In what follows, I seek to reflect theologically on remembering violence in light of current research on trauma and collective memory. I am interested in revisiting fragments from the Christian traditions that can be drawn into the conversation by sketching out the following areas as fruitful points of contact:

---

[38]   See Caruth, *Unclaimed Experience*, 62.

[39]   Ron Eyerman claims that slavery is a site of traumatic collective memory for African Americans, a site that needs constant reflection and reinterpretation. Slavery has become a habitus, in Bourdieu's sense, something »lived and living ... inherited and transmitted ... « Ron Eyerman, *Cultural Trauma: Slavery and the Formation of African American Identity* (Cambridge: Cambridge University Press, 2002), 188.

[40]   Cathy Caruth, *Trauma: Explorations in Memory* (Baltimore: John Hopkins University Press, 1995), 151.

[41]   Dirk Lange, »Trauma Theory and Liturgy: A Disruption of Ritual.« *Liturgical Ministry* 17 (2008): 128.

the understanding of anamnesis (remembrance) as it derives from the Eucharist, the inhabitation of Holy Saturday, and the invocation of the Holy Spirit as paraclete who helps the remaining community to remember and to remain in love.

ANAMNETIC PRACTICE

Through traumatic events, a linear sense of temporality is destroyed, as life cannot be ordered in a neat timeline anymore. The past is no longer separated from the present and the future. It is rather something from the past death experience that haunts the present and that affects how we can imagine the future. One's whole life and way of being is shaped by this powerful contact with death and by the force of its return. It is an experience of excess of death which cannot be controlled and domesticated. Some theologians suggest interpreting the Eucharist in light of this dimension of trauma theory.[42]

Many liturgical theologians assert a classical notion of anamnesis according to which the implosion of linear temporality stirs up the fullness of divine presence unbound by and simultaneously fully immersed in the past and the future God holds for God's creation. Eucharistic remembering leads, in this view, to an actualization of the Christ event (cross and resurrection) in its singularity.[43] In light of trauma theory, the iteration that happens in the ritual disrupts this illusion of actualization:

> The force of return – of something that cannot be grasped in the singular event – the continual irruption of that event in life, both individual and communal, is here opposed to simple imitation, repetition, and memorial. Something in this event – its singularity – cannot be captured by our memories, by any act of mimesis, imitation or remembrance. [...] The resistance to facile remembering is a dissemination of context and subject; we might say that it is a ›dis-membering‹ of personal identity, of life and knowledge, of body and blood. The event returns and irrupts in the present moment, in the present context through dissemination.[44]

In the Eucharist, we return to a site of state terror and torture by having a meal together. We do this by entering the chain of speech communion that be-

---

[42]   See Dirk Lange, *Trauma Recalled: Liturgy, Disruption, and Theology* (Minneapolis: Fortress Press, 2009).

[43]   See for a discussion on anamnesis Bruce Morrill, *Anamnesis as Dangerous Memory: Political and Liturgical Theology in Dialogue* (Collegeville: Liturgical Press, 2000).

[44]   Lange, *Trauma Recalled*, 140 and 142.

gins with Jesus' demand at the Last Supper, »Do this in remembrance of me«, which points to the Jewish practice of saying grace at the table and remembering the Exodus story, the liberation from slavery.

The narrative invites us into the night before the violence happens: »In the night when Jesus was betrayed, he took the bread . . .« It invites us into the space of dissemination: »Take, eat, this is my body given for you.« This invitation is not a glorification of violence; it is rather an invitation in the sharing of the eschatological body, since the story of violence told in the Eucharist is narrated from the hopeful perspective that God has disrupted the violence and the terror through the resurrection of Christ. I suggest understanding the Eucharist as a focal rite within the Christian faith, in which we are drawn into a story of divine redemption, which has at its heart the transformation of violence.[45] We return to a site of violence which is in many ways not accessible to us, which we cannot remember. We also return to the garden of the resurrection, which is in many ways not comprehensible to us and which is a frightening place, too, as the witnesses to the resurrection, such as Mary Magdalene and Peter, teach us.[46] This return is not happening in a triumphalist attitude that death is conquered; rather, the community gathered does a strange thing: People are having a meal together and believe that by doing so they commune with God. In light of trauma theory, we might understand the Eucharist as a practice which recognizes the reality of trauma inducing violence without giving it ultimate power. The site of violence cannot be represented in a simple, straightforward fashion in the act of remembrance. Here, through the medium of eating and drinking, a genre is created which holds the memory of memory. It is a space of reference, in which the force of the return, as reenacted violence, is disrupted. Instead, people are coming together to eat and drink and hear words that hint at love which gives itself radically to the other: »This is my body, take and eat.«

The Greek term *anamnesis* that is used in the New Testament in the context of the Last Supper scenes refers to a concept of remembering in which the linear perception of time implodes. By engaging in the ritual of eating and drinking, the tortured Christ is strangely made present as the Resurrected One. This presence holds both the indelible marks of vulnerability and violence as well as the transformative vision of resurrected life in the flesh. It is

---

[45]   See Andrea Bieler and Luise Schottroff, *The Eucharist: Bodies, Bread, and Resurrection* (Minneapolis: Fortress Press, 2007).

[46]   See Hans-Martin Gutmann in this volume, and Rambo, *Spirit and Trauma*, 83–99.

in this complex space that the encounter with God occurs, the most intimate form of communion: Christ's body in my body. Christ's body becoming the community's body.

REVISITING HOLY SATURDAY

»Witnessing to what does not go away [. . .].«[47]

Shelly Rambo calls this complex in-between-space the *middle* space. This is the space in which death and life are inextricably interwoven, a space in which resurrection can only be proclaimed when it testifies to the traces of death that remain. Here, the tale of redemption is not told in a linear fashion in which life triumphs over death as we march victoriously towards Easter. »Looking from the middle, we are oriented to suffering in a different way – always in its dislocation, its distance, and its fragmentation. This orientation calls for a theology of witness in which we cannot assume presence or straightforward reception of a violent event, but instead contend with excess of violence and its tenuous reception. Without witnessing to what does not go away, to what remains, theology fails to provide a sufficient account of redemption.«[48] In the aftermath of violence, Rambo calls for a *theology of remaining* which carves out a space for people who suffer from trauma, whose lives have forever changed as they have been touched by some sort of encounter with death.

Within the Christian liturgical calendar, it might be Holy Saturday which holds the middle space. While the liturgical reforms of the 20th century have recovered the Western liturgies of Holy Week, especially the Triduum, little attention is given to Holy Saturday. Triduum refers to the three days: Maundy Thursday, Good Friday and the Great Easter Vigil. If Holy Saturday is observed at all, it often happens only in very sparse forms.[49]

Holy Saturday, as Cornel West claims, is a highly neglected terrain within Christian theology. It is a puzzling day, especially for those who are obsessed with the linear narrative of salvation, which moves seamlessly from Good Fri-

---

[47]   Rambo, *Spirit and Trauma*, 79.

[48]   Rambo, *Spirit and Trauma*, 79.

[49]   For instance, the Book of Common Prayer provides readings that remember Jesus' burial, evoke a sense of mortality, and a solemn preparation for Easter. An optional hymn is suggested: »In the midst of life we are in death.« The Methodist Book of Worship offers a brief prayer for Holy Saturday. The Eastern Orthodox traditions however provide a more elaborate liturgy on Holy Saturday.

day to Easter. In that trajectory, identifying with Easter is about identifying with the winning team:

> That's why Easter Sunday the churches are full, but Good Friday they are empty. I'll show up when the winner pops up. But don't tell me about the main protagonist being treated like a political prisoner by the Roman Empire. Don't tell me about a senseless death based on injustice. And certainly don't tell me about the Saturday, in which, echoing Nietzsche, God is dead, even for Christians. You don't get too much theo-thanatology in Christian thought these days. But God is dead that Saturday, and there was no thought of a bounce back.[50]

From the perspective of trauma theory, Holy Saturday might be interpreted as the middle space: it is the time-space which occupies the aftermath of violence, when vision is obscured and life does not feel safe anymore. Holy Saturday is the time-space that many survivors of massive violence inhabit; it is the moment after the violence has erupted, the numb and disorienting time span when it is absolutely not clear how life flourishing could ever be envisioned again.

It is the time-space in which we are to do the impossible – to witness the death of Christ. One major interpretation of Holy Saturday derives from the harrowing of hell tradition, which depicts Christ's victorious descent to hell where he breaks the chains of death and saves the departed. It is echoed in the *Exsultet* (Rejoice), the hymn that is sung to bless the Paschal candle: »This is the night, when Christ broke the bonds of death and hell and rose victoriously from the grave.« Victory becomes a major image that arises from Holy Saturday and leads into the Easter Vigil.

Shelly Rambo invites us to discover another, more passive and subtle trace of the Holy Saturday tradition, which speaks to Christ's forsakenness, when the Word falls silent.[51] Holy Saturday, as the middle day between death and resurrection, inhabits the abyss of hell in which God's own self is taken over by death as utmost forsakenness, desolation and disconnect. The ethical responsibility that comes with the inhabitation of Holy Saturday requires a twofold witness: The first witness relates to how we see Christ and how the Divine is present and absent in and with him. It challenges the doctrine of *divine apathia* and turns it upside down, as we are urged to reflect on divine

---

[50]   Cornel West, »Readings and Conversations.« June 2003, http://podcast.lannan.org/2010/06/18/cornel-west-reading-25-june-2003-video/ (accessed October 12th, 2011).

[51]   Shelly Rambo engages here a critical dialogue with Adrienne von Speyr's and Hans Urs von Balthasar's theology of Holy Saturday.

vulnerability marked by the experience of violence and death. From the exchange between Mary Magdalene and the gardener, we can learn that en-
countering the Resurrected One leads into a space where the trauma that has
happened will not simply go away. It rather bleeds into the relationship and
the exchange with Jesus; it creates knowledge and a way of seeing which remains incomplete and is troublesome.[52] Reading the biblical witnesses this
way, an unexpected connection occurs: Mary's witness and the testimonies of
Elie Wiesel, Jean Améry, or more recently from the veterans of the Iraq war
share the space of traumatic knowing and insight in all its incompleteness.
What if we need to receive these testimonies as a necessary Holy Saturday
practice? What if they would illuminate for us today what Mary has encountered? In light of the insight that we are threatened with resurrection, as Julia Esquivel puts it, we might receive the stammering call to become witnesses of trauma in the aftermath of violence.[53] This is the other aspect of
witnessing which is grounded in an ethical responsibility that is geared towards Holy Saturday.

INVOKING THE PARACLETE

Shelly Rambo suggests, through her reading of the farewell discourse according to the gospel of John, that it is the middle Spirit who witnesses to
what remains in this in-between-place, between death and life:

> Looking through the lens of trauma, it is important to revisit the Spirit not as a
> figure who secures love between death and life but rather as one who witnesses
> to what remains – what persists – between them. This is the ever-greater Spirit
> of the middle, the fruit of love forged through death. The middle Spirit rewrites
> an understanding of love in significant ways, attesting to a form of divine pre-
> sence that is difficult to see, to feel and to touch. The Spirit provides a distinctive
> way of orienting oneself between death and life, a way of witnessing the fractured
> dimensions of word and body between death and life.[54]

The invocation of the Spirit in Christian liturgies is most often wrapped in images which depict her as a life-giving force that falls afresh on us, enlivens
and strengthens us. Spirit is then evoked in opposition to death. The Holy
Spirit is also evoked as divine force that provokes unexpected and unbound

---

52   See also Rivera, ›Ghostly Encounters‹, 128–129.

53   Julia Esquivel, *Threatened with Resurrection: Prayers and Poems from an Exiled
Guatemalan*, Spanish-English edition (Elgin: Brethren Press, 1982).

54   Rambo, *Spirit and Trauma*, 79.

speech; in the Pentecost event embodied in the outbursting multitude of languages. Spirit falling down in burning tongues facilitates the astounding comprehension of other tongues. In these examples, Spirit is portrayed as opposite to speechlessness, disconnect, and silence. She is rarely invoked as the divine energy that emerges from the wounds of trauma and that hovers over the time-space of Holy Saturday, enabling the community to bear witness to life in the aftermath of traumatizing violence.

The Spirit as paraclete, as depicted in the farewell discourses in the gospel of John, might help to broaden our invocations of the Holy Spirit in our practices of remembrance. Jesus promises that the paraclete will come after Jesus has left them and will enable them to become witnesses. This is promised to a community who has been reduced through outside pressure and internal conflict to ›bare life‹. This is how Tat-siong Benny Liew imagines the situation of John's community, surrounded by an all-encompassing threat of death.[55] After the violence, after Jesus has departed, new forms of violence arise. In this situation, it is the paraclete who inspires the witness to the death experiences surrounding the community. The paraclete becomes the carrier of memories of the martyrs emerging from the middle space between death and life. The paraclete will move the disciples to become witnesses (John 15: 26–27).[56]

Witnessing becomes a fragile practice: it needs to happen in the midst of threatening conflict:

> If the paraclete resides in them, this figure will place them at the cusp of death and life as witnesses … The paraclete bears witness to the things that Jesus did, and the paraclete will remain in and with them to remind them of these things. The disciples, in turn, are instructed to love and to witness. The presence of Jesus with them and the call to remain in him is delivered in a context of death. This death context not only indicates that they will be survivors – those who remain – but they will operate in the world in a particular way – remaining – in the aftermath of death.[57]

---

[55]   Tat-siong Benny Liew follows Giorgio Agamben's reflection on bare life. See »Living and Giving in the Shadow of Imperial Death.« *Journal of Race, Ethnicity and Religion* 1, no. 13.4 (December 2010): 1–58, http://www.raceandreligion.com/JRER/Volume_1_ (2010)_ files/Peace%20Liew.pdf (accessed February 12, 2011).

[56]   See Andrea Bieler and David Plüss, »Wenn der Paraklet kommt (Joh 15:26–16:4), Sonntag Exaudi.« *Göttinger Predigtmeditationen* 2 (2008): 271–277.

[57]   Rambo, *Spirit and Trauma,* 101 and 104.

In our practices of remembrance that seek to be attentive to the realities of trauma that surround us, we might consider invoking the paraclete as the middle Spirit who dwells in people and places who have to bear witness – trembling and in a tenuous fashion – to life and grace in the aftermath of violence.

CONCLUSION

Practical theological research which draws on critical practice theory needs to continuously delve into the analysis of acts of memory that are foundational for religious communities as well as for public discourse. How communities remember in the aftermath of violence is a vital issue for attending to the present and to the future. A critical analysis of the affective and the expressive media that are employed is crucial. As some of the essays in this volume demonstrate, churches oftentimes participate in the continuation of sectarian violence[58] or in acts of dismissive silencing[59] since they have failed to address their own complacency. It is, however, also the elusiveness of the phenomenon of memory that complicates the creation of practices that take the realities of trauma seriously into account.

In the last section of my essay, I have hinted at traditional biblical and liturgical resources that are in need of reframing so that the issues at hand can be addressed in new ways. Still, I also see the need for communities of faith to develop new rituals and to bond with artists and activists who seek to explore aesthetic expressions that address the aftermath of collective violence. If such connections are created, synergies might unfold, which spark glimpses of honesty and of hope.

---

[58] See Siobhán Garrigan's essay in the volume on Catholic and Protestant worship practices in Ireland and Northern Ireland.

[59] See Jean-Pierre Karegeye's essay in this volume on the genocide in Rwanda and the responses of the Roman Catholic church.

LITERATURE

Adorno, Theodor W. »Erziehung nach Auschwitz.« In *Erziehung zur Mündigkeit, Vorträge und Gespräche mit Hellmut Becker 1959–1969*, edited by Gerd Kadelbach, 92–109. Frankfurt a. Main: Suhrkamp, 1970.

Améry, Jean. *At the Mind's Limits: Contemplations by a Survivor on Auschwitz and Its Realities.* Bloomington: Indiana University Press, 1998. German edition: *Jenseits von Schuld und Sühne. Bewältigungsversuche eines Überwältigten.* Munich: Klett Cotta, 1966.

Arendt, Hannah. *Eichmann in Jerusalem: Report on the Banality of Evil.* New York: Penguin Classics, 2006.

Assmann, Jan. *Das kulturelle Gedächtnis: Schrift, Erinnerung und politische Identität in frühen Hochkulturen,* Munich: Beck, 1992.

Bal, Mieke. »Introduction.« In *Acts of Memory: Cultural Recall in the Present,* ed. Mieke Bal, Jonathan Crewe, and Leo Spitzer, vii–xvii. Hanover and London: Dartmouth College, 1999.

Bieler, Andrea and David Plüss. »Wenn der Paraklet kommt (Joh 15:26–16:4), Sonntag Exaudi.« *Göttinger Predigtmeditationen* 2 (2008): 271–277.

Bieler, Andrea and Luise Schottroff. *The Eucharist: Bodies, Bread, and Resurrection.* Minneapolis: Fortress Press, 2007.

Bourdieu, Pierre and Loïc J. D. Wacquant. *An Invitation to Reflexive Sociology.* Chicago: Chicago University Press, 1992.

Brendler, Konrad. »Identitätsformationen von Jugendlichen im Schatten der Schoah. Zur Wirkungsgeschichte der Schoah und den Chancen der Erinnerungsarbeit.« *In Zugänge zur Erinnerung. Bedingungen anamnetischer Erfahrung. Studien zur subjektorientierten Erinnerungsarbeit,* edited by Ottmar Fuchs, Reinhold Boschki, Britta Frede-Wenger. Münster: LitVerlag, 2000.

Caruth, Cathy. *Trauma: Explorations in Memory.* Baltimore: Johns Hopkins University Press, 1995.

Caruth, Cathy. *Unclaimed Experience: Trauma, Narrative, and History.* Baltimore: Johns Hopkins University Press, 1996.

Esquivel, Julia. *Threatened with Resurrection: Prayers and Poems from an Exiled Guatemalan,* Spanish-English edition. Elgin: Brethren Press, 1982.

Eyerman, Ron. *Cultural Trauma: Slavery and the Formation of African American Identity.* Cambridge: Cambridge University Press, 2002.

Lange, Dirk. »Trauma Theory and Liturgy: A Disruption of Ritual.« *Liturgical Ministry* 17 (2008): 127–132.

Lange, Dirk. *Trauma Recalled: Liturgy, Disruption and Theology.* Minneapolis: Fortress Press, 2009.

Liew, Tat-siong Benny. »Living and Giving in the Shadow of Imperial Death.« *Journal of Race, Ethnicity and Religion.* Vol. 1, issue 13.4 (December 2010): 1–58, http://www.race-andreligion.com/JRER/Volume_1_(2010)_files/Peace%20Liew.pdf (accessed February 12, 2011).

Lorey, David E. and William H. Beezley, (eds.). *Genocide, Collective Violence, and Popular*

Memory: The Politics of Remembrance in the Twentieth Century. Wilmington: SR Books, 2002.

Littell, Marcia Sachs and Sharon Weissman Gutman (eds.). *Liturgies on the Holocaust: An Interfaith Anthology.* Valley Forge: Trinity Press International, 1996.

Morrill, Bruce. *Anamnesis as Dangerous Memory: Political and Liturgical Theology in Dialogue.* Collegeville: Liturgical Press, 2000.

Oldenhage, Tania. »Walking the Way of the Cross: German Places, Church Traditions, and Holocaust Memories.« In *Religion, Violence, Memory, and Place,* ed. Oren Baruch Stier and J. Shawn Landres. Bloomington & Indianapolis: Indiana University Press, 2006.

Olick, Jeffrey K. *The Politics of Regret: On Collective Memory and Historical Responsibility.* New York: Routledge, 2007.

Rambo, Shelly. *Spirit and Trauma: A Theology of Remaining.* Louisville: Westminster John Knox, 2010.

Reichel, Peter. *Politik mit der Erinnerung: Gedächtnisorte im Streit um die nationalsozialistische Vergangenheit.* Munich: Carl Hanser Verlag, 1995.

Rivera, Mayra. »Ghostly Encounters: Spirits, Memory and the Holy Ghost.« In *Planetary Loves: Spivak, Postcoloniality and Theology,* eds. Stephen Moore and Mayra Rivera. New York: Fordham University Press, 2011, 118–135.

Volavkova, Hana (ed.). *I Never Saw Another Butterfly.* New York: McGraw-Hill Book, 1964.

Volf, Miroslav. *The End of Memory: Remembering Rightly in a Violent World.* Grand Rapids: Eerdmans, 2006.

Wermke, Michael. »Einführung.« In *Die Gegenwart des Holocaust. ›Erinnerung‹ als religionspädagogische Herausforderung.* Münster: LitVerlag, 1997.

West, Cornel. »Readings and Conversations.« June 2003, http://www.lannan.org/docs/cornel-west-030625-trans-read.pdf (accessed January 15, 2011).

Wiesel, Elie. *From the Kingdom of Memory: Reminiscences.* New York: Summit, 1990.

Wiesel, Elie. *Night.* New York: Bantam Books, 1982.

Wiesel, Elie. *The Accident,* trans. Anne Borchart. New York: Hill and Wang, 1962.

Missing Bodies, Conflicted Rituals: Performing Memory in Germany, Argentina, and Cambodia

Brigitte Sion

Introduction

The Holocaust, the Argentine Dirty War, the Cambodian genocide – three different cases of 20th-century genocide or mass murder that share a grim characteristic: the absence of the bodies of the victims, or the impossibility of identifying incomplete bodily remains. With rare exceptions, the exact circumstances of death, such as date, place, and cause, were never revealed; nor were the bodily remains accorded appropriate funerary rites. Funerary and mourning practices generally center on the body of the deceased, whether the remains are preserved, buried, cremated, embalmed, or eaten. Relatives and community members symbolically mark the departure of the deceased from the world of the living by disposing of the body. When bodily remains cannot be found or have been destroyed, the mourning process is compromised, and a social drama unfolds in the absence of the main character.

This essay focuses on national memorials erected to the victims of state-sponsored violence: the Memorial to the Murdered Jews of Europe in Berlin; the Monument to the Victims of State Terrorism within the Park of Memory in Buenos Aires, which commemorates thousands of kidnapped and »disappeared« people during the military dictatorship (1976–1983); and the Choeung Ek killing fields in Phnom-Penh, the main mass murder site of the Khmer Rouge genocide (1975–1979). I argue that while monuments carry a commemorative function, they may also induce a variety of rituals and practices that are far removed from memory but serve other agendas.

In contrast with the missing bodies during World War I, the bodies of those who were killed in the Holocaust, during the Argentine Dirty War, and in the Cambodian genocide were deliberately made to disappear. The Nazis cremated millions of corpses, while the Argentine victims were called ›*desa-*

parecidos‹ because their bodies were never to be found. In Cambodia, mass graves revealed dismembered bodies that could not be identified. In the words of General Jorge Rafael Videla, the military junta leader, »The *desaparecidos* are neither dead ... nor alive ... they simply are not.«[1] This conscious act of erasure has resulted in depriving victims of appropriate funerary rites, and relatives of a way to complete their mourning process. In other words, these situations created a mourning vacuum and a commemorative challenge.

It is the absence of bodies that distinguishes a memorial from a cemetery. A cemetery is marked by the physical presence of remains, by certainty, individuality, and funerary rites that focus on the place where the body was buried. In his speech at the unveiling of the Buenos Aires monument, Marcelo Brodsky insisted that the purpose of the memorial was »to create a place where families could exercise their right to grief and to memory.«[2] He focused on place, on the need to bring together victims and mourners in a location that both previously lacked. In the absence of a body to lay to rest, the ritual that marks the passing of the deceased out of the community of the living cannot be performed; mourners are stranded between the need to turn the page and a lingering doubt about the actual death of their loved one. In anthropologist Victor Turner's words, they remain »betwixt and between the positions assigned and arrayed by law, custom, convention, and ceremonial.«[3]

Funeral rites reflect this moment between the death of someone and the last resting place, a time when the deceased does not belong to the living anymore, but does not rest yet among the dead. In the case of absent bodily remains, this transitional rite of passage cannot be completed: The dead is in limbo, and so is the survivor, who remains in a liminal state between shock and closure, between hope and acceptance. Memorials address this »ambiguous loss«, which psychologist Pauline Boss defines as »the incomplete or uncertain loss.«[4]

---

[1]   Quoted by Sergio Sorin, »Argentina le pone nombre y apellido a sus desaparecidos.« *El Sitio*, February 17, 1999.

[2]   Marcelo Brodsky, »Génesis y evolución de una idea.« *Ramona: Revista de Artes Visuales* 9–10 (December 2000–March 2001), 6–7, http://www.ramona.org.ar/files/r9y10.pdf (accessed February 8, 2011).

[3]   Victor Turner, *The Ritual Process: Structure and Anti-Structure* (Chicago: Aldine Publishing Company, 1969), 95.

[4]   Pauline Boss, *Ambiguous Loss: Learning to Live with Unresolved Grief* (Cambridge: Harvard University Press, 1999), 3.

Memorials are a form of surrogation: »Into the cavities created by loss through death or other forms of departure, ... survivors attempt to fit satisfactory alternates«; performance »fills, by means of surrogation, a vacancy created by the absence of an original«,[5] in the words of Joseph Roach. In the case of missing bodies, a memorial can act as a surrogate for a grave and focal point for commemorative performances. However, as Roach explains, »the fit cannot be exact. The intended substitute either cannot fulfill expectations, creating a deficit, or actually exceeds them, creating a surplus.«[6] The memorials that I examine are fraught with precisely the tension between deficit and surplus, between underachieved memory and excess of interpretation.

One of the numerous challenges posed by such large-scale tragedies is the difficulty of honoring the thousands of victims, whose deaths were robbed of their individuality. How, in practical terms, can the individuality of their deaths be restored? How can one make an exhaustive list of victims, given the lack of documentation? How can they be remembered individually without creating a memorial as big as the crime? While the naming of victims is a traditional commemorative device, the practice is inadequate in the case of mass murder. The immensity of the tragedy precludes any attempt to record and remember each individual life in a single monument. Some memorials, particularly those dedicated to the Holocaust, have reverted to collective, symbolic, or partial memorialization: The Holocaust Museum in Washington is a general tribute to all victims; the New England Holocaust Memorial in Boston is a symbolic and abstract glass monument; the Shoah memorial in Paris is a wall listing only the names of the 76,000 Jews deported from France, based on German and Vichy archives.

THE MEMORIAL TO THE MURDERED JEWS OF EUROPE IN BERLIN

The design that was eventually selected for the Berlin memorial, the one proposed by American architect Peter Eisenman, does not shy away from being monumental, but does not attempt to individualize each death. Located in downtown Berlin, it consists of a gigantic field of 2,711 rectangular stelae of

---

[5]   Joseph Roach, *Cities of the Dead: Circum-Atlantic Performance* (New York: Columbia University Press, 1996), 36.

[6]   Roach, *Cities of the Dead*, 3.

different heights, through which visitors wander, and an underground Information Center, which presents a small but powerful exhibit about the Holocaust. The abstract stelae do not bear a name, a date, or any reference to the Holocaust. As Eisenman explains, »Today, an individual can no longer be certain to die an individual death, and architecture can no longer remember life as it once did. The markers that were formerly symbols of individual life and death must be changed, and this has a profound effect on the idea of memory and the monument.«[7] The architecture blurs the lines. The slabs are so similar to tombstones and the accumulation of stelae so mindful of a cemetery that visitors are confused, and some act as if in a cemetery. They walk slowly until they find an evocative pillar in the forest, and leave an object according to their spiritual tradition: Some take their hat off and light a red candle with engraved crosses on a slab, as they would in a church. Others cover their head and lay a stone on the flat surface, following Jewish tradition. Others leave a flower. The presence of objects associated with mourning and remembrance, along with the silent and somber attitude of these visitors, is an embodied performance of memory that clearly identifies the field of stelae as a memorial. However, the material traces they leave behind, such as candles, flowers, or stones are quickly removed by the housekeeping staff; as if, from the management's perspective, the stelae were to be admired as artwork, but not to be used as a memorial.

In spite of its nominal and geographical centrality, the Berlin Holocaust memorial has been ignored by elected officials, foreign dignitaries, the organized Jewish community, and other organizations for commemorative needs. Some fierce critics of the memorial feared that it would become a »wreath-dumping place« (*Kranzabwurfstelle*). They can be reassured: there is no date for wreaths to be brought, no space designed for this purpose, and no political impulse to commemorate the Holocaust at the Memorial. The design, without a focal point and without a space dedicated to gatherings, prevents any ceremonial use. It is an »anti-commemorative« memorial, both for collective and individual purposes. Individual commemorations performed with traditional objects relate to a time in the past, an approach criticized by Eisenman as »a nostalgia located in the past touched with a sentimentality that remembers things not as they were, but as we want to remember them.«[8] Meanwhile, official visits of foreign dignitaries continue to halt at the manda-

---

[7]   Peter Eisenman, »Memorial to the Murdered Jews of Europe.«, in *Materials on the Memorial to the Murdered Jews of Europe* (Berlin: Nicolai, 2005), 10.

[8]   Peter Eisenman, »Memorial to the Murdered Jews of Europe.«, 12.

Ritual objects at the Holocaust Memorial in Berlin. Photo: Brigitte Sion

tory station of the Neue Wache, the memorial broadly dedicated to »victims of war and tyranny«, with the laying of a wreath, a moment of silence, and brief closing of the edifice to the general public during the ceremony. Lack of interest in this memorial – even parties that supported it rarely use it – reflects perhaps what James Young had warned about Holocaust memorials in Germany: »The best German memorial to the Fascist era and its victims may not be a single memorial at all – but simply the never-to-be-resolved debate over which kind of memory to preserve, how to do it, in whose names, and to what end.«[9]

The public, however, reacted differently to the memorial. In spite of rules of conduct displayed in German at the corners of the field of stelae, many visitors jumped on the slabs, ate, drank, screamed, or sunbathed. Eisenman seemed to anticipate and even condone this behavior on German national television the night before the opening, when he said he was »now handing over the memorial to the German people and the population of Berlin. They will decide what to do with it. If they want to dance or have a picnic on the stelae, that's fine with me.« This statement is consistent with Eisenman's rejection of signage, fences, rules of conduct, or any normative markers. He also re-

---

[9]   James Young, *The Texture of Memory: Holocaust Memorials and Meaning* (New Haven: Yale University Press, 1993), 21.

sisted the Information Center and its didactic mission, but eventually agreed to it.

The field of stelae receives a lot of traffic, not of the best kind. A number of graffiti – swastikas, stars of David and short slogans – repeatedly deface the monument, but are swiftly removed by the maintenance staff. The memorial has been used as a urinal and a sex scene, according to media reports. In the summer of 2006, a wooden building was constructed on the east side of the Cora-Berliner-Strasse, for fast food stands, a souvenir store, a beer garden, and a terrace overlooking the field of stelae. On Hannah-Arendt-Strasse, the parking spots reserved for tourist buses are often full. A year after its opening, in 2006, the memorial had attracted 3.5 million people, and 500,000 had visited the Information Center, which was considered a major success. Six years later, the »Eisenman Memorial«, as it is commonly called, is first and foremost an architectural landmark of the New Berlin, a political legacy of the Kohl era, and a place of leisure. The numerous rituals taking place – play, socializing, buying and selling of commodities – are remote from commemorative practices.

In an interesting case of inversion, however, the Information Center does what the memorial does not. It is not by accident that it is called an »information center«, for it does provide information, which the memorial decidedly does not. Paradoxically, the informative display not only informs but also memorializes more effectively than the memorial itself. Whereas the monument refuses to individualize the dead, the Information Center emphasizes the uniqueness and diversity of lives lost in four different ways. The first room, the Room of Places, tells the story of a few individual Holocaust victims through quotes from diaries and letters, pictures, and other personal visual materials. On a frieze around the room, the fifteen countries from which Jews were deported are listed, together with the number of murdered victims. The second room, the Room of Families, reminds visitors of the geographic scope of the Holocaust: Nazis deported Jews from countries as far apart as Norway and Albania, from small Greek islands and remote Ukrainian villages, from big cities such as Vienna or Rome and *shtetls* such as Radzilow (Poland) and Stefanesti (Romania). The exhibit portrays the itinerary of one family from each of the 15 countries from which Jews were taken to their death. Each family member is identified by name, place and date of birth, occupation, and fate during the war; each person also appears in one or more photographs. Together, these family itineraries make up a social portrait of Holocaust victims that includes wealthy Berlin merchants and poor Polish peddlers, ultra-Orthodox men with beards and side curls, young women dressed in the latest

French fashion, children going to school, and the elderly playing cards. The third room, the Room of Names, is the most ambitious effort to give individualized expression to Holocaust remembrance. The room is dark; names appear as white, ghostly letters; the tone of voice is somber, solemn. The litany of names resembles a religious ceremony of remembrance. Visitors slow down, freeze, stare at the names, and listen to the life stories: a child from Dresden, a grandmother from Budapest, a student from Lyons, a singer from Venice. One more. It is hard to exit the room, to leave the ongoing performance, to interrupt the witnessing experience. It would take about seven years to listen to all the life stories. Nevertheless, visitors spend a few minutes, a few biographies, in this unexpectedly solemn setting. »Individual life stories are thereby lifted out of the anonymity of the enormous numbers of victims«,[10] writes Sibylle Quack, former director of the Memorial and curator of the exhibit. The voice gives body to the names and shines a light on individual fates by inscribing them into history with their birth and death dates, into a geography with their country of origin and destination of deportation, into society with their occupation, and into the Holocaust with their place of death and their identity as documented victim. In the dark underground, visitors have affective reactions to the displays: They are silent, they sob, clutch hands. They learn about the Holocaust through embodied experiences, which anthropologist Thomas Csordas calls »somatic modes of attention,« or »ways of attending to and with one's body in surroundings that include the embodied presence of others.«[11] Philosopher Edward Casey applied the embodied perspective to the study of memory, and showed how the body was »at once a transmitter of the inheritance of the external world and itself an inheritance for perception in the present.«[12] In other words, visitors of the Information Center remember in, by, and through their bodies.

The field of stelae and the Information Center are both designed as memorials to the Holocaust; the design located aboveground does not generate commemorative practices. I would thus argue that it is a failed memorial, but a successful work of public art. Simultaneously, the underground exhibit induces affective reactions of mourning and remembrance that can only be witnessed in this part of the memorial.

---

[10]   Sibylle Quack, »Creating an Exhibition about the Murder of European Jews.«, in *Materials on the Memorial to the Murdered Jews of Europe* (Berlin: Nicolai, 2005), 147.

[11]   Thomas Csordas, »Somatic Modes of Attention.« *Cultural Anthropology* 8 (1993): 138.

[12]   Edward S. Casey, *Remembering: A Phenomenological Study* (Bloomington: Indiana University Press, 1987), 174.

THE MONUMENT TO THE VICTIMS OF STATE TERRORISM IN BUENOS AIRES

While it may be somewhat easier to commemorate 30,000 individual disappeared than six million who perished in the Holocaust, the Argentine tragedy faces a similar challenge in addressing the discrepancy between an iconic number that is constantly used as a reference and the documented facts about victims. The iconic number is in dispute: The 1984 report of the CONADEP, the National Commission on Disappeared Persons, included an updated database of over 9,000 names; new ones continue to be added. Recent declassified documents in the United States point to 22,000 *desaparecidos*.[13] Rather than reverting to metaphorical, symbolic, or collective representation of victims, architect Alberto Varas decided to confront this discrepancy and embedded it in his design. The Monument to the Victims of State Terrorism was unveiled in 2007. It is a wall of names located along the River Plate, in the Park of Memory, which also hosts a dozen artworks associated with the *desaparecidos* and a documentation center. The 2-meter-high wall includes 30,000 individual 70-cm-long plaques made of Argentine porphyry. About two thirds of them remain empty, nameless, »thus commemorating the violent voiding of identity that was the torturers' explicit goal and preceded disappearance«,[14] writes Andreas Huyssen. Indeed, the empty plaques echo the empty graves – or the absence thereof – that characterize the tragedy of the *desaparecidos.* Framed by these empty plaques at the top and bottom of each wall panel, the names and ages of 8,718 victims appear etched in the stone, displayed by year of disappearance and alphabetically within each year. Journalist José Pablo Feinmann argues, »The accumulation of names has a visual power that numbers lack. It is one thing to say ›eight thousand‹, it is another to ›see‹ eight thousand names written on stone. This is an eerie, indelible view. It nears the horrific dimension with more power than an abstract number.«[15] Furthermore, the juxtaposition of names on the wall offers a diversified image of Argentina: a country of immigrants with Spanish, Russian, Italian, French, Arab, Scottish, Jewish, Basque, and Japanese names; a country of young people, many in their late teens and twenties; and a precocious

---

[13]   Hugo Alonada Mon, »El Ejército admitió 22.000 crímenes.« *La Nación*, March 24, 2006.

[14]   Andreas Huyssen, *Present Pasts: Urban Palimpsests and the Politics of Memory* (Stanford: Stanford University Press, 2003), 103.

[15]   José Pablo Feinmann, »El rio y la memoria.« *Página/12*, December 13, 1997.

Mother honoring her disappeared son at Buenos Aires Memorial. Photo: Brigitte Sion

birth rate, with as many as 500 pregnant women listed among the *desapare-cidos.*

The encounter with death is felt *ex negativo* in the living bodies of the visi-tors, who have to adjust their pace and their breathing, pause, and be physi-cally conscious of their presence in a site marked with absence. Visitors literally experience the memorial with their feet and with their hands. »I want to touch the name of my son«, said Tati Almeida, one of the Mothers of the Plaza de Mayo. »I want to touch it.«[16] On the day of the unveiling of the monu-ment, there were many mothers, fathers, siblings, and friends of *desapareci-dos* who stood for some long minutes in front of a wall panel, a hand or arm covering a name, stroking relief letters, a head bent low in prayer or medita-tion. As a surrogate for absent bodily remains and graves, these granite plaques invite a physical contact between deceased and mourner, probably the first tangible encounter since the disappearance, and the closest gesture to a physical, sensual, motherly embrace, not between two skins, but between skin and stone, life and death. Touching the letters »gives body« to a dead per-son reduced to a name, and infuses a name with memory through the medi-ation of the living body.

The Parque de la Memoria is intended as a place for families and sur-vivors to gather, collect their thoughts, and remember the *desaparecidos.* Ceremonies already took place by the River Plate, when the Monument was

---

[16]   Tati Almeida, »Quiero tocar el nombre de mi hijo ...« *Ramona* 9–10 (Buenos Aires, De-cember 2000-March 2001): 10.

still in construction. Human rights activist Patricia Valdez describes the first tribute to the *desaparecidos* in front of the river:

> A moving religious-ecumenical act that peaked when the attendees threw flowers in the water, final destination of a large number of desaparecidos. The River Plate can now be recognized as a ›historical site‹, where families of victims can convene, remember and ›lay‹ flowers on the place that has become the grave of many.[17]

Some relatives of *desaparecidos* have organized private ceremonies there, such as memorial services, or even funerals during which the ashes of a relative are scattered in the River Plate. This happened on March 9, 2008; the Foundation for Historical and Social Memory in Buenos Aires published a death announcement for Lola Weinschelbaum de Rubino, inviting relatives, friends, and comrades to a ceremony at the Parque de la Memoria. There, »according to her wishes, her ashes will be thrown into the River Plate to reunite symbolically with her daughter Raquel, who was detained and disappeared.«[18] This ritual was performed on the promenade along the river; other ceremonies take place in an area on the right edge of the park designed for larger gatherings, such as the International Day of the Disappeared (August 30) or the anniversary of the military coup (March 24). Before its completion, the Parque de la Memoria was a site of symbolic commemoration. Since its unveiling, it has also become a place to hold funerals for individuals who associate so strongly with the river and the name of their child on the wall that they voluntarily turn the memorial into their final place of rest, engendering new rituals for funerals and memorialization. The official competition guidelines for the Park's sculpture garden were unequivocal and decisive:

> The memorial park does not intend to heal wounds that cannot be healed, nor should it be a substitute for truth and justice. Nothing will give back true peace to those who could never find out the final destiny of their beloved ones, brutally tortured and murdered without trial. This park will stand as a testimony, a symbolic memento and homage to those whose lives were obliterated and who became known to the world as ›desaparecidos.‹[19]

---

[17]   Patricia Tappatá de Valdez, »El Parque de la Memoria en Buenos Aires.«, in *Monumentos, memoriales y marcas territoriales*, eds. Elizabeth Jelin and Victoria Langland (Madrid: Siglo XXI, 2003), 98.

[18]   »Lola Weinschelbaum de Rubino.«, email sent by Memoria Abierta to its mailing list, March 7, 2008.

[19]   *Escultura y Memoria: 665 Proyectos Presentados Al Concurso En Homenaje a Los De-*

Although the project started with grandiose ambitions as a national memorial, an architectural and artistic landmark, and a magnet to an otherwise peripheral area, the Park of Memory has remained a place mostly visited by Argentine nationals – survivors, relatives, students, and other visitors with a connection or an interest in recent history. At a time when the elderly Mothers of the Disappeared have stopped their weekly silent marches on the Plaza de Mayo, the Park of Memory has perhaps become the central memorial site for Argentina's *desaparecidos*, a site that invites transgenerational rituals of mourning and remembrance.

The double challenge of the enormity of the tragedy and the uncertainty surrounding the documentation of individual names and fate have forced the Berlin and the Buenos Aires memorials to combine both approaches rather than settle for either one alone. The Eisenman design offers monumentality and anonymity, while the underground exhibit focuses on intimacy and individuality. The Varas design blends an iconic number and individual names, while commemorating the absences created by the disappearances and the erasure of the crime, and identifying those victims whose fate could be documented. In Berlin and Buenos Aires, the national memorials were not erected on the exact site where murder occurred, but they are close and carry a strong symbolic association to the perpetrators: The Nazi chancellery and Hitler's bunker were located in the vicinity of the current Holocaust memorial, while the Wall of Names is near the ESMA, the naval academy and main torture center dubbed »the Argentine Auschwitz«, as well as the River Plate, where hundreds of disappeared were thrown to their deaths from military airplanes.

CHOEUNG EK GENOCIDAL CENTER IN PHNOM-PENH

In Cambodia, most memorials are site-specific mass graves, prisons, or ossuaries. Between 1975 and 1979, a Marxist dictatorship, the self-proclaimed »Democratic Kampuchea«, or Khmer Rouge regime, under the leadership of Pol Pot, caused the death of about 1.5 million people, or a quarter of the population. Thirty years later, memorialization of the genocide stands at the center of conflicted interests – the government's politics of reconciliation, Bud-

tenidos desaparecidos y Asesinados Por El Terrorismo De Estado En La Argentina (Buenos Aires: Comisión Pro Monumento a las Victimas del Terrorismo de Estado & Eudeba, 2000), 13.

dhist beliefs in Karma, economic development, mass tourism opportunities, international law, and national historical narratives.

There are over one hundred memorial sites related to the genocide in Cambodia, from mass graves to urns and ossuaries to public artworks, but most of them are scattered in the provinces and not easily identifiable by foreign visitors. This partially explains why local memorials have not generated much scholarship. Most attention has focused on the Tuol Sleng prison and the Choeung Ek killing fields, the first »genocide museums« that meant to display the crimes of the Khmer Rouge while primarily fulfilling a political agenda. In other words, Choeung Ek, our case study, did not become a tourism destination over time; curatorial and marketing strategies to attract visitors have been essential from its inception.

Located ten miles southeast of Phnom-Penh, Choeung Ek is described, on the official flyer, as »hell on earth in the 20th century«. A former orchard and Chinese cemetery, it was the main killing field where prisoners from Tuol Sleng prison were transported to be murdered between 1977 and 1978. When Vietnamese troops discovered the site, they found about 9,000 bodies in mass graves; many were headless, their hands tied, and naked; the separated heads were blindfolded. The skulls and bones showed traces of bullets, knives, and other forms of violence inflicted upon men, women, and children. Babies were thrown against trees and instantly killed. Choeung Ek opened to the public in 1989, after Lim Ourk was commissioned to build a monumental *stupa* where 8,000 skulls and bones would be preserved. A *stupa*, according to Rachel Hughes, is »a sacred structure that contains the remains of the deceased – especially those of greatly revered individuals – in Buddhist cultures. The construction of *stupa* is a significant activity that produces merit for the living and encourages the remembrance of the dead.«[20] This *stupa* is inspired by Khmer religious motifs, such as the snakes (*naga*) and lions that guard the edifice, and by traditional architecture – the roof and pediments resemble the Royal Palace in Phnom-Penh. However, contrary to *stupas* in other parts of the country, this one contains the anonymous remains of ordinary people.

Through the glass doors, one can see hundreds of skulls and human bones stacked almost to the top of the 62-meter-high structure. The glass doors are ajar, and the skulls stare at the visitors. Foreign tourists constitute over 90 percent of the total visitors, according to the 2007 and 2008 statistics

---

[20] Rachel Hughes: »Memory and Sovereignty in Post-1979 Cambodia: Choeung Ek and Local Genocide Memorials.«, in *Genocide in Cambodia and Rwanda: New Perspectives*, ed. Susan E. Cook (New Brunswick and London: Transaction Publishers, 2006), 261.

released by the administration of the memorial.[21] In line with this statistic, the development and management of the site seem to be entirely geared towards international tourism. The mission statement on the official flyer indicates, »Choeung Ek Killing Field became a historical museum for humankind and is one of the most popular attractions for both domestic and foreign tourists in Phnom-Penh.«[22] Since 1993 and the establishment of the Kingdom of Cambodia, the Killing Field has seen thousands of tourists from capitalist countries (Australia, Japan, South Korea, United States, France, Germany, etc.). Consequently, it has adapted its offering to mass tourism: a US $ 3 entrance fee charged to foreign visitors, guided tours, marketing with travel agents, pamphlets in various languages, bathrooms, a souvenir shop, a food and drink stand, and parking areas.

Choeung Ek has become a symbol for thanatourism, defined by A.V. Seaton as »traveling to a location wholly, or partially, motivated by the desire for actual or symbolic encounters with death, particularly, but not exclusively, violent death.«[23] Thanatourism is a subgenre of tourism, an industry usually dedicated to leisure, time out, and escape. Its goal is to market attractions and pleasurable experiences rather than moral uplift. Marketing a memorial requires a delicate negotiation between staying true to the serious purpose of the memorial and promoting it as an attractive destination that recounts a country's negative history. Choeung Ek is still struggling to find a sensitive balance.

The official management policy lists the following goals: »Preserve genocide history . . .; make Choeung Ek an international symbol of genocide; bring Choeung Ek to the attention of the world; make Choeung Ek a model for conservation.«[24] The means to achieve the goals include improving communication with tourists, generating income by attracting more tourists, finding

---

[21]   In 2007, there were 13,000 Cambodian and 181,000 foreign visitors; in 2008, 15,000 Cambodians and 195,000 foreigners. See the detail by month from 2005 to 2008 on the official website: »Statistics.« Choeung Ek Genocidal Center, http://www.cekillingfield.com/statistics.htm (accessed February 8, 2011).

[22]   See also »About Choeung Ek.« Choeung Ek Genocidal Center, http://www.cekillingfield.com/aboutchoeungek.htm (accessed February 8, 2011).

[23]   A. V. Seaton, »Guided by the Dark: From Thanatopsis to Thanatourism.« *International Journal of Heritage Studies* 2 (1996): 240.

[24]   *Management Policy for Choeung Ek Genocide Center,* document in Khmer given by Choeung Ek deputy director Ros Sophearavy on 8/12/2009 and translated into English by Sin Saroeun.

alternative sources of income aside from the entrance fee, and developing ties with other tourism sites such as the Tuol Sleng prison. The strategic plan recommends »the progressive enhancement of the facilities so as to increase income by providing resting chairs, a coffee shop, a restaurant, a souvenir and bookshop and toilets; the development of a calendar of special events, information projects, lectures that will eventually attract 1,000 visitors per day.«[25]

The notions of remembrance or memory are almost absent from the official document; so are Cambodian nationals who do not seem worthy of much attention, as opposed to paying international tourists.

This situation may have to do with the 2005 takeover of Choeung Ek by a Japanese corporation, JC Royal, which obtained from the Cambodian government a 30-year license to operate the site in exchange of an annual $ 15,000 fee and the award of a few scholarships to needy Cambodian students. The agreement between the government and the private company created a major controversy; to this day, the profit made from Choeung Ek remains a mystery, as are the operating budget and the number of scholarships allotted.[26] What is clear is that the killing fields are a source of profit, whose beneficiaries are neither survivors nor relatives of victims.

Visitors wander freely in the vast compound that includes excavated pits with signs bearing minimalist descriptions: »mass grave of 166 victims without heads«. There is no trail to follow, no itinerary. Some excavated pits are fenced, other graves are untouched, and people often walk on clothes and bone parts that stick out of the ground. Nobody pays attention to the rules displayed at the entrance, such as »please dress suitably while remaining at the center«, or »bones and other items in the center are not allowed to take out«. In fact, most foreign visitors wear light summer clothes, such as shorts and sleeveless T-shirts; some stand by the *stupa* drinking soda or smoking, while others touch the skulls through the open door.

The high point of Choeung Ek is not didactic, but visual – the *stupa* and its stacks of skulls at a hand's reach. Skulls are aestheticized – clean, neatly arranged in a window case – and their endless accumulation turns the victims into statistics. The shock value of this raw display lies both in the prox-

---

[25]   Ibid.

[26]   See, for example, the investigative article by Chhang Bopha, »›Killing Fields‹: pas de trace d'aménagement du site après trois ans de gestion privée,« *Ka-Set* (May 21, 2008), http://ka-set.info/actualites/khmers-rouges/cambodge-actualite-khmers-rouges-choeung-ek-killing-fields-memorial-080521.html (accessed February 10, 2011).

Stupa filled with human bones. Choeung Ek Killing Fields, Cambodia. Photo: Brigitte Sion

imity of death and in the objectification of human remains, in the tension between the educational agenda of the memorial site and the commodification
of genocide. A national debate arose after the discovery of thousands of
unidentified and often incomplete dead bodies: Should they be preserved?
Cremated? Buried? The government argued in favor of preserving and ex-
hibiting human remains as evidence of the crimes perpetrated by the Khmer
Rouge, and as a pedagogical resource to educate the Cambodian population.
This attitude served the propaganda of the time, which emphasized the
crimes of the Khmer Rouge regime so as to affirm the control of the country
by the »clean« PRK party.

The King held the opposite view:

> Sihanouk and prominent members of the Buddhist order have given vocal
> support to the idea that all the bones of the dead should be gathered together and
> given a mass incineration in tune with Buddhist values. The resulting ashes
> would then be enshrined in a national stupa envisaged as offering the possibility
> of rebirth both to the individual victims and the nation as a whole. In February
> 2004, the King made the following characteristically robust statement on his web-
> site: »What Buddhist man or woman accepts that, instead of incinerating their
> dead relatives, ... one displays their skulls and their skeletons to please ›voy-
> eurs‹?«[27]

---

[27]   Quoted in Ian Harris, *Buddhism under Pol Pot* (Phnom-Penh: Documentation Center
of Cambodia, 2007), 233.

According to Khmer Buddhism, »the souls of persons who die sudden deaths, considered to be untimely deaths, deaths which are not good, will remain around the place where they died. They will not be reborn as is ordinarily the case. Villagers fear these souls very much, fear that the spirits of those who died sudden deaths will haunt them or cause good people to fall ill.«[28] Traditionally, people who die suddenly or violently are cremated or buried as quickly as possible, on the site where they died. A violent death is particularly inauspicious; cremation immediately following death allows the spirit to move into the next karmic realm, instead of haunting the place of death forever. However, in the case of mass murder, where bodies were often dismembered, putrefied, impossible to identify, mixed with others in mass graves, and discovered years after the death, many Cambodians faced a religious dilemma and eventually seemed to support the preservation of skulls and human remains. »This support is reinforced by an underlying belief in Buddhist tradition that people can cremate only the remains of their family members. Because virtually no individuals in the country's killing fields have been identified from their remains, cremation could pose some obstacles in Cambodia.«[29]

If traditional rituals cannot be performed, one can understand that Cambodians have no personal or religious stake in the human remains on display at Choeung Ek. This would also explain the relative lack of interest from Cambodians for Choeung Ek as a memorial. »Both religious relics and bodies in museums are recontextualized human remains, removed from the graveyard or tomb, sites often associated with both literal and metaphorical pollution, into another sacred context where they are preserved for a different function«. Mary Brooks and Claire Rumsey observe:

> Museums objectify the bones conceptually for research and display. Whether the motivation is theological or analytical, macabre or morbid, the display of dead bodies is an increasingly contested issue. Displaying bodies can serve as connection of the past with the present, and the dead with the living, offering succor, solace, inspiration, or information, but it also renders them ambivalent, both ›persons and things‹.[30]

---

[28]   Phra Khru Anusaranasasanakiarti and Charles F. Keyes, »Funerary Rites and the Buddhist Meaning of Death: An Interpretative Text from Northern Thailand.« *Journal of the Siam Society* 68 (January 1980): 1–28.

[29]   Wynne Cougill, »Remains of the Dead: Buddhist Tradition, Evidence, and Memory.«, in *Night of the Khmer Rouge: Genocide and Justice in Cambodia*, ed. Jorge Daniel Veneciano and Alexander Hinton (Newark: Paul Robeson Gallery, 2007), 32–48.

The bones in Choeung Ek have lost their spiritual value and elicit only mild interest from locals. They serve a higher purpose as evidence or educational tool than as an improbable vehicle for karmic reincarnation and personal closure. For tourists, the skulls still carry a shock value, but it is sanitized by the transformation of human remains as objects on display behind glass.

However, in villages where people were killed and buried on premises, the bones retrieved from local mass graves have kept their spiritual connection. The whole community took part in the excavation and transfer of remains into a *stupa*, often near the village's temple. This participatory act was not always spontaneous and sometimes responded to repeated government calls, which asked »all local authorities at the province and municipal level [to] cooperate with relevant expert institutions in their areas to examine, restore and maintain all existing memorials, and to examine and research other remaining grave sites, so that all such places may be transformed into memorials.«[31] The excavation of pits and transfer of human remains into a *stupa* was not a sheer forensic act; it was a religious ritual that had to be performed by spiritual leaders.

In the years following Democratic Kampuchea, meeting the required quorum of monks to lead such ceremonies became a challenge. Over 60,000 monks had been killed or left Cambodia under Khmer Rouge rule. »Ordination in the early post-Khmer Rouge period proved difficult«, as Ian Harris remarks. »Some took to shaving their heads and wearing white and, in this way, Buddhist ceremonies, particularly those commemorating the dead, were performed.«[32] Both the responsibility of completing the physical transfer of bones and the religious rituals fell upon lay people – who were all survivors and mourners. As of 2007, the Documentation Center of Cambodia has identified close to 20,000 mass graves, as well as 81 memorial sites located throughout Cambodia.[33]

One such local memorial stands at Kampong Tralagh, in the Kampot province, southwest of Phnom-Penh, not far from the Vietnamese border.

---

30   Mary M. Brooks and Claire Rumsey, »The Body in the Museum,« in *Human Remains: Guide for Museums and Academic Institutions,* eds. Vicki Cassman, Nancy Odegaard, and Joseph Powell (Lanham: Altamira Press, 2006), 261.

31   Cited in Cougill, »Remains of the Dead.«, 40.

32   Ian Harris, »Buddhism in Extremis: The Case of Cambodia.«, in *Buddhism and Politics in Twentieth Century Asia,* ed. Ian Harris (London: Cassell, 1999), 54–78.

33   Veneciano and Hinton, *Night of the Khmer Rouge,* 109.

Most villagers work in the adjacent rice fields. In the heart of the village is a majestic pagoda, tall, old, well-kept, and beautifully decorated. Its typical Khmer architecture echoes the Royal Palace and the Choeung Ek *stupa*: the four receding roofs each have an ornate triangular pediment that is guarded by erect snakes. The white, gold, and orange pagoda is surrounded with lush greenery; the area is very quiet, even with workers toiling in rice fields.

A few feet away stands a much more modest edifice – a little house painted in white, with a traditional roof and erect snakes. It is small, almost invisible in the shadow of the impressive pagoda. The door is open. The single room is split into two, one side for skulls, one side for bones. Hundreds of bones ara piled up. There are dozens of those in Cambodia, often built near the pagoda so as to balance good and evil. The local ossuaries were built by villagers who have reclaimed their dead, their history, and their spiritual lives.

Penh Samarn, patriarch monk at the Kroch Seuch pagoda, who initiated the construction of such a memorial, combines a spiritual and a practical perspective.

> I do not want to lose the evidence, so that people from various places can come to pray and pay homage to the dead. ... I am thinking of having monks stay there and for people to come and pay homage because some souls of the dead have made their parents or children dream of them, and told them that they are wandering around and have not reincarnated in another world. I want to have monks meditating there so that the souls of the dead will rest in peace. In Buddhism, when someone dies and their mind is still with this world, then their souls wander around.[34]

Local villagers honor the dead on various occasions, often individually. In his film on the Tuol Sleng prison, *S-21*, Rithy Panh interviews the parents of a former Khmer Rouge soldier; they beg him to hold a religious ceremony to chase the evil spirits. »Hold a ceremony so that we never see those men again. Become a new man ... Tell the truth, then have a ceremony. Make an offering to the dead so that they find peace, so there is no more bad karma in the future. Ask the dead to remove the bad karma.«[35] A communal occasion to com-

---

[34] Cited in Cougill, »Remains of the Dead.«, 40.

[35] *S21: The Khmer Rouge Killing Machine*, DVD, directed by Rithy Panh (New York: First Run Features, 2003).

memorate the dead takes place on the Day of the Ancestors, *Phachum Benn*, a fifteen-day period that falls some time around September and October according to the lunar calendar, during which locals dedicate offerings to the spirits of the ancestors that they bring to temples and *stupas*.

No such ceremony takes place at Choeung Ek, which is ignored by Cambodians and government officials throughout the year. This reality confirms that Choeung Ek is not meant to be a memorial site, but an efficient moneymaker benefiting from international tourism. Officials considered piles of skulls and bones as a sheer commodity that, once publicly exhibited, covered up the involvement of former Khmer Rouge still active in public affairs and enjoying complete impunity. They established artificial commemorations that did not acknowledge the suffering of the Cambodian people, the responsibility of the State in the genocide, or the need for mourning rituals, moral and material reparations, and complete accountability. Instead, Choeung Ek induces another kind of performance: it generates income, absolves the government composed of former Khmer Rouge, and satisfies the international community by acknowledging past crimes publicly.

At the end of the 20th century, the most violent in the history of humanity, memorialization efforts have also seen an evolution in their architecture, mission, and actual usage by the public. Our three case studies have shown that memorials have agency of different kinds – inviting visitors to play or pray, admire or acquire an object, take a picture or leave a flower. The conflicted forms of engagement with memorials also depend on the type of visitors, Germans and tourists in Berlin, locals associated with the tragedy in Buenos Aires, Western tourists in Phnom-Penh, and villagers in Cambodian provinces. Given their agency, fluidity, and ambiguous identity, it would not be surprising to see all three memorials transform again, in a give-and-take performance of remembrance and oblivion.

Literature

Alonada Mon, Hugo. »El Ejército admitió 22.000 crímenes.« *La Nación*, March 24, 2006.

Anusaranasasanakiarti, Phra Khru, and Charles F. Keyes. »Funerary Rites and the Buddhist Meaning of Death: An Interpretative Text from Northern Thailand.« *Journal of the Siam Society* 68, no. 1 (January 1980): 1–28.

Boss, Pauline. *Ambiguous Loss: Learning to Live with Unresolved Grief.* Cambridge: Harvard University Press, 1999.

Brodsky, Marcelo. »Génesis y evolución de una idea.« *Ramona: Revista de Artes Visuales*, 9–10, (December 2000-March 2001), 6–7. http://www.ramona.org.ar/files/r9y10.pdf (accessed February 8, 2011).

Brooks, Mary M., and Claire Rumsey. »The Body in the Museum.« In *Human Remains: Guide for Museums and Academic Institutions*, eds. Vicki Cassman, Nancy Odegaard, and Joseph Powell. Lanham: Altamira Press, 2006.

Casey, Edward S. *Remembering: A Phenomenological Study.* Bloomington: Indiana University Press, 1987.

Cougill, Wynne. »Remains of the Dead: Buddhist Tradition, Evidence, and Memory.« In *Night of the Khmer Rouge: Genocide and Justice in Cambodia*, edited by Jorge Daniel Veneciano and Alexander Hinton, 32–48. Newark: Paul Robeson Gallery, 2007.

Csordas, Thomas J. »Somatic Modes of Attention.« *Cultural Anthropology* 8, no. 2 (1993): 135–156.

Eisenman, Peter. »Memorial to the Murdered Jews of Europe.« In *Materials on the Memorial to the Murdered Jews of Europe.* Berlin: Nicolai, 2005.

Escultura y Memoria: 665 Proyectos Presentados Al Concurso En Homenaje a Los Detenidos desaparecidos y Asesinados Por El Terrorismo De Estado En La Argentina. Buenos Aires: Comisión Pro Monumento a las Victimas del Terrorismo de Estado & Eudeba, 2000.

Feinmann, José Pablo. »El Rio y La Memoria.« *Página/12*, (December 13, 1997).

Harris, Ian. »Buddhism in Extremis: The Case of Cambodia.« In *Buddhism and Politics in Twentieth Century Asia*, edited by Ian Harris, 54–78. London: Cassell, 1999.

Harris, Ian. *Buddhism under Pol Pot.* Phnom-Penh: Documentation Center of Cambodia, 2007.

Hughes, Rachel. »Memory and Sovereignty in Post-1979 Cambodia, Choeung Ek and Local Genocide Memorials.« In *Genocide in Cambodia and Rwanda: New Perspectives*, edited by Susan E. Cook, 257–279. New Brunswick and London: Transaction Publishers, 2006.

Huyssen, Andreas. *Present Pasts: Urban Palimpsests and the Politics of Memory.* Stanford: Stanford University Press, 2003.

Panh, Rithy: *S21: The Khmer Rouge Killing Machine*, DVD, (New York: First Run Features, 2003).

Quack, Sibylle and Dagmar von Wilcken. »Creating an Exhibition about the Murder of European Jews.« In *Materials on the Memorial to the Murdered Jews of Europe*, 40–48. Berlin: Nicolai, 2005.

Roach, Joseph. *Cities of the Dead: Circum-Atlantic Performance.* New York: Columbia University Press, 1996.

Seaton, Anthony V. »Guided by the Dark: From Thanatopsis to Thanatourism.« *International Journal of Heritage Studies* 2 (1996): 234–244.

Sorin, Sergio. »Argentina le pone nombre y apellido a sus desaparecidos.« *El Sitio,* February 17, 1999.

Turner, Victor. *The Ritual Process: Structure and Anti-Structure.* Chicago: Aldine Publishing Company, 1969.

Tappatá de Valdez, Patricia. »El Parque de la Memoria en Buenos Aires.« In *Monumentos, memoriales y marcas territoriales,* edited by Elizabeth Jelin and Victoria Langland, 97–11. Madrid: Siglo XXI, 2003.

Young, James. *The Texture of Memory: Holocaust Memorials and Meaning.* New Haven: Yale University Press, 1993.

Religion, Politics, and Genocide in Rwanda

Jean-Pierre Karegeye

General Considerations

From April to July 1994, an estimated one million people were killed in Rwanda. More than 10,000 were killed every single day for three months. This mass killing was not the product of an emotional reaction. It was systematically planned by the Rwandan State. Certain political parties and the administration were committed to exterminating the Tutsi population. This genocide happened in one of the most Christianized countries in the world. It has marked the history of the Catholic Church in Rwanda. After a century of evangelization, Christians killed, enthusiastically or forcedly, other Christians seeking refuge in churches during the genocide. In 1994, victims hoped they would find a sanctuary in the church, while perpetrators turned over crosses, destroyed sacred images, smashed altars and trampled hosts. More than one million people were atrociously massacred, more than 300 religious and priests, including three bishops, were also killed. How, in one of the most Christianized countries in Africa, was genocide made possible? How could a country being reputed as Christian, with a Catholic majority, be unable to resist forces of hatred and self-destruction? Most importantly, how did moral Christian teaching and faith touch and transform concrete challenges of the surrounding human tragedy?

Through textual analysis, this essay tries to explore the influence of the political discourse that sponsored mass violence on Rwandan Catholic bishops' letters and messages during the war. I claim that the rhetoric of unity, peace, reconciliation, and development employed by the bishops became finally a means of implicit support of a political rhetoric that prepared the stage for genocide.

The bishops' writings function like a parchment or »palimpsest«.[1] Just unroll it and discover other texts from which it derived. One can distinguish at least three narrative voices within the bishops' letters and messages. They conceal voices such as the one by President Habyarimana, which may be called ›hypotext‹[2] or ›pro-text‹. It is used as a common source for pastoral letters and the official media. The second voice reflects the usual expression of faithfulness to the Gospel and the teachings of the Church. The third narrative voice constitutes the ›paratext‹; it can be discovered in »The Collection of Letters and Messages of the Catholic Bishops Conference in Rwanda, published during wartime (1990–1994)« and in the »Presentation« delivered by Reverend Ladislas Habimana, then secretary for the Conference of Catholic Bishops in Rwanda.

CITATION AS MIMESIS

The »Collection of Letters and Messages of the Catholic Bishops Conference in Rwanda published during wartime (1990–1994)« hinges on three letters concerning »unity«, written at the time of the visit of Pope John Paul II to Rwanda on September 7–9, 1990. These are followed by a group of ten letters and messages between November 7, 1990 and December 21, 1995, covering the war period, and a letter dated January 13, 1995 on pastoral priorities after the war. The *Recueil des Lettres et Messages (R.L.M) de la Conférence des Evêques Catholiques du Rwanda publiés pendant la guerre*[3] has been used as a source of quotations by the Secretariat General during the Catholic Conference of Bishops from Rwanda, published by Pallotti Press in 1995. The discourses the bishops engaged in between 1990 and 1994 appear in certain places to be a re-writing of the Head of State's speech. Interest is raised by the text of the preface: »This volume wants to provide an answer to the public expectation that wants and has the right to know what the Rwanda Catholic

---

[1]   Meaning borrowed from Gérard Genette in *Palimpsests: Literature in the Second Degree* (Lincoln: University of Nebraska Press, 1997).

[2]   Hypotext refers to the fourth type of transtextuality, in which Genette distinguishes a hypertext and hypotext: »By hypertextuality, I mean any relationship uniting a text B (which I shall call the hypertext) to an early text A (I shall, of course, call it the hypotext)«, Genette, *Palimpsests,* 5.

[3]   In the following (R.L.M) will stand for the abbreviation of *Recueil des Lettres et Messages de la Conférence des Evêques.*

Episcopate has said during the war.« (R.L.M, 4–5) Why and how do the bishops mention the Head of State? What do the bishops' quotations say? The quest takes place through an explicative study of the text. Intertextuality will serve as a reading screen, as connections between political and religious texts are explored.[4] In my intertextual reading, the presence of political texts in the bishops' letters is exposed. These texts appear as a hypertext deriving from changing the political speech of President Habyarimana, the hypotext.

In preparation for the Pope's visit to Rwanda, the bishops, in February 1990, published the letter »Christ our Unity«:

> What we want is peace and unity between citizens of our country. The Head of State said: We do not tolerate quarrels and hatred, we do not tolerate nepotism or favoritism, and we do not tolerate false rumors that destroy. (R.L.M, 13)

Which leads to the following outline recording the sequence of events:

Bishops	President Habyarimana
What we want	The Head of State said
is peace and unity	We do not tolerate quarrels and hatred

The title of the letter refers to Christ as founder of unity among the Rwandan people. However, the incursion of the speech of the President of the Republic allows the latter to occupy some categories proper to »Christ our Unity.« Habyarimana is mentioned instead of the Gospel and of the traditional teachings of the Church. The Episcopal letter affirms what the Head of State said. Both texts have the same meaning; they differ only in the way they are ex-

---

[4]   In Julia Kristeva's understanding, as Abrams wrote, the term »intertextuality« means »the multiple ways in which any one literary text is made up of other texts, by means of its open or covert citations and allusions, its repetitions and transformations of the formal and substantive features of earlier texts, any text is in fact an »intertext« – the site of an intersection of numberless other texts, and existing only through its relations to other texts.« See Meyer Howard Abrams, *A Glossary of Literary Terms*, 7th edition, (Fort Worth: Harcourt Brace College Publishers, 1999), 317. Gérard Genette prefers the term »transtextuality«, by which he understands »all that sets the text in relationship, whether obvious or concealed, with other texts.« See Gérard Genette, *Palimpsests*, 1. For Genette, »intertextuality« is one of the five types of transtextual relationships (intertextuality, paratext, metatextuality, hypertextuality, and architextuality).

pressed (positive form: peace and unity; negative form: no quarrels, hatred, favoritism and false rumors). The bishops' text establishes its authority from the reference to the speech of the Head of State. The negative form gives authority to the word of the Chief. The affirmative form suggests that the speech of the bishops obeys the directive from the political power. The imperfect tense used in the verbal expression »said« shows that the political speech by the Head of State precedes the one of the bishops. It places the Head of State in a role of welcoming a host and bestows on him a religious status. The direct quotation updates the Chief's thought. It also appears in the present tense used in the bishops' speech. The verbal form »What we want« expresses a wish, an intention, but also an affirmation for peace and unity. Relating to the use of »said« by the Head of State, the expression »What we want« indicates an adhesion, an approval, a participation in the text of the Head of State. Why does the church articulate the meaning of peace and unity taken from the political speech? In fact it means »to obey the words of order indicated by the National Republican Movement for Development, M.R.N.D., and using the slogan: peace, unity and development ... of the status of peace (in the sense of consensus, order, absence of all contradiction), of unity (fight against the centrifuge force) and the development (preliminary and ultimate justification of everything).«[5] Between 1990 and 1994, the trope of »unity and reconciliation« leads to a coalition against a common enemy, the Tutsi.

The press and extremist political parties adopted the concepts of unity and reconciliation indicated in various reports of statements from those with political power. *Kangura Magazine*, No. 46, saluted »Radio Télévision Libre des Mille Collines« (R.T.L.M) as »a symbol of unity by the Hutu people«. Hatred against Tutsis, massacres, and genocide became semantic elements or topics of discourse for themes of unity and reconciliation. These tropes were pivotal for the founding of the Coalition for the Defense of the Republic (C.D.R.) and the »Interahamwe« (those who attack together) in 1992, as key steps in the preparation of genocide. The substantive »coalition« and the adverb »together« contain the idea of unity. The words »peace and unity« are religious concepts but find their meaning in political discourse. The words of the President established a criterion of expression. Since the pre-text »Christ our Unity« is used, Habyarimana becomes the reference.

---

[5]   Thierry De Smedt, »Comme un homme privé du sommeil. Et si la difficulté d'expression artistique était aussi à l'origine du génocide rwandais.« *Dialogue*, No. 202 (January–February 1998): 90.

In linguistics, a term has no meaning; it has only usage. This reflects the notion of the arbitrary nature of signs or better, the relation between the signifier and the meaning codified by the usage. In this case, an implicit contract is developed between what stands for politics and what stands for religion. Thus, the bishops deploy and define the semantic field of »peace« and »unity« emerging from the universe of the political speech by the President of the Republic. The words »peace«, »development«, and »unity« are code words in the M.R.N.D. universe, and lead the recipient to believe that, thanks to the President, Rwanda »has enjoyed, perhaps for the first time in its existence, an uninterrupted period of peace and unity.«[6]

There is apparently in these intertextual (transtextual) references an attempt to legitimize the Chief of State by rejecting the accusations brought against his regime by the international press and open letters from Tutsi refugees of 1959, namely addressed to Pope John Paul II before his visit to Rwanda. The title of the letter »Christ our Unity« seems to allocate to the Head of State the symbol of unity:

> Dear brothers in Christ,
> When we reflect on what destroyed unity among the Rwanda people, let us not forget the positive accomplishments that reinforce it. Everybody recalls that the President of our country has declared: »We refuse nepotism and the monopolizing of some people.« On all levels, the country endeavors an equitable distribution at the place of work and school. The leaders do the best they can to help the inhabitants of Rwanda to get along with each other: they give us roads, newspapers, various meeting places, M.R.N.D. institutions, workers associations and women's promotion. A lot of initiative has been undertaken in order to bring government and administration closer, and rich and poor getting along. (R.L.M, 9–10)

The invocation »Dear brothers in Christ« emanates from the spoken word of the Head of State. A possible identification does exist at the textual level between »Christ« and »The President of our country.« The content of »Christ our Unity« is being read through the project presented by the political party in power. The receiver »Dear brothers in Christ« loses its Christian identity and becomes anonymous: »Everybody remembers what the Head of State said.«

---

[6]   President Habyarimana in his speech for the 28th anniversary of Independence cited in Ministry of Foreign Affairs and of International Cooperation, *Livre Blanc. Sur l'agression dont le Rwanda a été victime* (Kigali: Imprimerie nationale, 1990), 28. In the same book, one can read the M.R.N.D objective to »gather all the Rwanda population within a same political formation, pursuing a threefold objective: peace, unity and development« (20).

The word »Christ« has been erased and gives way to the spoken word of the President. The pronoun »everybody« encompasses all of the population of Rwanda, including non-Christians. The »everybody knows« includes the text of the President in the classification of general truth and needs no demonstration. With the knowledge of »everybody«, any demonstration or proof is a tautology. The words of the Chief do not leave room for discussion. The pastoral letter defends the regime and refutes accusations brought against it by way of diminishing criticism: »When we reflect on what consumes unity among the Rwanda people, let us not forget the accomplishments that reinforce it.«

The bishops' text is based on the speech of the Head of State. Unity finds its foundation in the Head of State's declaration. The verbal form »has declared«, introducing the President's quotation, seems to be in the text of the bishops, an act of perlocution, provoking, or leading to unity through the mere fact of expressing it. This link between »say« and »do« suggests the creative word of God in Genesis. The President's citation shows no references. It is the general truth. The law of ethnic balance is recognized and presented in a positive way by the bishops: »the equitable distribution at work and in school«. In the same letter about unity, and closer to the top, the bishops confirm their adhesion to an ethnic balance:

> However some Rwandans reject these teachings and pursue maintaining the ethnic rivalry in all various speeches and schemes. One hears, at times, people complain, that due to their ethnic origin, employment, or admission to school has been refused to them. They are either deprived of an advantage or justice has not been impartial in its treatment toward them … You do not ignore the fact that the law of ethnic balance on employment and school is aiming at correcting this inequality that favoring one, to the detriment of the other. It is evident that such policy cannot please everybody, and is unable to produce all the results they were hoping to gain. Let us not forget that its aim, which is also ours, is to distribute with equity the opportunity to secure employment or to be accepted in school, without taking into consideration the ethnic background, but putting the emphasis on the competition of each individual. (R.L.M, 11–12)

The »you do not ignore« is a variant of »everybody knows about it« forces the reader to not question the policy of ethnic balance. This knowledge is evident. The *Kinyarwanda* text of the bishops uses the affirmative form »*muzi ko*«, »you know that«. At the form level, two contrary propositions are made on ethnic balance. The first starts: »[Ethnic] balance is destined to correct this inequality that may be in favor of one at the detriment of the other.« This statement reads logically, as a universal affirmative clause (A). The predicate »is«

refers to the ethnic idea already shown in the subject »ethnic balance«. The second clause »... Its aim, also ours ... on the competence of each individual« may be put into writing as: »The ethnic balance does not take ethnicity into consideration.« It becomes a universal negative clause (E). The two clauses A and E on ethnic balance cannot be true at the same time: To affirm and to negate the primacy of ethnicity in the same discourse is invalid.

In the second clause, the malaise is already visible between the subject »ethnicity« and a predicate that refutes »ethnicity«. Grammatically speaking, can a verb put the subject and its predicate into conflict? What derives from this quotation is the dangerous acceptance of the ethnic balance principle by the Church. The latter justifies itself in correcting inequalities: »Its aim is also ours« points out the complicity of church and state. The balance presents itself as a facet of unity between the people of Rwanda.

It was thus an anachronism to talk about correcting the inequalities. At what point in time can we place the injustices? The *Ten Commandments* published in the No. 6 of *Kangura*, dated December 1990, have probably resulted from »ethnic balance« radicalism. The 6th Commandment says: »The teaching sector (schoolchildren, students, and teachers) has to have a Hutu majority.« The 7th Commandment says: »The Rwanda Army Forces have to be exclusively Hutu.« The ethnic balance would be the labor of some missionaries; various sources attributed the notion to Reverend Naveau, former principal at the »Christ-Roi« College in Nyanza. He founded the »Public Salvation Committee« in order to denounce the »social short-sightedness« of the Hutu who allow the education of Tutsi without restriction.

The translation of a text is not an original text: It is a new text presented to the reader. It is a citation among others. The French text of the bishops proceeds by omission and modification of certain sequences of the *Kinyarwanda* text »*Kristu, bumwe, bwacu. Igice cya mbere. Ubumwe.*« (Christ our Unity – First Part: Unity):

> However, some Rwandans did not understand the teachings and advice from their political leaders; on the contrary, they pursued their racial discrimination (ethnic) by the use of their words and actions. At times, one hears someone complain of being a victim of his race (ethnicity) such as being refused work or a promotion, being unjustly treated in a court of justice, or not being admitted in a school. You know that the policy of ethnic balance in employment and schools aims at correcting this racial discrimination (ethnic) that is giving preference to some by leaving out others. It is understandable that this policy does neither please any nor lead to a perfect balance. (R.L.M, 13)

The *Kinyarwanda* text addresses those who believe they are victims of ethnic or racial discrimination, implied Tutsis. The quote »advice from their political leaders« does not appear in the French text of the bishops. The French translation does not clearly mention to whom these »teachings« are being applied. In any case, the words »teaching« and »counsel« give »ethnic balance« a doctrinal meaning in the practice of justice and unity. To complain (*Gu-taka*) of »ethnic balance« is contrary to the concept of unity. The notion of justice presupposes equal anonymity beyond social, regional, and ethnic adherence. Unity linked to the Head of State becomes a political power system:

> Representatives of authority do not cease to appease quarrels and hatred based on ethnic origins. They remind us constantly that our country will not progress unless unified efforts are being exercised by all its children. The Church does not cease preaching unity and good [relationships] between the children of God, even if they are from a different ethnic, ideological and religious level. (R.L.M, 11)

On a paradigmatic situation, this speech would present itself as follows:

1) Those who represent authority	1') The Church
2) **Do not cease** to appease quarrels and hatred based on ethnic origins/bring up constantly	2') **Does not cease** to preach unity and goodwill
3) All (the) children (in the country)	3') God's children

The verbal form »do (does) not cease« indicates insistency, a permanent action that is also shown in »bring up constantly«. The occurrence of the verbal form »do/does not cease« (2 and 2') brings together the Church's intent and political power. The couple »State/Church« (1 and 1') appears in the first paragraph of the introduction in the book by the bishops: »We also wish to underline the efforts of those who are real agents of unity in our country and in Church.« (R.L.M, 9) The identification is revealed in »on its part«. In »remind us«, the Church is contained in »us« and places itself in a subordinate position.

At the beginning of the war, the Church expressed its support to the political power. Bonaventure Habimana, Secretary General at that time of the M.R.N.D, is correct in his sentiment when addressing Pope John Paul II, who met with dignitaries on September 7, 1990. He talks about the »quality in relations existing between the Rwanda Republic and the Catholic Church« and »relations« that led to a gratifying development« of »flowers and friendship«.[7]

During wartime, the Catholic Church translated published remarks made by the President of the Republic and the Ministry of Foreign Affairs into religious words. Press articles and university professors' articles echoed the thoughts of the leader on the subject of war. In a bishops' letter, dated November 7, 1990, »Happy Are the Artisans of Peace, For They Will Be Called Sons of God«, it was said:

> As everybody knows, on last October 1st, from the Northern district region Byumba, our beloved country was victim of an army aggression coming from Uganda, and of infiltrations inside of the country up to the Capital of Kigali. This unfortunate event has brought up again, the refugee problem, and poses, unfortunately, once more, the question of national unity … We disapprove strongly of the war situation that has been inflicted upon Rwanda … it is important to clarify matters, on one hand, our country has been attacked by armed assailants, including not only refugees, but also Ugandan military forces. On the other hand, the refugee question was being studied a long time ago at the regional level and by the United Nations High Commissioner for refugees, and was about to be resolved. The armed attack perpetrated by the assailants has unfortunately compromised the current steps. (R.L.M, 121–122)

This abstract of the letter by the bishops at the beginning of the war is based on the version of the party in power and imposes it as truth in itself. This is indicated by the phrase »as one knows«, which recalls »as everybody knows«; »you do not ignore«; »you do not forget«; »everybody remembers« – expressions used in the speech introduction made by the President in the bishops' letters. This truth, in the first place, consists of an interpretation of a historical fact (beginning of war, October 1st) which occurs as an aggression against Rwanda, with the M.R.N.D appearing like a victim.

The term of affection »our beloved country« conflates the party or political system with the fatherland. Among causes due to war is the refugee question, which is minimized and presented as a problem about to be resolved. The

---

7   »Présidence de La République Rwandaise avec la collaboration du comité pour la visite du pape de l'Eglise catholique au Rwanda,« in *Discours prononcés à l'occasion de la visite du pape Jean-Paul II au Rwanda* (Kigali: Pallotti Press, 1990), 14.

bishops are also using the same words as the the President of the Republic and the Ministry of Defense. It can be noticed in the use of »armed assailants«, »Uganda military«, »armed aggression«, »refugee question ... about to be resolved«, and »infiltration«. A literary trade is taking place (or a textual solidarity) between the press, the Church, and official discourse. In January, 1991, the Rwandan Ministry of Foreign Affairs and International Cooperation published *Livre Blanc sur l' agression armée dont le Rwanda a été victime à partir du 1er Octobre 1990*. The title of this book recalls an excerpt of a letter by the bishops, dated November 7, 1990: »This last October 1st ... our beloved country has been the victim of an armed aggression.«

The »hypotext« was a radio message delivered over radio Kigali on October 5, 1990, whereby the Head of State talks about »assailants, infiltration, and rebels in Kigali districts ... about arms hidden by the enemy in the capital and its surroundings, which were seized, and most of the invaders located.«[8]

The statement »rebels in the capital of Kigali« in the President's speech is anterior to the statement by the bishops, »infiltrations inside of the country up to the capital of Kigali«. It was thus established among numerous sources that the famous »attack during the 4 to 5 October night« was a montage serving as a pretext to arrest the Tutsi population. In a document signed by 117 missionaries and other expatriates, the term »infiltration« was also used: »Has it been clearly explained that the shootings over Kigali were not coming from the army that sought to penetrate from the East, but came from little groups infiltrated in the city?«[9]

---

[8]   Excerpts of this speech have been used by Goretti Uwimana in her article »President Habyarimana's Indignation Against the Disinformation Campaign,« *La Relève*, no. 143–144 (October 1990): 19–25. The paper carried a large title on the front page: »Inyenzi version 90«. Inyenzi means cockroaches.

[9]   »Expatriates Bear Testimony: Wrath During Wartime.« *La Relève*, no. 145 (October 26–November 1, 1990): 9. In 1994, the word »wrath« became a reason that lead to genocide. In the same text, missionaries seemed surprised that genocide had not yet taken place in 1990: »But current events are hopeful up till now, even if characteristics of a recent crisis do not allow reaching a too hasty conclusion: Hope derives from the fact that at no time pogrom took place: a tentative systematic liquidation of Tutsis, although the assailant is rather akin to this ethnic group«. (10) Has the kick off act been given? In case the text by missionaries is leaning toward hope and expectation, what follows in the text, »does not allow a hasty drawing to any conclusion«, opens the gap to genocide. The link established between »assailant« – with all meaning given to that word – and the Tutsi is a sort of delivery. The conjunction »although (*bien que*)« does also translate into »but also«, and »in

It thus follows that the arrest of »suspects« should not be linked to proof of the Rwandan Patriotic Army's intervention. The excerpt on intervention by the bishops concerning the war cited above, »As everybody knows … the armed attack perpetrated by the assailants, has unfortunately compromised the current steps,« can be divided into two sections: The first, from »As everybody knows« to »inflicted upon Rwanda«, tries to establish facts in a narrative style. The second part, »it is important … the current steps«, rewrites the first part in an argumentative style, wherein the bishops assume position by appropriating themselves the M.R.N.D version.

The speech of the Head of State on October 5, 1990 has seemingly become a source of concepts and information to the Christian message, as shown in the grid on p. 93.

Three considerations can be drawn from these statements. The first consideration comes from the affirmation according to which Rwanda has been attacked by Rwandan refugees and the Ugandan military. The press and the bishops use the term »assailants« in naming the Rwandan Patriotic Front. The Ministry of Foreign Affairs applies a flexible language »armed elements in the provenance of Uganda.« Uganda is being implicated in the three texts. Resemblance is shown between the governmental texts and Pastoral Letters to present the war situation. (»**it is** important **to clarify**« (R.L.M.) and »**It is** thus **clear**« (*Livre Blanc* …). Lexical and verbal congruency is shown in underlined elements. The second consideration is concerned with the refugee problem, which must not serve as a pretext to the attack by assailants inasmuch as exchanges between government and international entities were about to reach a solution The press talks about »an immediate way out being made available in view to achieve a voluntary repatriation.« To the bishops, the problem »was about to be resolved.« The government sector feels that »the results were promising.«

The third consideration presents war as a hindrance to the refugee problem. The bishops believe that »The armed attack by the assailants has unfortunately compromised the current steps.« In parallel, political power discourse refers to the attack that »has interrupted and even almost annihilated efforts deployed by the Rwandan government.« Support to the Habyarimana

---

spite of « indicates concession in »pogrom at no time has taken place, or a tentative of systematic liquidation of the Tutsi.« Does genocide against Tutsi side with the right, the privilege of a political power? Grammatically speaking, »although« is used as a concessive meaning only in the link that exists between pogrom, liquidation of Tutsis, and akin to the ethnic group of the assailant. Four years later the concession has been lifted.

The Press (*La Relève*, N. 143–144, 1990)	The Bishops (R.L.M)	The Government (*Le Livre Blanc*)
1) During the morning of October 1st, 1990, Rwanda has been attacked by assailants including Rwandan refugees, members of the Uganda army who rallied with Uganda elements, members of this army. (2)	1') It is important to clarify matters on one hand: our country has been attacked by armed assailants, including not only refugees, but also Ugandan military forces. (122)	1") It is thus clear that the attack on October 1, 1990, perpetrated against Rwanda by armed elements. (25)
2) Rwandese authorities have never forgotten the situation refugees found themselves in. HCR and the Kampala Government cannot, within their soul and conscience, deny this fact. Refugees themselves knew that an immediate way out was being made available in view to achieve a voluntary repatriation. (2)	2') On the other hand, the refugee question was being studied a long time ago at the regional level and by the United Nations High Commissioner for refugees, and was about to be resolved. (122)	2") The attack … has prevented negotiations in process that were pertaining to the Rwandan refugee question, results of which were promising. (25)
3) High level contacts took place between Rwanda and the high commissioner on refugees. We were almost on the way to find a solution with a durable outcome. (8)	3') The armed attack by the assailants has unfortunately compromised the current steps. (122)	3") War imposed on Rwanda on October 1st, 1990, by RPF has interrupted and even almost annihilated efforts deployed by the Rwandan government and pertaining to finding a satisfactory solution to problem of Rwandan refugees. (25)

system from bishops appears as concern to tell the truth. However, during wartime, taking sides »for« is, above all, taking sides »against«:

President of the Republic (*La Releve*, n.143–144, 1990, 7)	Catholic Bishops letter of Nov 7, 1990, in R.L.M, 123–124.	Government (*Le Livre Blanc*)
Aggression against our country is not only of military nature. It also rests on international media manipulation and disinformation ... We were surprised by the violent manipulations, being prepared a long time ago, as we know now, by certain media from the Occident and not in the least minimal. Our country is still being subjected to attacks and calumnies, to systematic lies, that we can only qualify as diabolic in nature.	In these difficult times, it is our duty to remain in solidarity for the defense of the truth. False information and rumors and libel and lies have taken place in Rwanda ... We strongly deplore disinformation, cleverly and maliciously organized by those who have attacked Rwanda on certain facts and events, as some of the media have reverberated. Happy are the promoters of peace.	Everybody was under a shock, not only caused by military aggression, led with large means, but also by a campaign of intoxication, cleverly prepared and orchestrated by the aggressors and their international mass media allies. (11) Among arms used, other than military armament, there is the intoxicated opinion of international press. (184) Before attack took place, they (Tutsi population) proceeded carefully in manipulating international opinion. (28)

In a pastoral letter by the bishops dated November 7, 1990, the Rwandan Patriotic Front, referred to as »those who attacked Rwanda«, was being identified with the reverse of moral values like false alarm, rumors, slander, lies, and disinformation. In short, all that is contrary to the truth emanates from the Rwandan Patriotic Front. One can thus come to the conclusion that the party in power is keeper and holder of truth and morality. It is the same truth and values that the Church wants to defend.

All of the three texts question the international press, which was supposedly manipulated by aggressors. Disinformation or propaganda enters into the aggressors' game. Words used to express them are the same: »prepared manipulations« (President), »disinformation, cleverly and maliciously organized by those who attacked Rwanda« (bishops), or »intoxication cleverly prepared and organized by the aggressors and their allies« (*Le Livre Blanc*).

The Episcopal Conference and the Ministry of Foreign Affairs attach the same meaning to »disinformation« and »intoxication«. They all use the adverb »cleverly« with the exception of the bishops, a negative connotation is expressed by the adverb »maliciously« which brings to mind the adjective »evil«, applied ethnologically to the Tutsi population and functioning in other cases as an attribute of the devil. This is close to the speech of the President who uses the adjective »diabolical« in qualifying lies of the »enemy«. A caricature of the F.P.R presented it with horns and a tail. The words »disinformation« and »lies« in the speech by the President are also brought up in the speech by the bishops. The word »lies« reinforces the link with the devil.

The word »slander« in the presidential speech is replaced by its synonym »defamation« in the bishops' speech. In the French text, they add »false rumors« and »rumors« in order to reinforce its meaning. Information enters the battlefield. The President sets the tone when speaking about authors of attacks and libels. The bishops express it by a nominal syntax form: »Those who have attacked Rwanda«. The government talks about »arms being utilized«. In the Pastoral Letters, President Habyarimana becomes a general symbol of peace and unity. He offers a model of development.

> In a letter dated March 31, 1991, »Truth Will Render You Free Men« the bishops denounced the abuses of multiparty democracy and eulogize the state party in paraphrasing the objectives of M.R.N.D., which are unity, peace and development: As of founding of a unique Party, political power has endeavored to lead Rwanda in unity and peace in its way of development. By doing so, its urban and rural society has reached beautiful achievements. (R.L.M, 154).

The R.L.M. kept silent about some discourses made during the time of the genocide. A void exists between November 10, 1993 and December 21, 1994. In his April 9, 1994 appeal, the President of the Episcopal Conference introduced genocide as a »strike from pain and sorrow ... to avenge the President« and exhorted the population to support the government that was accountable for genocide. He repeated the statement in a letter dated May 18, 1994:

> Massacres do no longer take place in our zone. There is much talk about it from the part of the F.P.R that has shot the fleeing population and tortured those that were caught. War should end and then there would be no isolated killings and no banditry in the hills. The course of this war has turned into an ethnic matter, in which both ethnicities face and kill each other ... The President's death, attributed to the F.P.R, has intensified ethnic hatred and provoked massacres.[10]

---

[10]   Letter by Bishop Thaddeus Nsengiyumva, President of the Episcopal Conference of Rwanda from the Kabgayi diocese in *La Documentation Catholique* 2096 (June 19, 1994): 585. On Kabgayi massacres that he minimizes, see African Rights, *Rwanda: Death, Despair and Defiance* (London, 1995): 708–718.

Besides this interpretation we can find explicit glorification of the killings, for instance in the writings of Reverend Maindron, who sees in the genocide a sign of love to the President:

> This war wanted to replace the despotism of President Habyarimana, who, as declared by false rumors, was not liked in his country, and by all his akazu followers. At his death, the way people reacted shows more than a plebiscite, but how much Habyarimana was popular.[11]

There was also a courageous text by Cardinal Etchegaray: »Cease-fire means here cease the machete, cease the spear; each Rwandan is called to tell the truth.«[12] After genocide, the pattern has been broken. In a letter dated December 21, 1994: »Love thy neighbor« was lacking a textual ally. We do not find references to statements from political officials anymore. However, when considering the text in a psycho-critic manner, as in a dream, the text by the bishops can participate in the life of the unconscious.[13] Refusal of genocide connotes presence of the father (political influence). The terms »massacres and wars« (R.L.M, 283), »big ordeal«, »disasters«, »misfortunes« (R.L.M, 284), »dead end« (R.L.M, 286), »murderous tragedies« (R.L.M, 287), »Rwanda tragedy« (R.L.M, 291) and »endless conflicts based on power« (RLM, 291) are registered in a logic of quotation.

Instead of words by the President, an engagement with the Gospel should have raised the question of unity, peace, and reconciliation and have an impact in the life of people. Such engagement could have denounced injustices, protested exclusions of an ethnic nature, and offered a better way of behavior and conduct. In other words, the message of love by Jesus Christ did not become the absolute reference by which the Rwandan Christian was called to examine, rethink, and assume her/his »ethnic being« and life.

It seems that the Rwandan drama took place in a crossroads of ambiguities of some bishops' messages in the midst of war and genocide with the previous Habyarimana political power and ideology. It thus became difficult to draw a line between religious and political discourse. The future of »new evangelization«, of a message of hope against genocide and war crimes, necessarily presupposes the relocation of religious language.

---

[11]   G. Maindron, »Rwanda: A Horror.« *Dialogue* 177 (August-September, 1994): 55.

[12]   »Message by Cardinal Roger Etchegaray to the Rwanda People.« *Documentation Catholique* 2099 (August 7 and 21, 1994): 733.

[13]   Regarding an interpretation of text as a dream, see François Pire, »Psycho-critics.«, in *Method of Text*, ed. Maurice Delacroix (Paris: Duculot, 1995), 266–275.

RELOCATION OF RELIGIOUS LANGUAGE

A meeting was held on July 26, 1994 at Bujumbura in Burundi, which was attended by various religious communities working in Rwanda. The ensuing report stated the following:

> Our church has professed the language of the M.R.N.D. during 20 years. The same mistakes should no longer be repeated. The major challenge is to take politics out of the church. The church should not be affiliated with any political party in order to be the reliable voice of the people ... what is certain, is that should the church have fulfilled its prophetic mission, things would not have happened that way.[14]

Strong interaction in political and religious speeches facilitated the way to genocide. Texts indeed produced their effect. Eight years following genocide, terms like »interethnic war« and »double genocide« persist in some religious writings.

The introduction and the speech appeal in a clever way to reason and memory: the place of recognition for a true word being used as dogma. The quoted speech of the President integrated into bishops' letters was *ipso facto* transformed into affirmations of faith, inasmuch as it was not simply a quotation giving information on war; it was a discourse that committed the recipient. Indeed, a language of faith referred to events or truths and implied commitment (self-involving), expressed in performative acts the bishops engaged in.

Self-implication suggests a reply, an involvement on the part of the reader regarding the speech of the President. This can be found in various texts used by the bishops. The latter are already involved in »those who represent authority do not cease their endeavors in appeasing quarrels and hatred ... for its part, the Church does not cease preaching for unity«; »various civil and religious authorities do not cease ...«; »We, your bishops, support wholly communal works ...«; »let us not forget that its (ethnic balance policy) aim, is also ours ...«. We find declamatory acts of language being applied in words expressed by the President. After quoting the President, the speech by the bishops becomes a repetition explaining or adding a religious coloring to the already existing political propaganda.

---

[14]   Sister Marie Paule LEBEL (her report), Meeting 7/26/1994 held at the Xaverian community in Bujumbura during the visit of Father Henri Hosser of Rwanda. Bulletin copy.

However, Pope John Paul II's writings may be an interesting topic for further studies since they opened the scope of the Christian response to Rwandan genocide. From the Gemelli Hospital in May 15, 1994, he was the first to claim that genocide was occurring in Rwanda and stigmatized the involvement of Catholics:

> It is a question of a true and authentic genocide, for which, unfortunately, Catholics are also responsible. I am close to these people in their suffering and I would like to address again the conscience of all those who planned this massacre and carried it out. They are carrying this country toward the abyss! All of them must answer to history and to God for their crimes. Enough blood! God expects from all the people of Rwanda, together with their neighboring countries, a moral reawakening: the courage of pardon and brotherhood.[15]

In this quotation, the use of the word genocide was important since many countries were calling it an interethnic war. In his other writings, the Pope calls for justice and Christian forgiveness. The theme of reconciliation is dominant in the Pope's address to the Rwandans. He spoke strongly against »all members of the church« involved in the 1994 genocide against the Tutsi people. But he said clearly that the Church as such has no responsibility: »The Church as such cannot be held responsible for the faults of her members who acted against the law of the Gospel; they will be called to account for their acts.«[16] John Paul II used biblical quotations to reinforce the theme of reconciliation after the genocide. In his letter to the Archbishop of Kigali, he also insisted on reconciliation and peace, speaking of the mercy of God in »all situations.«

What place does the Gospel have in life? The current pope, Benedict XVI, then President of the Congregation for the Faith Doctrine, issued this complaint:

> It is shameful to us that Catholic countries like Rwanda and Burundi have become the theater of the worst atrocities. We have thus to reflect in depth and find out what we have to do so that the Gospel has a stronger grip in social life.[17]

---

[15]   Luigi Accattoli, *When a Pope Asks Forgiveness* (Pauline Book Media: Boston, 1998), 213–214.

[16]   Acattoli, *When a Pope Asks Forgiveness*, 216.

[17]   Cardinal Joseph Ratzinger (Talks with Peter Seewald), *Le Sel de la Terre. Le Christianisme et l'Eglise Catholique au Seuil du Troisième Millénaire* (Paris: Flammarion/Cerf, 1997), 146. A declaration that contrasts with the one of the Rwandan bishops: »Several times, we have asked for help, and you never did pay any attention.« (R.L.M., 283)

How and why do »Catholic countries like Rwanda and Burundi . . . become the theater of the worst atrocities«? At least five dimensions shape the discourse around this question that need to be considered. First, to elucidate the ›how‹ and ›why‹ of genocide in a Christian country, two schemes of explanation compete with each other. One scheme considers the efforts by the missionaries and colonial powers regarding genocide as a failure. Some missionaries, clergy, and politicians created or adopted a discourse with a constant reference to »racial categorization« of Rwandan people. This is then considered the main source of Rwandan misfortune. This discourse of racial categorization will still remain for a long time and may only lead to violence. Therefore, genocide becomes a logical end result of church and state attitudes toward Rwandan people. The second scheme of explanation hints at the depth of Christian conviction. It assumes that evangelization took place only on the surface, leaving unchanged the existing Rwandan premises of hatred, as each local church bears the sins of the society where she is located. Sins like pedophilia, prostitution, exploitation, injustice, apartheid, racism, and genocide are related to the moral structures of each society.

A third thread of explanation explores »biopower« assumed by the state that is placed beyond the domain of ethics and religion. The state considers the right to live as a mere favor. In this vein, the systematic extermination of ethnic groups or members of oppositional political parties is understood as an ordinary and exemplary sanction against »enemies«. The exercise of the power to decide over life and death can also be perceived as a stratagem, or just an available means, to keep or to conquer political power. Then, how can a Christian defend his or her faith and moral principles before a totalitarian state? Some Christians were in an overpowering situation of submission. Can religion impel people to choose to suffer death rather than renounce religious and ethical norms?

A third argument perceives the participation of Christians in massacres as a result of manipulation. Then, it seems that certain numbers of perpetrators believed that they acted according to the moral and Christian values of self-defense and of a struggle against evil.

A fourth dimension of the debate is concerned with the question how the sin of genocide shapes the official Catholic Church discourse with regard to priests who were involved in the killings. How can we explain the strange situation of priests involved in the crimes of genocide who are still running parishes in Western countries? Why does the Vatican protect them against any legal proceedings? The Church's attitude towards genocide seems to suggest that the hierarchy of religious values is not usually in proportion to the hierarchy of moral standards. Genocide in Rwanda against the Tutsis constitutes a position of rupture and marks thus the bankruptcy of old religious discourses. Violence may not have its inception in religion as such, but the use of religious language vindicates violence and turns it into a moral and/or religious value.

Fifth, it is obvious that, during genocide, many Christians lost insight into what it means to live as disciples of Christ. The Rwandan bishops seem not to have faced the intricate dilemma (to kill or to be killed) of ordinary people. Their discourses were not the result of political intimidation but of a »friendship« between state and church. A clear message of peace and love could have indicted some Christians who freely and enthusiastically participated in killings. In distancing itself from the Rwandan genocidal regime, the Church would have had the chance to cut off the moral support to political violence. Unfortunately, this did not happen.

NOT A CONCLUSION

It is certainly difficult to make a moral system work in extraordinary circumstances, where moral or religious issues may go beyond a personal choice or responsibility. Nevertheless, religious discourse should build the foundation for a new language that deals with mass violence, and define a horizon that breaks the »logic« that has welcomed various structures of violence. The theoretical task also calls for a critique of concepts and methods in African theology. If genocide or mass violence comes into focus in African theology, then, there is a need to liberate (not to reject) this theology from *adapting* or *translating* Greco-Roman traditions and mummified African traditions. In a very particular way, there is a need for »decentralizing« theological language and approaches. The huge task of African theology after the genocide will consist of extending its reflection through dialogue with other disciplines in social sciences and the humanities rather than to limit itself within Western philosophical concepts and history.

Genocide or mass violence has to become a new ›locus theologicae‹. It seems that the works of pioneers such as the Congolese Vincent Mulago and the Rwandan Alexis Kagame, have remained unfortunately dependent on the language and discourse they have criticized in their own comparative approach. In general, the idea of »African culture and values« seems to magnify and romanticize the African continent. The concept of *negritude* that is implied in this discourse has been criticized by the Nigerian writer and Nobel

Prize winner Wole Soyinka. Soyinka has challenged the concept of *negritude* in referring to genocide in Rwanda. His remarks are applicable to some African theological studies:

> We can talk about negritude, but then how to explain the massacre in Rwanda, is this negritude? You see, it is of such painful problems that we must confront, that the negritude should evoke! And not the romantic atmosphere and idyllic that surrounded it at his apparition.[18]

Theology, as well as other disciplines based on rehabilitation of African traditions, seem to be tarnished today by genocide and mass violence of Africans against Africans in Africa. From an epistemological standpoint, the emergence of a new thought affirms the necessity to endow disciplines with tools and approaches that engage in depth the African crises. Today, there is a need for theological reflections that do not romanticize »the African experience«, nor pity the misfortune of Africa. Without neglecting new approaches in African Theology, among them the Theology of Reconstruction, researchers rather need to attend to the brutal realities of the Rwandan genocide, and how the church and ordinary people have been implicated in the violence. This is a radical challenge that calls for a shift in our ways of doing theology and research in Africa.

LITERATURE

Abrams, Meyer Howard. *A Glossary of Literary Terms*, 7th edition. Fort Worth: Harcourt Brace College Publishers, 1999.

Accattoli, Luigi. *When a Pope Asks Forgiveness*. Boston: Pauline Book Media, 1998.

African Rights, Rwanda. *Death, Despair, and Defiance*. London, African Rights, 1995.

Bishop Thaddeus Nsengiyumva, President of Episcopal Conference of Rwanda »A Letter from the Kabgayi Diocese.« In *La Documentation Catholique* 2096, 585. June 19, 1994.

De Smedt, Thierry. »Comme un homme privé du sommeil. Et si la difficulté d'expression artistique était aussi à l'origine du génocide rwandais.« *Dialogue*, No. 202 (January-February 1998): 85–96.

Etchegaray, Cardinal Roger. »Message to the Rwanda People.« La *Documentation Catholique* 2099, 733. August 7 and 21, 1994.

Genette, Gérard. *Palimpsests: Literature in the Second Degree*. Lincoln: University of Nebraska Press, 1997.

---

[18] Boniface Mongo-M'Boussa, *Désir d'Afrique* (Paris: Gallimard, 2002), 68.

Maindron, Gabriel. »Rwanda: A Horror.« *Dialogue* 177 (August-September, 1994): 1–168.

Ministry of Foreign Affairs and of International Cooperation. *Livre Blanc. Sur l'agression dont le Rwanda a été victime.* Kigali: Imprimerie nationale, 1990.

Mongo-M'Boussa, Boniface. *Désir d'Afrique.* Paris: Gallimard, 2002.

Pire, François. »Psycho-critics.« In *Method of Text,* edited by Maurice Delacroix, 266–275. Paris: Duculot, 1995.

»Présidence de La République Rwandaise avec la collaboration du comité pour la visite du pape de l'Eglise catholique au Rwanda.« In *Discours prononcés à l'occasion de la visite du pape Jean-Paul II au Rwanda.* Kigali: Pallotti Press, 1990. See also http://www.afrik-abibliothek.de/asp/BuchSelect.asp?par=ID&val=3849 (accessed June 20, 2011).

Ratzinger, Cardinal Joseph. *Le Sel de la Terre. Le Christianisme et l'Eglise Catholique au Seuil du Troisième Millénaire.* Paris: Flammarion/Cerf, 1997.

Recueil des Lettres et Messages de la Conférence des Evêques. Pallotti Press, 1995.

Uwimana, Goretti. »President Habyarimana's Indignation Against the Disinformation Campaign.« *La Relève,* no. 143–144 (October 1990): 19–25.

Surviving the War in Liberia

Sabine Förster

Introduction

During the so-called civil war in Liberia among MODEL, LURD, and Govern-ment troops,[1] all factions used elements of traditional religion to give the fighters the feeling of power and strength. They used masks; boys dressed like girls with long hair and marked symbols into their skin. They believed that these rites would make them invulnerable against shots and also invisible. Also, the gruesome style of killing showed traits of ritualized behaviour, in-cluding the mutilation and desecration of dead bodies. Later, one could not even distinguish between the different factions – even the fighters themselves could not; most of the young people wore jeans and white or red T-shirts, like civilians. It was also difficult to distinguish any more between combatants and civilians, between war and criminal acts. Two hundred fifty thousand people were killed during the fourteen-year-long war from 1989–2003. Today, the whole country still seems traumatized. Many people feel victimized. The most widespread and lasting effect of this long war is the exacerbation of con-flicts between males and females expressed in gender-based violence and rape.

In the following, I would like to highlight different aspects of this situa-tion by means of four different pictures that may yield some insight into an otherwise confusing matter. I have chosen pictures that show different groups afflicted by the war. They serve as portraits of the systematic violence pres-ent in the country as a whole. At the same time, they should be seen as a re-minder that there is an individual fate behind each person and that generali-

---

[1]   MODEL: Movement for Democracy in Liberia (South Eastern Region, Joe Willie), LURD: Liberians United for Reconciliation and Democracy (Sekou Conneh, supported by New Guinea), Government fighters (Taylor troops).

zation of and stigmatisation about people involved needs to be overcome in order to arrive at meaningful insights.

In West African civil wars, as the one in Liberia, warlords like Charles Taylor were able to recruit large numbers of young men for fighting by promising them a better future. These young men were suffering from poverty and unemployment and shared utterly bleak prospects of advancing in their communities. He used their sense of outrage against injustice and exploitation for his own purposes. In a paradoxical manner, the (often forcibly) recruited troops acted both as perpetrators and victims of systematic violence. Systematically abused and wilfully made addicted to alcohol and other drugs, they internalized a concept of masculinity that consisted of excessive violence. Gruesome killings, the raping of girls, pregnant women, or mothers as well as looting were thus regarded as means to improve ferocity and obedience. Warlords became the supreme role model for young people. These developments were underlined by claims of their leaders – Charles Taylor of Liberia or Foday Sankoh of Sierra Leone – to be »Men of God« and elected by God to perform God's duties. Their followers took on ›jungle names‹ like General Power, General Peabutter, Gunfire, Jungle Fire, Bush Lover. These meant more than just names to their bearers; they were regarded as a different entity from their usual selves. Unspeakable crimes committed under their ›jungle names‹ had little or no moral consequence to them. »I killed

Getty images picture no. 2345963

Picture 1: Combatants in Liberia, 2003.

people and it doesn't stick to me. I still go to heaven.« When returning home to his suffering family, the same man who had raped, killed, and tortured left the »Bush Lover« behind and went on to support his family with looted items. In that context, Stephen Ellis's statement in *The Mask of Anarchy* must give pause to anyone looking at the conflict from a Christian perspective:

> It appears that Christian teaching is particularly attractive to any ex-fighter who wishes to make a radical break with his or her past, perhaps because of the Christian belief that the Holy Spirit is universal in nature and can enter anybody to provide instant transformation. The ex combatants after the war were attracted by the Christian belief that all evil is the work of the Devil … that old self, they now believe, was actually an agent of Satan …[2]

The most famous example is Prince Johnson, who fought in the very first beginning with Taylor, then built his own faction, tortured, mutilated and finally murdered President Doe and documented his horrific acts in a movie. After the war, he returned to Liberia from Nigeria as a pastor and self-proclaimed prophet, and currently holds the position of a senator of the Liberian Parliament, intending to run for the presidency in 2011.

FEMALE PERSPECTIVES ON SURVIVING VIOLENCE:
VICTIMS AND VICTIMIZERS

I will approach this topic from the perspective of women involved in war and violence in Liberia.While the vast majority of women were victims of violence, others were perpetrators (of violence), and some were both: victims and victimizers.

Among the most fiercely fighting troops during the last war period was a women unit called »The Women's Artillery Commandos«, led by General »Black Diamond«. Her followers irritated social gender stereotypes, as they made a point of styling themselves for battle with polished fingernails and trendy dresses. In a peculiar way, it seems war offered them an opportunity to emancipate from the oppression and discrimination they suffered in their communities and homes. Irma Specht points out:

> Girls interviewed gave two main feminist reasons for taking arms: the first was to protect themselves and other women from (particularly sexual) violence, and

---

[2]   Stephen Ellis, *The Mask of Anarchy* (London: Hurst & Co., 2001), 268.

Getty images picture no. 2394873

Picture 2: Colonel ›Black Diamond‹ of the LURD.

[secondly] to avenge such violence … Civilian girls were left with no other option than to flee or to join the fighting forces themselves, if they wanted to escape rape.[3]

Of course, the endemic, extreme poverty of Liberia played into the hands of chaos and mayhem. In the absence of public order, the attraction to resort to violence as a means of survival grew ever greater. People took to guns for a bag of grain or a pair of shoes. Some young women followed the militias more or less voluntarily to escape poverty, forced marriages, or to seek protection while escaping domestic violence. Others also sought revenge for their own suffering, being raped or witnessing the torturing and killing of loved ones. Plenty of girls and women were abducted into armed groups to provide sexual services to the commanders and fighters of the armed groups, to entertain troops and carry commanders' belongings and ammunition, to cook and farm.

This happened among both government and rebel troops. The similar experiences the women shared led to a kind of solidarity between the female commanders on both sides during the fighting. In an interview by Irmela Specht, [4] one female commander stated that when she captured a girl from the

---

[3]   Irma Specht and Larry Affree, *Red Shoes: Experiences of Girl-Combatants in Liberia* (Geneva: International Labor Office, 2006), 28.
[4]   Specht and Affree, *Red Shoes*, 76–77.

other faction, she was not able to kill her because she knew the other girl had gone through the same experience of rape as she had. As Nastassja Hoffet concludes:

> During and after the war, girls experience a larger spectrum of problems than boys do, ranging from physical attacks, sexual harassment and exploitation and early marriages with commanders in armed forces to more household responsibilities, unsafe work, health complications and early pregnancy.[5]

Right after the fighting in Liberia had ended in 2003, I frequently went with a friend of mine to a place in Monrovia, where about eighty female ex-combatants lived with their children. They lived in mere ruins. Throughout the country, thousands of refugees and »Internally Displaced People« (IDP) were living on fields, for example, under a tree, or on the roadside. But one thing was unusual: Whereas in my previous encounters with IDPs, they had directly approached me for help, these women were too afraid to take such initiative. Most of them were fighters or ex-fighters and were very uncertain and fearful about their prospects. Left behind, abandoned from their »bush husbands«, and facing possible prosecution, they did not know what to do. There was no place for them to go.

When disarmament by the UN started, their »bush husbands« disappeared, leaving the girls and women behind. Bereft of their weapons and with their supposed or actual commanders gone, the women were not considered combatants anymore, which meant that they did not go through the formal demobilization process, which would have given them access to skill trainings, trade or schooling. Moving on was not a viable option. Going back, however, was likewise rendered impossible to them. Some of the women intended to return to their parents' village. When they did, however, it became apparent that they had left the society's norms behind when they had gone into battle. They often showed aggressive behavior they had learned in the war, provoking others, using offensive language, smoking, using drugs, and generally violating gender norms.[6] As they felt more and more isolated and unaccepted, many reacted violently in order to gain respect, albeit out of fear, following the logic of »If you don't accept me, fear me.« Of course, this kind of behaviour convinced their respective communities all the more that these women pre-

---

5   Nastassja Hoffet, *Girl Soldiers Used Up, Then Thrown Away* (UN, March 12, 2009).

6   See Susan McKay, »How Do you Mend Broken Hearts? Gender, War and Impact on Girls in Fighting Forces.«, in *Handbook of International Disaster Psychology,* eds. Gerard A. Jacobs and Gilbert Reyes (Westport: Praeger, 2006) 45–60.

sented a threat to social peace and were best excluded from community life. The result was that most of those ex-combatants returning home encountered a spiral of social exclusion. While men returning from battle – regardless of the post-traumatic symptoms they may show (aggressiveness, depression, etc.) were considered ›normal‹, women had breached a taboo. »For a girl to do difficult things like killings and maiming is unthinkable. It is much more unthinkable than it is for a boy.«[7] Other women managed to abandon their ›bush‹-behaviour and became pregnant to identify themselves as women; however, they then did not know how to take care of the child.[8]

As a result, after the war ended, formerly tough female fighters were either treated as outcasts or pushed back into traditional roles. Programs for female combatants were often reduced to soap making, hairdressing, sewing and baking, pushing them back into the traditional roles they wanted to escape by having taken the gun in the first place. Those ex-combatants were most disappointed after they had returned their arms.[9] Of the 140 women surveyed in an interview by the United Institute for Peace in 2008, over 20 percent could envision fighting again for material goods. In contrast, only about 11 percent of men gave a similar response. Often they are facing stigmatization, which hinders their efforts to return to a peaceful life.[10] As a result, most former girl soldiers – whether they were recruited or abducted; whether they served as combatants or simply in support roles – try to hide their experiences emotionally because of shame and guilt, but also out of fear of rejection and violence. They are afraid of not being able to marry and have normal family lives. This indicates the need for senzitisation and education in communities to help decrease the stigma and to educate against domestic violence.

For any religious intervention and potential influence in this situation, one can identify three main issues that hinder a *healing of relations*: (1) the loss of values, (2) the conflict between the traditional and the modern role of women as they pertain to the war and its aftermath, and (3) the traumatic

---

[7]   Jane Morse, »Reintegration often Tougher for Girl Child Soldiers: Stigma, Secrecy Create Extra Burdens« *America Gov. Archive*, May 8, 2008. See http://www.america.gov/st/ democracyhr-english/2008/May/20080508144836ajesrom0.4115412.html (accessed on June 20, 2011).

[8]   See Carolyn R. Spellings, »Scratching the Surface: A Comparison of Girl Soldiers from Three Geographic Regions of the World,« *International Education* 38, no. 1 (2008), http://trace.tennessee.edu/internationaleducation/vol38/iss1/14 (accessed April 5, 2011).

[9]   See Richard Hill, *Special Report* (United States Institute for Peace, 2008).

[10]   Hill, *Special Report*, 5.

experiences as such. In Liberia, the issue of stigmatization presented an additional severe barrier to the healing process:

> There is an underlying expectation that ex-combatants must change and adapt …
> Most girls feel that they are basically alone with their experiences. They try to
> come to terms with their past by meeting former comrades. They find comfort in
> sharing their memories of hardship and suffering in the fighting forces, as they
> did during the war. This maintains strong bonds and interdependence between
> girl ex-combatants.[11]

Sitting together, sharing their experiences, and meeting other women with similar experiences, these women may be able to overcome their feelings of isolation, shame, and stigmatization eventually. It is crucial for any aid programs directed at these women to help them regain their dignity and humanize their relationships to themselves and to others, and to enable them to fight against rape and gender-based violence without taking the law (and guns) into their own hands.

Getty images picture no. 2425160

Picture 3: Fleeing women.

---

[11] Specht and Affree, *Red Shoes*, 76.

When I spoke to women who had been forced to flee their villages, and asked them how they survived, most of them said something like this: We were running, running, and running. Fight or flight – that was the option. But later, after the war, you need different skills other than being able to run and hide, and poverty and trauma become stress factors again.

Peacetime raises new challenges. Depression and suicidal ideation can break through as life becomes less tough.[12]

»Let's Pray the Devil Back to Hell«: Cathartic Worship

I remember a Thanksgiving service in a camp for Internally Displaced People (IDP) where parishioners were asked to talk about what has happened to them and to thank God for survival. It was very touching to hear about their experiences and fearful moments. In the end they were thanking God for their survival, and the congregation intensified this praise by songs, prayer, and dancing. Sometimes the people were not able to continue with stories or their voices became very low. One woman was telling her story in song. As she did, others from the congregation joined in to comfort her, to give her the feeling she was not alone in this situation. There was also an old woman among them, telling her story of how she had to watch her family being abducted by rebels and how they were then forced to carry the looted items to the rebel camp. She herself had managed to hide and was confined to looking on fearfully at what was going on, not knowing what to do. As she spoke, she became overwhelmed by her memories, and she was losing the thread of her story, repeating phrases over and over. This created some disturbance among the parishioners. »You see how I feel«, the women was saying, »fear is still in me. And fear is still here in this place.« It seemed the old woman and her incessant fearful emotions were overstressing the parishioners. They wanted to escape the sphere of spreading fear. I was surprised, then, to see some women starting to sing, standing up and surrounding the woman as they sang, in fact keeping her and her emotions in a circle. By doing so, they helped her come back to the reality of the here and now and find a way out of the fear.

---

[12]   See Judith Baessler, »Surviving the Past,« in IRIN News, November 10, 2010, http://www.irinnews.org/IndepthMain.aspx?InDepthID=87&ReportID=91038, (accessed April 5, 2011).

The service was seen as a place for the parishioners to talk about what had happened to them during the war. The congregation serves as a space of resonance for their stories, as people become witnesses to one another. In fellowship, the uniqueness of each individual fate is recognized. By offering a sheltered space to speak out and make their suffering public, the congregation is able to at least partially break the emotional isolation, which is among the most important steps for overcoming trauma. The very experience of individuals being part of a greater community is also important in this regard. People are reassured that they do not have to bear the burden of their memories alone. It may be that parishes are in a particularly capable position for this kind of support, as they offer familiar surroundings to their parishioners that are commonly associated with strong positive memories and collective festivities. In this way, the service helped to free participants from hate, from suffering, and from the idea of revenge. It became a place to experience strength and solidarity and new hope to overcome the situation, to remember accustomed traditions and rites and past instances of divine consolation and intervention. »Let's pray the devil back to hell!« This is what the people shouted again and again. And they all knew whom they meant by the devil: any gunman or gunwoman who did harm them. It may seem a paradox that by creating an occasion for praise and thankfulness, the service succeeded in helping the people feel like human beings (again), no longer occupied by the horrible things they went through. From personal observation, I learned that the shared experience of suffering and surviving the war formed a strong – yet subliminal – form of solidarity that proved stronger than former feuds and rivalries. As people shared their experiences, consoled each other spiritually in empathy and solidarity, and gave thanks for survival in worship and praise, formerly destroyed social networks were re-established. In this way it becomes possible to put down hate and revenge and open their eyes to the future as people join in prayer to call to God for help.

In this context, I was reminded of the *community psychology* described by Martín-Baró, a liberation psychologist of the last century.[13] What I witnessed during my stay in Liberia in 2003 could be seen as *community counseling*. Here, the community works as the therapist with the resources at hand; in a christological twist, it also serves as an intermediary network between God and the congregation, capable to bear (and contain) unsolved fragments of hate, of broken relations, and of unhealed wounds.

---

[13]   See Ignacio Martín-Baró, *Writings for a Liberation Psychology* (Cambridge: Harvard University Press, 1994).

Picture 4: Women in White.

Interestingly, the healing churches and prayer centers are springing up in every Monrovian neighbourhood. Liberians are increasingly putting their faith in spiritual salvation. »Spirituality is one of the biggest assets that Liberians have to cope with what had happened«, says psychologist Baessler in research published in 2008.[14] »It's a way of letting go of the atrocities and moving forward. The war lasted too long and too many bad things happened. It doesn't mean you are okay, it just means you go on living as best you can.«

THE WOMEN IN WHITE: AN INTERRELIGIOUS WOMEN'S PEACE MOVEMENT

An inspiring example of such a group that wanted to ›move forward‹ can certainly be found in the Women in White. The group started with prayers in the small chapel of the Lutheran Compound where I lived, and where Leymah Gbowee of the trauma healing program of the Lutheran Church and Lutheran World Federation (LCL/LWF) was working at the time. From the very begin-

---

[14] See Judith Baessler, »Surviving the Past.«, in IRIN News, November 10, 2010, http://www.irinnews.org/IndepthMain.aspx?InDepthID=87&ReportID=91038, (accessed April 5, 2011).

ning until the end of my work in Liberia, I was involved with the movement. Every Tuesday they gathered and demanded peace and a cease-fire. Just standing up and voicing their demands helped them not to feel like mere victims of violence. As their movement grew and the public became more aware of this grassroots-resistance movement, a documentary film was produced by Gini Reticker and Abigail E. Disney, entitled »Pray the Devil Back to Hell«. The title is drawn from a quote by Leymah Gbowee about Charles Taylor and the rebels, who, in the words of Leymah Gbowee, could »pray the devil out of hell«. In order to fully understand the scope of the quote, one must be aware of the fact that both sides were (supposedly) religious. The rebels were predominantly Muslim, while Taylor justified many of his crimes with Christian »teachings«. As a consequence, the Women in White saw it as their responsibility in this inter-faith coalition to pray the devil (of war) right back to hell. »We are tired of war!« This was their message. They reminded everyone willing to pay attention – conflict parties as well as the global public – that there were humans, civilians, suffering for the greed and vanity of warlords on both sides. Bob Marley's song »Get up! Stand up!« served as their informal anthem.

Women's peace activism was built on the experience that systematic violence against women in their homes, in the camps, in society – such as rape, forced prostitution, mutilation – was an expression of a deep-rooted disregard for women in their society. The women were suffering from broken relations between males and females due to the war. In their actions, they developed strength and power by using women's numerical strength and their ability to mobilize. Women from all levels of Liberian society were recruited from displaced camps, churches, markets, schools, ordinary jobs, and NGOs:

> For many women the Mass Action was a training camp; it proved what women could do in big numbers, voices and strength, and catapulted women from behind-the-scenes victims to frontline soldiers for peace, bridging a divide between the more educated »elite« and women from grassroots communities.[15]

At first no one took the Mass Action seriously, but the women became a constant presence on the streets in Monrovia – and later on throughout the country. Women carried placards and posters every day, rain or shine. Muslim and Christian women, dressed in white, came together to pray at the airfield. Bishops and Imams came to show their solidarity. The campaign chose

---

[15]   Abigail E. Disney and Gini Reticker, *Pray the Devil Back to Hell* (New York: Fork Films, 2008).

a simple and effective message: »We want peace; no more war.« And when the situation got worse, they answered with a sex-strike, saying to their husbands: »If you want to enjoy life, stop war and killing!« Though all women were committed to the campaign, the greatest sacrifice came from women who had lost loved ones or had been displaced or separated from their families. They said: »We have nothing to lose; we are ready to do what it takes to end this war.« All these women gave an impressive human face to the conflict. They all were dressed in white: no makeup, no jewels, only plain white clothes. They were seen everywhere, and in this they impressed the people. According to them, what really gave them power and courage were ›the dress‹, fasting and praying, putting their voices together, singing and dancing with tears and hope, standing and sitting in a circle. The longer they stuck together, the more they felt their responsibility and their importance. They transformed their individual experience into a common concern. Their presence and their message, »We want peace, no more war!«, soon became a universal mantra and song. »Keep your boys at home«, they asked every family so as to prevent them from being abducted by rebels. Soon, the movement became interreligious: »Does the bullet know who is a Christian and who is a Muslim? Can bullets pick and choose?« This is how Vaibah, one of the organizers, convinced sceptical Christian women. The Women in White acted as messengers between the various factions with their demands to stop fighting. There were also services being held; a famous one occurred in St. Peter's Lutheran Church at the beginning of 2003. From there, they were sending messages and appeals to their religious and political leaders from all factions, Traditional, Muslim, and Christian.

The relentless singing of (usually spiritual, but also improvisational) songs and hymns evolved as a means to strengthen the fleeing people, also among the Women in White wherever they gathered. In song, they were able to voice their dark experiences in the bush, and the subsequent and often unsuccessful search for their relatives. They kept themselves going through anecdotes and songs. Reading psalms and feeling at home in Bible stories; they had the feeling God was keeping them at going on even when they felt depressed. In an internal report on their activities, they explain that preserving the psychological well-being of women in the campaign was as important as the goal itself: the well-being and caring for the peace women.

Especially in Accra, where the peace talks were being held in 2003, the women who had left their families behind were under enormous stress. The outcome of the talks seemed uncertain at best; many were worried about the success of their campaigning for peace. The women responded by deciding that they needed to adapt to harsher nonviolent strategies. The women insisted that men not leave until they took the process seriously and committed themselves to reaching an agreement. They protested passionately, holding up placards saying »Killers of our people – no impunity this time«, »Butchers and murderers of the Liberian people stop!«, and »How many babies do you intend to slaughter?« This presence of the women demonstrating at the talks removed the focus from the warring factions to the real people affected by the conflict. Many people joined. The incentive to join the peace women were these: to get free from suffering caused by poverty and violence, to leave behind the status of a passive victim, to leave behind humiliation and disregard, which in turn stimulated violence and revenge.

A common challenge when dealing with victims of violence (often women, elderly, and children) is that after their initial suffering, they are at risk of being victimized once more by being seen as a helpless object, a needy recipient of help. Engaging with the Women in White gave many a new sense and meaning in life; the fellowship of the women was marked by reliable values. Furthermore, they were offered an opportunity to take responsibility for themselves and also for each other. Being able to protest alongside others also gave them a measure of control over living conditions within their community that were previously unimaginable.[16]

Nevertheless, emotional and physical scars of war prevail. There is still great need for training programs on all levels and for all groups of society that help participants deal with feelings like anger, aggression, depression, and conflict resolution. The role of the church as a grassroots community with widespread infrastructure and high acceptance levels should not be underestimated in this regard.

MEN AS CHANGE AGENTS

After the war, plenty of placards were seen along the road, saying, »Don't rape the women!« and »No violence against women!« In 2008, there were special rape courts installed. Nevertheless, according to reports from Liberia, the country is still experiencing extraordinarily high rates of rape and sexual assault. To change or to heal the deep-seated aggressiveness in the relationship

---

[16] Hans-Martin Gutmann identifies these experiences as »moments of gratitude«. See his essay in this volume.

between men and women is still one of the main objectives nowadays. In order to achieve this goal, it will be necessary to develop different role models for men, providing them with alternative ways of self-affirmation other than getting power by force and showing masculinity by violence, force, and sexual abuse.

> Networking women and non-governmental organizations that promote gender equality and social justice is effective. Recognition of women's rights, protection of women and children against sexual and domestic violence, and punishment of offenders can counteract sexist and proprietorial models of masculinity. This requires that sexism and organized crimes such as trafficking in human beings and forced prostitution be condemned by the society. [17]

It is only possible and realistic to develop peace after violence by overcoming this image of masculinity and developing a new orientation for males. To achieve this, *change agents* are needed who refuse violent ways of conflict-solving. They could define their masculine identity by engaging in human dignity, human rights, justice, and partnership. They could be religious leaders and authorities, priests (like Bishop Francis in Liberia), Imams, local authorities, and leaders of civil groups. It could also take just a single man to oppose violent behavior in his group and side with the women, as the following astounding anecdotes show.

During the course of the peace talks in 2003 in Accra, the Women in White were blocking the hall to demand a result of the talks and an end to the tiring bargaining among the different factions. General Abubakar, who was heading the peace talks, shouted into the microphone: »Oh my God, the peace hall has been seized by General Leymah and her troops!« Using the words »General« and »her troops«, he made them equal adversaries, on the same level as warlords. As the warlords and their delegations were becoming rude to them, he addressed the men sharply:

> Sit down! Go in! If you are a real man you won't be killing your people! That's why these women treat you like boys. Go back and I dare anyone to leave this hall until we negotiated with these women.[18]

---

[17]   Rita Schäfer, »Masculinity and Civil Wars in Africa,« in: *GTZ Dokumentation* (Eschborn: Gesellschaft für Technische Zusammenarbeit, 2009), 8.

[18]   Abigail E. Disney and Gini Reticker, *Pray the Devil Back to Hell* (New York: Fork Films, 2008).

My friend William Saa met another change agent in 2009 on his way to Voin-jama in Lofa. Several cars were stuck in the mud. While trying to get out of the mud, one of the other men approached him and identified himself as a general fighter also on his way to Lofa. He went on to confess that he did not know how to settle after the war and how to be accepted in the community. Some time later, they met again in Voinjama, where the general was invited to participate in a trauma healing program. Since finishing the program, he has been working with young boys in the town to help them reintegrate into their community, using the special link between the combatants and their commander:

a) The youth accepted him because he was a commander; and the com-manding structures they were used to during the war could be used for a peaceful purpose.
b) He himself got a responsible position and felt he was needed. His influence on the youth could be used for stopping their threats to people. He knew how to deal with them, taking care of law and order in town and helping to solve conflicts.
c) The ex-general became a »re-educator« because the young boys who trou-bled the town listened to him. He is a respected person now in the whole community.

In typical fashion, the new perspective on life brought with it a new name. As he was formerly known locally as the »Master General«, he later was known as »Master General for Peace«! His ability and capacity as a leader, but also his feeling of »uselessness«, was used for a peace purpose.

Despite such inspiring stories, it is understood that true change for the country will only be achieved if the profoundly unjust social and economic sit-uation can be overcome, and injustice and inequality among men and be-tween men and women can be improved. Beside the aforementioned examples of a change in attitudes on a local level, there has also been a powerful politi-cal statement on the national, if not global scale. Since the year 2007 (a ver-dict due within this year), former President Charles Taylor has been trialed at the international court of justice at The Hague. Meanwhile, Ellen Johnson-Sirleaf, as the first woman president in Africa, leads a tough presidency and develops hopeful perspectives for the country.

In traditional, hierarchical, and male-dominated structures, it is difficult to deal with weakness and failure due to the fear of losing face. There is also a need to deepen the theological reflection in Liberia to question the image of God and its effect on men and women. What does it mean: God the Almighty? Before and during the war, it was connected with power and violence. To gain a different understanding of God, one also needs to involve Christ as the divine but crucified and suffering Jesus – Jesus as the wounded healer! Jesus as your brother! In the process of peace building, one has to start with the wounded healer. Remembering the story of Cain and Abel, I ask: Where were the sisters in this story? Is there only victim and victimizer?

Having survived violence and war, it is impossible to come up with a shared and general narrative or perspective for victims and victimizers. If a whole country is destroyed by war and violence, reconstruction and safety in the country are needed, parallel to necessary reconstruction and creating safety for individuals. This will take time. And just as individuals may need to turn to inner resources to help them deal with their past, a society torn by conflict may also need to turn to its healing resources from within – community-based organisations, like churches, and well-recognized and accepted role models and leaders. It is important to strengthen such organizations and structures – for, as one participant of a consultation on Migration in Hamburg in 2010 put it, »In times of peace you can do a lot by interaction. If there is no peace, you need a history of interaction.«

Literature

Baessler, Judith. »Surviving the Past.« *IRIN News*, November 10, 2010. http://www.irinnews.org/IndepthMain.aspx?InDepthID=87&ReportID=91038 (accessed April 5, 2011).

Disney, Abigail E. and Gini Reticker. *Pray the Devil Back to Hell*. New York: Fork Films, 2008.

Ellis, Stephen. *The Mask of Anarchy*. London: Hurst & Co., 2001.

Hill, Richard, Gwendolyn Taylor and Jonathan Temin. »Would You Fight Again?« *Special Report* no. 211. Washington: United States Institute for Peace, 2008. http://www.usip.org/files/resources/sr211.pdf (accessed April 5, 2011).

Hoffet, Nastassja. »Girl Soldiers Used Up, Then Thrown Away.« *Inter Press Service*, March 12, 2009. http://ipsnews.net/news.asp?idnews=46085 (accessed April 5, 2011).

Martín-Baró, Ignacio. *Writings for a Liberation Psychology*. Cambridge: Harvard University Press, 1994.

McKay, Susan. »How Do You Mend Broken Hearts? Gender, War and Impact on Girls in Fighting Forces.« In *Handbook of International Disaster Psychology*, Vol 4, edited by Gerard A. Jacobs and Gilbert Reyes, 45–60, Westport: Praeger, 2006.

Schäfer, Rita. »Masculinity and Civil Wars in Africa.« *GTZ Documentation*, Eschborn: Gesellschaft für Technische Zusammenarbeit, 2009.

Specht, Irma and Larry Affree. *Red Shoes: Experiences of Girl-Combatants in Liberia.* Geneva: International Labour Office, 2006.

Spellings, Carolyn R. »Scratching the Surface: A Comparison of Girl Soldiers from Three Geographic Regions of the World.« *International Education* 38, no. 1, 21–39. http://trace. tennessee.edu/internationaleducation/vol38/iss1/14 (accessed April 5, 2011).

Truth and Reconciliation Commission of Liberia, Final Report. Monrovia: TRC, 2009. http://trcofliberia.org/reports/final-report (accessed April 5, 2011).

After Violence and the Anzac Tradition

Phillip Tolliday

Introduction

The relevance of exploring what I shall denote as the ›Anzac Myth‹ in relation to this volume's theme of *After Violence* is that it serves to demonstrate how a false or ideologically constructed memory of the past may indeed legitimate violence. This essay is essentially about how we choose to remember the past and the part that the story of Anzac has come to play in our corporate memory.[1]

I had been attending Anzac Day marches on April 25th since I was about seven years old, beginning during the mid-1960s. My parents gave me no encouragement to do so, and they themselves never attended. Year in and year out, in what was often cold, wet, and windy weather, I would stand on the footpath in Sturt Street, Ballarat, watching as the old men from the First World War, followed by their younger counterparts from the Second World War, made their way down the street toward the cenotaph.

I had an uncle who had served in Tobruk, El Alamein and New Guinea, and a great uncle who had been posted as ›missing‹ after the first push on the Hindenburg Line in 1917. Some might suggest – rightly – that I had a highly romanticized view of Anzac Day. At this time, during the 1960s and 1970s as Australians found themselves in an unpopular war in Vietnam, it seemed as

---

[1]   The word ›Anzac‹ was originally an acronym that arose during the First World War. It stood for Australian and New Zealand Army Corps and was stenciled on equipment sent to the Gallipoli campaign in 1915. It was at Gallipoli that Australian and New Zealand troops were first called ›ANZACS‹. However the name soon evolved into a proper noun and is also used adjectivally. The first Anzac commemoration took place in 1916 and has continued uninterrupted to the present.

if Anzac Day might come to an end. As public opinion shifted against the war in Vietnam and as Australia morphed into a more multi-cultural society with looser links to its imperial past, it was thought that Anzac Day and the alleged ideals for which it stood had perhaps outlived their usefulness. From a personal perspective I noted how the old men grew frailer and even the younger ones became old, and I adopted, albeit reluctantly, the view that all things must pass – including Anzac Day.

Yet sometime in the early 1990s, something changed, and those who had forecast – with joy or regret – the inevitable demise of Anzac Day were proven wrong. By the time the last soldiers of the Western Front had died and taken their personal history with them, Australians witnessed a resurgence of interest in the Anzac story. Many greeted this resurgence with joy, others with a sense of grave disquiet, and here I confess to belong to the latter category. For the last several years I have not attended the March. There are no longer any soldiers from the Great War and the ranks from the Second World War have thinned so considerably and rapidly that within ten years they too will have all but vanished. In their place now march grandchildren, keeping up, we are told, the traditions and spirit of Anzac. But as personal memory disappears and gradually slips into history, and as what I knew and experienced as Anzac Day becomes lodged in the irrecoverable past, it is perhaps timely to inquire about this comparatively recent and stridently proclaimed phenomenon: the *spirit* of the Anzac tradition.

This *spirit* of Anzac now seems to be invoked in a range of areas, including sporting events, the management of natural disasters such as floods and bushfires, the sending of Australian troops into Iraq and Afghanistan, in support of almost any argument to buttress national identity, and, in recent years, the Federal Government's values and ethics education in schools. This is a recent phenomenon, certainly not older than 1990. It is, I will suggest, a remembering of a past we never had and a construction of a present which, unleashed from the proper constraints of history and memory, threatens to ignore portions of our history which are violent and with which we as a nation have not yet come to terms.

When people think of Australia, they often have in mind its rugged natural environment. Rarely do we make the news on the world stage unless it is because of some natural disaster such as bushfire or flood. We are not, I think, perceived as a militaristic country but rather as a peaceful and peace-loving one. Indeed, that is one of the reasons why large numbers of refugees fleeing from war-torn countries have been attracted to Australia. And yet we must ask whether this pacific picture is not somewhat idealized. I will suggest that this picture is a view of the way we never were and that the Anzac myth, instead of mourning violence and war, as was its original intention, has now gained a triumphal, indeed celebratory note, which is untrue to the history to which it allegedly points.

The Ethical Imperative of History

»Historical communities, as Ricoeur repeatedly shows, are constituted in great part by the stories they recount to themselves and to others.« Thus it follows that »identity is a form of memory. Or as Hegel put it, *das Wesen ist das Gewesene.*«[2] Most nations have a founding story or narrative, and from it they generate their self-understanding. However, sometimes there is more than one possible narrative on which a nation may choose to pin its identity. Moreover, a particular narrative understanding may be contested, and the question of which narrative shall be the dominant one is driven by multiple interests, some of which are difficult to unmask.

Kearney argues that each nation or society discovers that at its root it is an »imagined community«, which means that, in terms of narrative construction, it is a community that can be, somewhat, at least, »reinvented and reconstructed.« His conclusion is salutary and should give us pause for thought.

> After such a discovery of one's narrative identity, it is more difficult to make the mistake of taking oneself *literally*, of assuming that one's collective identity *goes without* saying. This is why, at least in principle, the tendency of a nation toward xenophobic or insular nationalism can be resisted by its own narrative resources to imagine itself otherwise – either through its own eyes or those of others.[3]

In other words, Kearney and Ricoeur are arguing that nations and societies make choices about the founding narratives they will tell and the national identity that shall be constructed thereby.

We shall see in greater detail just how the so-called ›history wars‹ of the 1990s led to a re-casting of the Anzac story in a way that would emphasize some facets of our history while quietly eliding others. But at this point, I simply want to note that this re-casting took place at roughly the same time that personal memory was fading and the imperial ties with England that had

---

2   Richard Kearney, *On Paul Ricoeur: The Owl of Minerva* (Ashgate: Aldershot, 2004), 104.
3   Kearney, *On Paul Ricoeur*, 105, emphasis in the original.

been an essential part of the Anzac story were being slowly eviscerated. This fading of memory gave room for ideological imagination.

If, as we suggested above, history is a construction of identity formation, it invites us to pose the question about the nature of history. If history is immutable, a bare recounting of objective, discrete, and indubitable facts, then the corporate or national identity built upon it will be similarly inevitable and immutable. But if, at the opposite end of the spectrum, the practice of history is construed to be nothing other than the constructive use of the human imagination, then the identity, or more accurately *identities*, which are built upon it will be as flexible and polyvalent as the imaginative construals that gave birth to them. Though these visions of history lie at opposite ends of the spectrum, they share in common an assumption that history is not, and indeed cannot, be an ethical task. It is, however, that assumption that I reject here.

We may agree with Hayden White when he claims that every historical narrative has as »its latent or manifest purpose the desire to moralise the events of which it treats.«[4] Those who argue for history as a simple recounting of facts testify to the latent dimension of White's claim, while historians who come from the constructivist background, such as White himself and Roland Barthes, exemplify the manifest characteristic to which he gestures. There are two points to be noted here. The first is that whether acknowledged or not, the writing of history is an ethical task and responsibility. The second is that if every narrative seeks to moralise the events about which it speaks, how are we to ensure that such moralizing happens justly? It is somewhat ironic that White and Barthes, in arguing for only a most tenuous connection between narrative and the events to which it bears witness, end up with the possibility of severing any ethical connection to history. If, as they seem to suggest, historical narrative is characterized by »irrepresentability and irreference«, then it might appear to put in question »the power of narrative to retrieve historically real events for our ethical consideration in the here and now.«[5] A more considered appropriation of White's claim might lead us to wonder whether White also strives for a form of objectivity, albeit from his perspective of a constructivist imagination.

---

[4]   Hayden White, »The Value of Narrativity in the Representation of Reality,« in *The Content of the Form: Narrative Discourse and Historical Representation* (Baltimore: Johns Hopkins University, 1987), 14.

[5]   Kearney, *On Paul Ricoeur*, 103.

As we noted above, communities come to know themselves in the stories they tell about themselves. Such narrative memories are never innocent – there is too much at stake to permit that to happen. Instead, there is a continual »conflict of interpretations« where every history is told from »a certain perspective and in the light of a specific prejudice (at least in Gadamer's sense).«[6] We do well to apply a Ricoeurean hermeneutic of suspicion to our historical narratives, for, as Kearney reminds us, »memory is not always on the side of the Angels. It can as easily lead to false consciousness and ideological closure as to openness and tolerance.«[7]

The ethical dimension of history cannot be severed from an ethics of memory, and one of the critical functions of narrative memory identified by Ricoeur is that it involves and evokes empathy. A characteristic of empathy is that it seeks to identify with and include as many people as possible in order to participate in what Kearney calls »a common moral sense«.

> In this manner, narrative imagination can assist a certain universalization of remembrance. Here our own memories – personal and communal – can be shared and exchanged with others of very different times and places. The familiar and the foreign can change hands.[8]

Thus, as I shall show later in the essay, Prime Minister Howard could recognize and appreciate the truth of this universalization in the myth of Anzac, but he could not recognize it in the demand from many Australians to apologise to the Stolen Generations and on behalf of the nation to express sorrow for the violence done to Aboriginal communities. Many put the Prime Minister's intractability down to political machinations, but might it be that Ricoeur and Kearney are closer to the truth when they speak about the connection between memory and empathy? Is empathy one of the ways in which we may assure ourselves that memory is not playing us false?

The faculty of human imagination is an essential ingredient in memory and history. Yet the problem of the similarity and difference between memory and imagination has been one that has haunted Western thinking about memory, history, and writing ever since the ancient Greeks. Ricoeur has been especially sensitive to this problematic and follows Aristotle that »all memory is of the past.«[9] This seemingly unremarkable observation permits us to see

---

[6] Kearney, *On Paul Ricoeur*, 105.

[7] Kearney, *On Paul Ricoeur*, 105.

[8] Kearney, *On Paul Ricoeur*, 107, emphasis in the original.

[9] Ricoeur, *Memory, History, Forgetting* (Chicago: University of Chicago Press, 2006), 6.

that although Ricoeur endorses a conflict of interpretations and thus of national narratives, he is far from being a relativist. There could, he says, »be no *good* use of memory if there were no aspect of truth.«[10] In that sense, he agrees with the nineteenth century German school of history, which claimed that we have to tell things as they really happened.[11]

Typically, memory and imagination have been posed as referring to the real and the unreal past in a Sartrean fashion. There is some plausibility to this because part of the role of imagination is to bring us »outside of the real world – into unreal or possible worlds.« But it also has a second function, which is to »put memories *before our eyes.*«[12] And it is at this point that Ricoeur enlists the assistance of testimony as the connection between imagination and memory/history.

> Testimony is the ultimate link between imagination and memory, because the witness says, ›I was part of the story. I was there.‹ At the same time, the witness tells a story that is a living presentation, and therefore deploys the capacity of imagination to place the events before our eyes, as if we were there.[13]

It is noteworthy that, with regard to the Anzac story, the narrative begins to change at around the same time as personal testimonies diminish. Yet the late 1980s and 1990s witnessed a fever of activity to publish memoirs and stories before the old soldiers finally died and took their stories with them.

But is testimony no less liable to ideological distortion than memory or imagination? Testimony is based on a blending of »believing-that and trusting-in ... Testimony does not exclude criticism.«[14] Ricoeur's response is to say that all testimony is inevitably selective, but this does not mean that some critical safeguards cannot be applied. The critical historian must, he says, »give expression to the voices of those who have been abused, the victims of intentional exclusion.« And while the historian's voice is selective, it is »far less selective than the dominant class.«[15] We will do well to keep this advice in mind as we unravel how a new re-telling of the Anzac story has effectively become our new national narrative and one in which the competing inter-

---

[10] Kearney, *On Paul Ricoeur*, 154, emphasis in the original.

[11] Classically expressed by von Ranke: *wie es eigentlich gewesen.*

[12] Kearney, *On Paul Ricoeur*, 155.

[13] Kearney, *On Paul Ricoeur*, 155.

[14] Michael Johnson, »Review Article: Memory, History, Forgetting, by Paul Ricoeur«, *Anglican Theological Review*, 89,1: Winter 2007, 109.

[15] Kearney, *On Paul Ricoeur*, 156.

pretations of the ›history-wars‹ about our Aboriginal history were effectively elided.

ANZAC – OUR NATIONAL NARRATIVE?

Henry Reynolds, interviewing some senior high school students, asked why they thought Anzac Day was important.[16] He received two answers. The first was that the young soldiers had »shown a spirit that was inimitably Australian.« The second was that »the Anzac landing had made Australia a nation.«[17] Though disappointed by their answers, he found it representative of many students and therefore unsurprising. This was the answer they were expected to give, for this was the answer that was the common currency of leaders of all political persuasions and many academics. The leading military historian Peter Stanley had argued that the Gallipoli campaign »occupies a central place in Australia's national mythology, identity and memory. The landing on the Peninsula has been portrayed by commentators across the political spectrum as representing the place and time when Australia became a nation.«[18]

This view of history is manifestly untrue, and yet it is so pervasive as to be largely unquestioned. Australia became a nation in 1901, but such a momentous event, in which we devised our own constitution, did not happen *de novo*. Was the first one hundred years of white settlement merely window dressing? Was there nothing, asks Reynolds, »that happened within the Australian colonies before 1915 that had the importance of the Anzac landing?« From much of what is said and taught today, one might think not. But, as Reynolds shows in a remarkable *tour de force*, such rhetoric cannot stand up to the scrutiny of history.

> Could the Commonwealth of Australia fairly be described as an inadequate nation? By any measure it was a remarkably successful society; the envy of many countries in the contemporary world. It was peaceful, well governed and pro-

---

16 Note the way the question is asked. It assumes the day is important. During the 1960s and 1970s such an assumption would have been far from self-evident.

17 Henry Reynolds, »Are Nations Really Made in War?« in *What's Wrong With Anzac? The Militarisation of Australian History*, eds. Marilyn Lake and Henry Reynolds (Sydney: University of New South Wales Press, 2010), 24.

18 Deborah Gare and David Ritter, *Making Australian History* (Melbourne: Thompson Press, 2008), 311.

sperous. The average family was better nourished, housed and educated than in almost any other society. For more than half a century the self- governing colonies had developed their economies and their institutions and had introduced progressive reforms which had placed them at the forefront of democratic advance. The tradition was carried through into the first years of the new Commonwealth, which introduced women's rights, a living wage, old age pensions and kindred measures which pioneered the welfare state. This story of progressive, innovative legislation was recognized by well-informed contemporaries in Britain, continental Europe and North America. And at the time the White Australia Policy that underpinned these advances was widely admired and emulated.[19]

Australia did not, somehow, whether really or spiritually, come into being as a nation in 1915, or if it did, then that momentous fact remains unnoticed by such critical historians as Manning Clark in his five volume history of Australia. It would, after all, be a very peculiar national narrative that was so embedded in the background of British Imperialism. As Reynolds points out, Australia, though a Commonwealth, was not an independent nation state either before or after 1915.

> The national government had no say in the decision as to where the Australian Imperial Force (AIF) would go, who it would fight and for what reasons of state they would kill and be killed. Australia couldn't even choose its own enemies.[20]

More disturbingly, from the perspective of the conference theme of *After Violence,* Reynolds raises two critical questions. The first is whether nations that have lived in peace somehow lack something important. And secondly, how does violence contribute to a nation's spirit or identity? Although there were always voices of caution that advised against Australia becoming involved in Imperial wars, these Colonial Cassandras, as Reynolds calls them, were never more than a dissenting minority. Instead, it was a combination of social Darwinism and Edwardian militaristic values that carried the day. After 1915, one of Australia's celebrated poets wrote:

> The mettle that a race can show
> Is proved with shot and shell,
> And now we know what nations know
> And feel what nations feel.[21]

---

[19] Reynolds, »Are Nations Really Made in War?«, 26

[20] Reynolds, »Are Nations Really Made in War?«, 27.

[21] Andrew Barton ›Banjo‹ Paterson in Gavin Souter, *Lion and Kangaroo: Australia 1901–1919: The Rise of a Nation* (Sydney: Collins Press, 1976), 229.

These ideas were the common currency of the time, and Australia was merely going along with a dominant tide of opinion. English militarist Lord Frederick Roberts wrote:

> A nation is in risk of running to seed. And when the war is a just one ... its benefit to the nation is great. It is an appeal to the manhood and the virtue of the people. It prevents decadence and effeminacy. It corrects the selfishness and querulousness which are inevitably bred by a long peace ... A nation needs to be tried by fire – needs to be put on trial every now and then, and tested by the laws which govern this planet ... the law I mean, particularly, that only the efficient survive.[22]

It is hard to see the difference between this and the notorious Prussian militarist Heinrich von Treitschke, who argued that »only in war does a nation become a nation.«[23]

Pacifists of the day argued that far from war ensuring the survival of the fittest, it actually resulted in the destruction, crippling, and maiming of many of the fittest. But though the pacifists' arguments were strong, most people seemed not to find them compelling. Instead, an argument was made for the purifying qualities of armed conflict. War, it was claimed, would make the nation more earnest while at the same time removing mutual distrust and commercial dishonesty. In other words, conflict would sow a common purpose to our national identity and make us of one heart and mind. And it was with such hopes in mind that in the early years of the War the Prime Minister, W. M. Hughes argued:

> Since it has evoked this pure and noble spirit who shall say that this dreadful war is wholly an evil? Into a world saturated with a lust of material things, which had elevated self into a deity, which had made wealth the standard of greatness, comes the sweet purifying breath of self sacrifice.[24]

But at the very time the Prime Minister was expressing these views, the country was locked in a bitterly sectarian debate over the merits of conscription, thereby demonstrating that the War was fracturing society more than welding it together.

---

22   Reynolds, »Are Nations Really Made in War?«, 34.

23   Adam Gowans, ed., *Heinrich von Treitschke: Selections From His Lectures on Politics* (London: Gowans & Gray, 1914), 24. Later historians would seek to distance themselves from from von Treitschke's ideas, particularly his notorious claim later reproduced by the Nazis that »the Jews are our Misfortune.«

24   Reynolds, »Are Nations Really Made in War?«, 31.

These thoughts were common enough throughout the late nineteenth and early twentieth century; however, the disturbing prospect is that they remain part of the way in which Australians seek to understand themselves today. We are no longer tied to an Imperial Britain, and we are a modern multicultural society; therefore, it is all the more concerning that these values of a long outmoded society continue to be extremely influential. In the next section I shall look at the way in which the education of our children plays a role in perpetuating some of these ideas, but in finishing this particular theme, I want to outline some of the ways in which Edwardian militarism was transformed and transported through Australian culture.

By the end of the Great War it seemed that much of the jingoistic Edwardian militarism had collapsed. But in Australia, the Anzac legend attempted to glorify the tragedy of war. Robin Gerster has pointed out some of the ways in which war correspondents such as CEW Bean had portrayed armed conflict as though it were »an exhilarating, if dangerous, adventure.« The prose of many correspondents was replete with sporting metaphors, suggesting that Australians »excelled, even reveled in battle and that the war hero was the apotheosis of Australian manhood.«[25]

In the years between the First and Second World Wars there was a continual struggle between anti-war publications and those who, believing themselves to be on the side of the angels, as it were, proposed a system of censorship to be directed against those who, in their view, sought to »defame Australian soldiers.«[26]

In 1936, when it was evident to many that the world was about to be dragged into yet another major conflict, the magazine *Reveille* advertised twelve volumes on the Great War. It proclaimed: *Epic Stories that Touch the Heartstrings! Volumes that can be handed down to your Children's Children! Send for them Now and so Salute the Modern Odysseus.* The total cost for this package was three pounds and twelve shillings – a considerable amount of money for a country just beginning to come out of the Great Depression.

But neither should we miss the allusion to Homer and *The Odyssey* in these epic stories for, as Gerster commented, the Anzacs, as well as having »grown strong through generations of combat with the Australian bush, had now somehow atavistically inherited the transcendent qualities of the heroes of the legendary Trojan battlefield so tantalizingly close to Gallipoli

---

[25] Reynolds, »Are Nations Really Made in War?«, 42.

[26] Robin Gerster, *Big-Noting: The Heroic Theme in Australian War Writing* (Melbourne: Melbourne University Press, 1987), 118.

itself.«[27] This connection with the heroic theme of Greek mythology was also noted in a book written by R. Hugh Knyvett, entitled ›*Over There*‹ *with the Australians*. Published in 1918, Knyvett, a junior officer, and prior to the war, a clergyman, boasted that »the exploits of the Australians made the deeds of the heroes of past times pale into insignificance.« But at the same time, as he recorded his feelings on returning to Australia, he noted that he felt just like »the old King of Ithaca who had wandered for many years in many lands, but at last had returned home, and soon would have Penelope in his arms.«[28]

However, the homecoming for many soldiers was somewhat different from that of Odysseus. On return to Australia, they were confronted with a society that was polarized and in which some were caught up in clashes of mob violence in riots that broke out in Melbourne and Brisbane. Though seldom acknowledged, it is nonetheless true that »more strike days were lost in 1919 than in any year until the 1970s.«[29] War, it seems, had not had the pacific and unifying effect that had been supposed.

Opposition and struggle were also key features of how Anzac Day should be commemorated and just what part it ought to play in Australian national consciousness. Thus, in 1922, the National Congress of the conservative Returned Sailors and Soldiers Imperial League of Australia (RSSILA) resolved that »Anzac Day should be known as Australia's National Day and be observed with a statutory public holiday on April 25th ›to combine the memory of the Fallen with rejoicing at the birth of Australia as a nation‹, and ›to inculcate into the rising generation the highest national ideals.‹«[30]

If we grant, as the evidence suggests, that the commemoration of Anzac Day has a contested background, and if we attend to the fact that during the 1960s and 1970s it seemed as if the commemoration might come to an end, how do we then account for its contemporary pervasive influence and popularity?

---

[27] Gerster, *Big-Noting*, 2.

[28] Gerster, *Big-Noting*, 3.

[29] Alistair Thomson, *Anzac Memories: Living with the Legend* (Melbourne: Oxford University Press, 1996), 115.

[30] As cited by Peter Sekuless and Jacqueline Rees, *Lest We Forget*, (Dee Why, NSW: Rigby Press, 1986), 47–48.

The 1990s and Afterwards

In 1990, on the 75th anniversary of the Gallipoli landing, Bob Hawke became the first Australian Prime Minister to preside over the dawn service at Anzac Cove. Although numbers of attendees at Anzac Day commemorations were beginning to increase prior to this time, Hawke's action marks the symbolic moment of Anzac resurgence. Twenty years later we find that »twenty-first century Australians have embraced the Anzac legend as their most powerful myth of nationhood.«[31] Indeed, it has now become the litmus test for courage, suffering, endurance and rejoicing, which is one of the reasons why we hear of the ›Anzac spirit‹ when there are national tragedies such as bushfires and, more recently, floods.

It was true that, by the 1990s, the steady demise of ex-servicemen made it easier for contemporary Australians »to commemorate war in their own image.«[32] And this, of course, was to raise the problematic explored by Ricoeur as to how we might differentiate memory and imagination.[33] Thus it was argued that, as personal memory of the events of Anzac faded, it was now possible to construct a past which might be more conformable with the present and the future that we sought to imagine for ourselves.

A second explanation for the resurgence of Anzac Day claimed that Australians had an urgent need for a »civil religion« in a post-Christian society no longer able to »deliver ancient certainties to young people in search of nourishment for their spirit.«[34] Many Australians might demur at the suggestion that Anzac represents a civil religion, but if that may be understood to describe a »view of national life that fuses together understandings of religion, nation, destiny and providence«, then it will not be too far from the truth.[35]

McKenna argues that each of these explanations contains important insights, but taken alone, or even together, they cannot explain the contempo-

---

[31]   Mark McKenna, »Anzac Day: How did it Become Australia's National Day?«, in *What's Wrong with Anzac? The Militarisation of Australian History*, eds. Marilyn Lake and Henry Reynolds (Sydney: University of New South Wales, 2010), 111.

[32]   McKenna, »Anzac Day«, 112.

[33]   Paul Ricoeur, *Memory, History, Forgetting* (Chicago: University of Chicago Press, 2006).

[34]   Ken Inglis, *Sacred Places: War Memorials in the Australian Landscape* (Carlton: Melbourne University Press, 2008), 572.

[35]   For this definition of a civil religion, which is based on the work of Robert Bellah, see John Maiden, *National Religion and the Prayer Book Controversy, 1927–1928* (Woodbridge: Boydell Press, 2009), 14.

rary and pervasive influence of the Anzac myth. In order to find that answer, we must look to the politics of nationalism in the 1980s.

Australia had traditionally traced its beginning back to white settlement in 1788. It was, of course, well known that white people did not arrive in a deserted land. Instead, they found large communities of indigenous people, and white settlement was conducted in the context of what was often violent dispossession of indigenous settlements. The anniversary of white settlement in Australia is known as Australia Day and is celebrated on January 26th. As preparations grew near to celebrate the bi-centenary in 1988, the foreshadowed celebrations were hampered by two things: The first of these was that there was a lack of enthusiasm for Australia Day and an increasing lack of understanding as to the events that it sought to celebrate. The second reason was that, from the late 1970s, there had been growing a strong Aboriginal protest movement, which expressed itself succinctly and powerfully in its slogan: »White Australia has a Black History.«

The bi-centennial celebrations went forward under the heading of »Celebration of a Nation«, but this white history now being contested as Australia Day was mocked as »Invasion Day«. This was the beginning of the so-called *History Wars,* which would continue for a further twenty years. A re-enactment of the First Fleet, which had been scheduled for the bi-centenary, was abandoned, and in its place the federal government sponsored a Tall Ships expo. This was »a multi-cultural theme which would eventually see so many ships in Sydney Harbour on January 26th 1988, that no one could be sure exactly what was being celebrated.«[36] The uncertainty about just what was being celebrated or the ethical question about whether anything should have been celebrated at all on January 26th seemed to disclose an ideological and cultural vacuum at the heart of Australian self-understanding.

It was as a response to this ideological vacuum that voices were raised in favour of Anzac Day as Australia's national day. We have already noted how the League of the RSSILA had, in 1922, gestured toward this conclusion. In 1980, Vernon Wilkes, a former attorney-general, suggested that Anzac Day was the one day of the year »when the whole nation knows what it is celebrating.«[37] As Australia Day became more contested and views about its celebration more polarized, so Anzac Day came to be seen as less complicated – for everyone understood what it was about – and less divisive – for it was able

---

[36]   McKenna, »Anzac Day.«,115.

[37]   McKenna, »Anzac Day.«,116.

to elide the Black History that seemed to unmask our pretensions about nationhood.

When Prime Minister Hawke addressed the nation at the bi-centenary in 1988, he spoke of how Australia was a nation of immigrants; however, he did not mention the dispossession of Aboriginal Australians. It was a silence of which many, including the Prime Minister, would have been aware. So McKenna is correct in his assessment that, 18 months later, as the first Prime Minister to conduct the dawn service at Gallipoli, Hawke felt a sense of relief that:

> Here at last, was a day that could be shaped into a true source of national communion. The blood spilt in the frontier wars, the taking of Aboriginal land without consent or compensation, the physical and cultural decline of Aboriginal communities, and the political demands of Aboriginal activists, none of these need haunt or spoil the commemoration of Anzac Day. [And he adds with biting incisiveness:] For Anzac Cove, not Sydney Cove, was where the right kind of Australian blood had been shed.[38]

Prime Minister Hawke had set something in motion that was continued by John Howard's conservative government. It was during Howard's time in office that the history wars began to become more strident. Historians had brought evidence to light about Aboriginal children being taken from their parents without consent or due process. These were the ›Stolen Generations‹. A significant cross section of Australians began to demand that the government apologize for its treatment of Aboriginal people. But Howard refused and argued that present governments had »no need to atone for policies which had been introduced by previous administrations.«[39] And in a curious but nonetheless revealing logical maneuver he argued that what had happened in the past could not be linked to the present generation of Australians. However, that linkage was precisely what he claimed could and should happen in the case of the Anzac story. One of the ways in which the Howard government sought to facilitate this link was through education in schools.

---

[38] McKenna, »Anzac Day«, 121.
[39] McKenna, »Anzac Day«, 124.

CORRUPTING THE YOUNG?

From the late 1990s, the federal government, largely through the instrument of the Department of Veterans Affairs (DVA), began to promote and militarise the teaching of history in schools. In 2007-8, the DVA received nearly six million dollars to assist primary and secondary schools with curriculum materials and prizes including trips to some of the World War One battlefields.

> Whether it is the job of the federal Department of Veterans Affairs to prescribe schoolchildren's understanding of national history is surely debatable. Whether it should link these history lessons to the definition and promotion of national values is surely more questionable still.[40]

Throughout the 1990s and into the new millennium, government funding toward the DVA and the War Memorial in Canberra continued to expand. In 1999, the federal government sponsored an initiative called *Australians at War* for the cost of five million dollars. It had four major aims:

1. To mark the centenary of Federation by documenting Australia's involvement in major wars and conflicts during the past 100 years;
2. To explore how the Australian experience of war has helped to shape the nation;
3. To communicate this heritage to all Australians, especially young people; and
4. To provide a continuing resource for educational and community purposes.[41]

Schoolchildren were asked to research an ancestor who had fought in a previous war. But of course, given the reality of Australia's multi-culturalism, we can but wonder how first and second generation migrant children fulfilled this task. A range of programs and curriculum materials were disseminated to schools in the first ten years of the new millennium. Many of these were sophisticated web resources but they aimed to promote not so much a sense of history in the minds of attentive students, but rather notions of debt. Young people were encouraged to be involved in activities that »reinforced the no-

---

[40] Marilyn Lake, »How Do Schoolchildren Learn About the Spirit of Anzac?«, in *What's Wrong With Anzac? The Militarisation of Australian History*, eds. Marilyn Lake and Henry Reynolds (Sydney: University of New South Wales Press, 2010), 138.

[41] Lake, »How Do Schoolchildren Learn About the Spirit of Anzac?«, 144-145.

tion of the debt we all owe for our freedom and democracy.« And as students imbibed the lesson, they were able to respond to those who asked them that we owed everything to the Anzacs because, »If they weren't fighting Gallipoli, we wouldn't be where we are today.«[42] Here we can see the reason why Henry Reynolds was dismayed but hardly surprised when he asked students why they thought Anzac Day was important.

Marilyn Lake is correct to be concerned about the extensive remit of the DVA. After an exhaustive survey of the funding given to the promotion of the Anzac myth, she points out that the remarkable and indeed disturbing feature of all this is not that the DVA believes in the centrality of war to Australian history, for that, after all, might have been expected. Rather, the remarkable feature is that the DVA

> is funded so lavishly to make this case to schoolchildren and the larger community and that a federal department, established to take care of the needs of veterans and tend their graves, plays such a large role in the teaching of history in the primary and secondary schools.[43]

It is difficult to avoid the conclusion that children are being exposed to a well-orchestrated and munificently funded education program that seeks to introduce them to an understanding of nationhood that is not only selective but exercises that selection in a way that removes much of our imperial past while at the same time playing down many of the important and positive characteristics of late nineteenth-century Australia which culminated in Federation in 1901.

Conclusion

By 2007, the Howard government had been so successful in using Anzac Day as a vehicle for national self-congratulation that it was able to spill over into his Australia Day speech »in which he declared without irony: ›We think we're pretty good and we are.‹«[44] But were we as good as the Prime Minister seemed to think? I will close with one example – the White Australia policy.

---

[42] Anna Clark, *History's Children: History Wars in the Classroom* (Sydney: University of New South Wales Press, 2008), 47.

[43] Lake, »How do Schoolchildren Learn About the Spirit of Anzac?«, 153–154.

[44] McKenna, »Anzac Day«,127.

When Federation was proclaimed in 1901, it came with what would later become infamous as the White Australia policy. This policy prevented any non-white person from immigrating to Australia, and it remained in force until 1973. It was an unashamedly racist policy and yet one which was the envy of at least some countries around the world. But my point in introducing it here is simply to indicate that this was the world in which the original events of Anzac were framed. We cannot simply lift these men out of their context and remake them in our own image. Many of them were convinced of white supremacy. And when Prime Minister W. Hughes returned to Australia after the signing of the Treaty of Versailles in 1919, he was congratulated by members of the RSSILA for his successful fight to keep Australia white. He declared to Parliament: »White Australia is yours. You may do with it what you please; but at any rate, the soldiers have achieved the victory, and my colleagues and I have brought that principle back to you from the Conference.«[45]

Significant numbers of people born after 1973 have no memory or knowledge of such a policy. They hear instead a rhetoric of freedom and tolerance grounded in the resurgence of the Anzac myth and in moments of disquiet and puzzlement wonder how this fits with the bipartisan federal government support for detention centres that serve to dissuade refugees from coming to Australia. Their puzzlement might be alleviated somewhat if they realized that the freedoms for which the Anzacs fought were essentially male, imperial and white. That does not make the Anzacs particularly iniquitous, but it might prevent us from elevating them to a god-like status, and that might be salutary for a nation that wishes to commemorate the destructiveness of violence rather than run the risk of celebrating it.

LITERATURE

Clark, Anna. *History's Children: History Wars in the Classroom.* Sydney: University of New South Wales Press, 2008.

Gare, Deborah and David Ritter, *Making Australian History.* Melbourne: Thompson Press, 2008.

Gerster, Robin. *Big-Noting: The Heroic Theme in Australian War Writing.* Melbourne: Melbourne University Press, 1987.

---

[45] Marilyn Lake and Henry Reynolds, *Drawing the Global Colour Line: White Men's Countries and the Question of Racial Equality* (Melbourne: Melbourne University Press, 2008), 308–309.

Gowans, Adam, ed., *Heinrich von Treitschke: Selections From His Lectures on Politics*. London: Gowans & Gray, 1914.

Inglis, Ken. *Sacred Places: War Memorials in the Australian Landscape*. Carlton: Melbourne University Press, 2008.

Johnson, Michael. »Review Article: Memory, History, Forgetting, by Paul Ricoeur.« *Anglican Theological Review* 89:1:Winter 2007, 105–112.

Kearney, Richard. *On Paul Ricoeur: The Owl of Minerva*. Ashgate: Aldershot, 2004.

Lake, Marilyn and Henry Reynolds. *Drawing the Global Colour Line: White Men's Countries and the Question of Racial Equality*. Melbourne: Melbourne University Press, 2008.

Lake, Marilyn. »How do Schoolchildren Learn About the Spirit of Anzac?« In *What's Wrong With Anzac? The Militarisation of Australian History*, edited by Marilyn Lake and Henry Reynolds, 135–156. Sydney: University of New South Wales Press, 2010.

Maiden, John. *National Religion and the Prayer Book Controversy 1927–1928*. Woodbridge: Boydell Press, 2009.

McKenna, Mark. »Anzac Day: How did it Become Australia's National Day?« In: *What's Wrong with Anzac? The Militarisation of Australian History*, edited by Marilyn Lake and Henry Reynolds, 110–134. Sydney: University of New South Wales, 2010.

Reynolds, Henry. »Are Nations Really Made in War?« In *What's Wrong With Anzac? The Militarisation of Australian History*, edited by Marilyn Lake and Henry Reynolds, 24–44. Sydney: University of New South Wales Press, 2010.

Ricoeur, Paul. *Memory, History, Forgetting*. Chicago: University of Chicago Press, 2006.

Sekuless, Peter and Jacqueline Rees. *Lest We Forget*: Dee Why, NSW: Rigby Press, 1986.

Souter, Gavin. *Lion and Kangaroo: Australia 1901–1919: The Rise of a Nation*. Sydney: Collins Press, 1976.

Thomson, Alistair. *Anzac Memories: Living with the Legend*. Melbourne: Oxford University Press, 1996.

White, Hayden, »The Value of Narrativity in the Representation of Reality.« In *The Content of the Form: Narrative Discourse and Historical Representation*, 1–26. Baltimore: Johns Hopkins University, 1987.

AFTER VIOLENCE: NARRATIVES OF GRACE IN THE MIDST OF TRAUMA

Hans-Martin Gutmann

DISRUPTING VIOLENCE

In 2009, I published an essay with the title »Gewaltunterbrechung«[1], in which I argue that mutual religious commitment can support people *not* to give in to the fascination of violent reciprocity. By mutual religious commitment I mean acts of solidarity and dedication to others and to the Divine which emerge from the intense immersion in one's own religious tradition. I engage the concept of disruption of violence through mutual religious commitment with the focus on the instant *before* violence breaks out, thus with an eye on possible ways of prevention. I have recognized the powerful impact of connecting individuals both with a nexus of interactions and trustworthy relations as well as with Biblical stories, symbols, and rituals that give witness to the transformation of violence into grace. All of these can inspire ways of action marked by solidarity instead of mimetic violence. I focus on insights and examples from my own Christian (Lutheran) background, hoping to encourage others to explore resources within their own religious traditions that might inspire the interruption of violence. The eventual goal is to encourage people of faith to collect those resources and make them accessible as stories, symbols, rituals, or political statements, both within their respective contexts.

The time structure of violence is of particular interest to me. I am particularly concerned with those moments when established codes of conduct and common ways of behavior are being shattered. In the ecstatic moments when violence explodes as a fascinating force, perpetrators seek to experience personal transgression and grandiosity. The aim is to attain and exercise power

---

[1] Hans-Martin Gutmann, *Gewaltunterbrechung. Warum Religion Gewalt nicht hervorbringt, sondern bindet. Ein Einspruch* (Gütersloh: Gütersloher Verlagshaus, 2009).

over others – to manifest this power by the destruction of their bodies while at the same time showing a complete lack of compassion or empathy for their suffering. For the perpetrators, the moment of violence can be an ecstatic, vibrant trip, during which they may be utterly different from how they usually behave. Their violent selves may be transformed so much as to be unrecognizable to their usual selves.

My research focuses on exploring resources and possibilities of mutual religious commitment. How can the mimetic power of reciprocity work to evoke the gift of grace instead of reciprocal violence? What alternative ways exist to experience transgression and grandiosity – not by the destruction of the other, but by experiences of the abundance of life and the fateful experience of divine grace? Where are spaces for the formation of empathy and compassion?

Victims of violence experience the violation of their bodily and mental integrity, which, if they can escape or survive, usually causes deep posttraumatic damages. With regard to those suffering from violence, I sought to discover alternative responses to the experience of violence. What are the decisive factors for victims not to end up in physical and psychological separation and dissociation, mimetically perpetuating violent reciprocity (as depression against themselves or violence against others)? What are resources that help to facilitate mourning and grief and support victims to achieve a new sense of life?

Various scholars have convincingly argued that mutually *exclusive* religious commitment may aggravate large-scale conflicts between nation states or large ethnic or social groups.[2] My study, in contrast, focuses rather on examining individual biographies and social environments, encompassing the traditional realms, the »Lebenswelten« of familial relationships, friendships, and neighborhoods. It seems appropriate to also regard communities shaped by new media like Twitter, social networks, or MMORPGs (massive multiplayer online role play games) as possible spheres of individual experience in this context.

---

[2]   Wolfgang Sofsky, *Traktat über die Gewalt* (Frankfurt a. M.: Fischer, 1996); Hans G. Kippenberg, *Gewalt als Gottesdienst. Religionskriege im Zeitalter der Globalisierung* (Munich: C. H. Beck, 2008); Mark Juergensmeyer, *Die Globalisierung religiöser Gewalt. Von christlichen Milizen bis al-Qaida* (Hamburg: Hamburger Edition, 2009); Pamela J. Stewart and Andrew Strathern, *Violence: Theory and Ethnography* (London: Continuum Publishing for Athlone Press, 2002); René Girard, *Das Heilige und die Gewalt* (Munich: Benzinger, 1972). I thank Theodor Ahrens for our discussions of these works.

Is it possible to define markers of Protestant religiosity in this context? In a pluralistic Protestantism, the answers will be manifold. My perspective is this: Mutual religious commitment gravitates towards the faith of justification by grace alone – both as a set of inner convictions and attitudes and as an outward mode of social behavior. The gift of God's grace can neither be earned nor justified nor sufficiently and conclusively matched by human efforts. This promise is encountered and realized in what I have come to call moments of gratitude – dense moments of bliss and abundance. In such moments, people come to look upon their life with a feeling of thankfulness and appreciation. They are assured of themselves, of their individual selves existing in the fatefulness and connectedness of their being. Life turns into an overflow of grace. It is presumably a feature of human existence – regardless of a particular religious orientation – to draw from such fragmentary and vulnerable moments of bliss.

The communication of the Gospel in sermon and liturgy, pastoral care, and social or political action may create spaces for this existential experience to happen. It may be realized in personal encounters, performances, metaphors, stories, rituals, symbols, or music. Ideally, exposure to the Biblical narrative allows access to those fundamentally human moments of gratitude. The perception of life as gift holds the potential to liberate the individual from fantasies of retribution. The promise of the Gospel resounds in faith in the fact that God wants to see our lives flourishing. It encompasses not only a spiritual and psychological but also a physical awareness as tensions are eased, breathing becomes deep, and release is deeply felt at the very core of the body.

AFTER VIOLENCE: VICTIMS AND PERPRETATORS

In the following, I will shift my focus from the moment before violence breaks out to the aftermath of collective violence by seeking to perceive those who suffered violence, who have been harmed or even destroyed in their physical and mental integrity. What does it mean to pay attention to those whose loved ones have been killed, raped, or beaten, who have witnessed devastating images of violence, whose living environments have been wiped out and social surroundings have been destroyed? What kind of spaces of imagination need to unfold for victims of violence to regain assurance and composure so that they are not in turn caught by the fascination of violence? What does it take to disrupt the compulsion to mimetically pass on the experienced violence to others, and thus not to become a perpetrator oneself in the process?

Also, the offenders must be kept in view. Especially in the German context of the 20th century, the importance of understanding what happens to the offenders has to be underscored. When approaching this topic, it is still helpful to refer to the groundbreaking analysis by Alexander and Margarete Mitscherlich. They published their study in the 1960s, roughly twenty years after the end of the Nazi regime. They sought to comprehend why large parts of the German population did not become offenders by coercion and oppressive force but rather willingly surrendered control to the »Führer« in a state of fascination, seemingly oblivious to the terrible consequences of the war of aggression and mass murder, resulting in their very own ruin. Margarete and Alexander Mitscherlich based their analysis of the German inability to grieve[3] on the psychoanalytical approach of Sigmund Freud. They asked how and why the »Führer« could wield such power over the people, a power dissolving all the usual stabilizing achievements of the self in terms of rational and ethical orientation. The Mitscherlichs mused that the majority of Germans had identified themselves with the figure of the »Führer« so intensely that, after his disgraceful downfall and the discovery of the genocidal reality of their beloved nation, the inner psychological instance of the ideal self had been harmed severely, resulting in collective denial and shame but prohibiting grief and compassion. Until the late 1960s, a public addressing of and discussion of the issue were rendered impossible by a state of denial usually associated (in Freudian theory) with the prevention of melancholy. After having imputed all mental energies of the self-ideal onto the »Führer« for the duration of his rule, his defeat caused a feeling of complete loss of the people's selves. In light of the Freudian school of thought, this collective fascination with the »Führer«, which provoked very destructive forms of violent reciprocity, can be viewed as a form of collective infatuation, a form of amalgamation of the concepts of ideal self on the one hand and the image of the chosen ideal (in this case, the »Führer«) on the other.

Not only victims of violence but offenders, too, are traumatized by the experience of violence. They are bound by guilt, no matter how much they want to block it from their memory or consciousness. Paul Ricoeur reminds us of the time dimension of guilt.[4] Just as anxiety may firmly tie somebody to the – dreaded – future, guilt has a way of fixing ties to the past. With regard

---

[3]   Alexander and Margarete Mitscherlich, *Die Unfähigkeit zu trauern. Grundlagen kollektiven Verhaltens* (Munich: Piper, 1967).

[4]   Paul Ricoeur, *Das Rätsel der Vergangenheit. Erinnern – Vergessen – Verzeihen,* (Göttingen: Wallstein Verlag, 2002, 3rd. ed.), 56.

to their respective time structure, *guilt* and *debt* are direct opposites of each other. While debts must be made up, »repaid« by the debtor, and will result in a loss of honor and status for him if he fails to do so, *guilt* refers to an affair which, as a matter of principle, cannot be made up for by the guilty. Forgiving is never a matter of the offender, but first and foremost one of the victim of violence. The guilty cannot escape these ties to the past, neither the obligation to remember nor the prohibition to forget. As a consequence, wherever guilt is incurred, the ties to the past are tightened. Guilt is impossible to make up through reciprocal transaction. Guilt exists where the mechanism of reciprocity grinds to a halt. There are no adequate retributions for guilt, even if an act of violence led to both debt and guilt. This insight has been maintained in the discussion about reparations between Germany and Israel and, generally, with regard to the atrocities of the Shoah, but has been taken up more recently in the debates on acceptable avengement of sexual abuse. Only the victims have the power and ability to forgive – not the offenders.[5]

Whereas with economic debts there may be opportunities for forms of true generosity that, as acts of grace, escape the usual obligation to reciprocity, there is no such easy way out with guilt.[6] Here, generosity on the side of the guilty is rendered impossible. On the side of the victim, any form of generous forgiveness comes with the ambiguity of cheap grace, of forgiving all too easily, and the resulting risk of humiliating the victims again by letting offenders off too easily.

---

[5]   Ricoeur, *Das Rätsel der Vergangenheit*, 145.

[6]   Marcel Mauss, »Die Gabe. Form und Funktion des Austauschs in archaischen Gesellschaften«, *Soziologie und Anthropologie*, vol. 2, (Berlin: Verlag Ullstein, 1978; Bernhard Waldenfels, »Das Un-Ding der Gabe«, Bernhard Waldenfels et al. (eds.), *Einsätze des Denkens, Zur Philosophie von Jacques Derrida* (Frankfurt a. M.: Suhrkamp, 1997) 385–409; Jacques Derrida, *Ethik der Gabe* (Berlin: Akademie Verlag 1993); Magdalene L. Frettlöh, »Der Charme der gerechten Gabe,« Jürgen Ebach et al. (eds.), ›*Leget Anmut in das Geben‹. Zum Verhältnis von Ökonomie und Theologie*, Jabboq, vol. 1, (Gütersloh: Gütersloher Verlagshaus, 2001), 105–161; Theodor Ahrens, »Ungeschuldetes Geben,« *Gegebenheiten. Missionswissenschaftliche Studien* (Frankfurt a. M.: Lembeck Verlag, 2005), 192–203.

COUNSELING IN THE AFTERMATH OF TRAUMATIZING VIOLENCE

Let me now turn to the victims of violence, to men, women, and children who have suffered violence. Much has been learned about their perspectives from clinical therapy and pastoral care. Blocking and suppressing, negating and forgetting are to be understood as seemingly helpful measures of protection of the self which tragically fail to deliver on their promise over time. They do not present viable long-term perspectives.[7] Individuals entangled in such strategies require a considerable part of their energies to keep up their defenses. Long after the actual suffering from violence, victims often are deprived of vital energy by the dynamics of trauma, which then can lead to further disarray with regard to social relationships, personal health and wealth. Worse yet, despite all their efforts, their mental armor is readily pierced by images, sounds, or personal encounters which bring back the traumatizing images and experiences in the *here and now*. Such triggers are incontrollable and cause victims to relive the traumatizing situation again and again. This may also happen in a therapeutic setting or in pastoral care; this is why it is of utmost importance to avoid direct confrontation with the traumatizing event. Counseling along the lines of »having to get back on the horse that threw you« may cause victims to be overwhelmed by memories of the violent situation.

In therapeutic work with people who have suffered from traumatizing violence, a model has been established, defining different stages of integration of the violent event into a personal biography. In this context, Luise Reddemann, a German expert on trauma therapy, has proposed the following stages: 1. Finding inner stability, 2. Feeling at home inside your body (elements of bodywork), 3. Facing the terror, 4. Accepting and integrating the personal history. During all stages, the method of *imagination* plays a key role.[8] In a real-life situation, each stage may take weeks or months, if not years.

During the first phase, the building of a therapeutic relationship between counselor and traumatized is essential. In order to offset the oftentimes low self-esteem of trauma patients, it is important to take stock of those resources

---

[7]   See Luise Reddemann, *Imagination als heilsame Kraft. Zur Behandlung von Traumafolgen mit ressourcenorientierten Verfahren* (Stuttgart: Klett-Cotta, 2010), 15; Ursula Gast, Elisabeth Christa Markert, Klaus Onnasch, and Thomas Schollas, *Trauma und Trauer. Impulse aus christlicher Spiritualität und Neurobiologie* (Stuttgart: Klett-Cotta, 2009).

[8]   See Reddemann, *Imagination als heilsame Kraft.*

for healing that already exist. It may be worthwhile to ask the patient to write a list of everything he or she *can* do, even seemingly ordinary tasks. For patients, it can be an astonishing discovery how these things may help them already. Another exercise can be the packing of a ›toolbox‹ – imagining a box or suitcase which you pack with anything that has been helpful in other difficult situations – pictures of loved ones, pleasant fragrances, music that is consoling, activities which make you feel good (dancing, exercising, etc.). Another recommended exercise would be to develop a counter-image against the terrifying memories or images – the picture of being carried and caressed by the mother as a child, of intense friendships in their youth, etc. There is no ›set‹ of appropriate images, the vital criterion here being that it suits the particular person. The practice and exercise of mindfulness also plays an integral part in this first phase. Sitting quietly, feeling in contact with the floor, feeling the motions of the body as I breathe. When I consciously go through my body – how does it feel, how do my limbs feel, muscles, ligaments, from head to toe? By such exercises, one gets acquainted with the »inner observer«. It is a milestone for the development of the self to realize that one is not simply identical with one's emotions, but that there is something within that simply observes. This discovery can be of tremendous importance to the traumatized. They become aware of an inner differentiation which enables them to distance themselves from certain experiences. The impact of a bodywork-approach can be tremendous. Realizing the strengths and limitations of one's body and acquiring a feeling of integrity with one's own physical being is pivotal. Through exercises of mindfulness and imagination, a process is set in motion to find images that offset the images of terror. One such exercise is the development of the »inner shelter«. As Luise Reddemann puts it, »let thoughts or images well up of a place where you feel comfortable and sheltered. Mark this place out and characterize it so that it suits you – you define what people or what kinds of beings should inhabit it [...].«[9]

Another important lesson is learned from the contrary: developing a *gestalt* for uncomfortable or oppressing images or memories, and allowing a place for them while at the same time being able to distance oneself from those images. Being able to step back from such images and to ask, »What do you want to teach me?« can restore a degree of control to the traumatized. Lastly, the patients learn to bring to mind former, joyful states of the self: the child playing in the street, the successful student, the expectant father or

---

[9]   Reddemann, *Imagination als heilsame Kraft*, 45.

mother, etc. They are invited to ask those selves to help their current selves overcome the trauma.

The second phase centers on feeling at home inside one's body and treating it accordingly. The aforementioned exercises in mindfulness are a prerequisite in this regard. Luise Reddemann draws on different traditions and contexts in her recommendations for this second stage. Autogenic training, Breema-bodywork of the Persian-Kurdic tradition, or Qui-Gong from traditional Chinese medicine may serve as examples. Others could be added. The combination and crossing over of different traditions is intentional – they are all welcomed as resources. The fundamental idea is that all of these practices develop their healing potential over time, through repetition and persistent training.

It is only now, in the third phase, that actual confrontation with the terror becomes the center of attention. Established techniques of mindfulness and distancing are picked up, extended, and intensified. The screening technique may be used to illustrate this: Counselor and counselee sit together, and the counselee shows the images welling up inside him or her to the counselor on an imaginary screen, which they are able to ›switch off‹ at will. Anything that goes too far or hurts too much can also be put inside an »inner vault« to be taken out again for re-evaluation at a later stage. Advancing the technique of the »inner observer«, the counselee is now able to face and confront the moment of violence itself, while at the same time distancing him- or herself sufficiently so as not to be overwhelmed by the violent images and feelings. The aim is to achieve a protected re-appropriation of the self *in* the violent situation without being dragged back into trauma.

During the last stage, which may last quite long (sometimes for the rest of a person's life), the task is to integrate and accept one's personal history. Again, exercises in mindfulness and imagination are used but also complemented by music or art therapy and the development of appropriate symbols and rituals to further aid the processes of grieving, departure, and, lastly, embracing life again.

In accordance with theories on processes of grief and mourning in other (non-violent) contexts, it seems adequate to view these stages not to be in a linear sequence, but rather to form a repetitive or cyclical progress, during which one may have to go back at some point to re-examine an aspect again, until at last departure and integration are achieved.[10]

---

[10] See Yorick Spiegel, *Der Prozess des Trauerns. Analyse und Beratung* (Munich: Kaiser, 1989), 7; Jorgos Canacakis, *Ich sehe deine Tränen. Trauern, Klagen, Leben können*

Mutual religious commitment can have a positive impact on people not only before the outbreak of violence (in the form of prevention) or in the moment of violence (by evoking my individual ›moment of gratitude‹). In the aftermath of violence, too, mutual religious commitment may be transformative. In working with traumatized people, Christian spirituality has come to be viewed as an important resource by counselors. The authors of the book *Trauma und Trauer (Trauma and Grief)*[11], who work in the fields of systemic counseling and pastoral caregiving, suggest a new approach to the New Testament and especially the stories around the passion of Christ. Stories that depict Jesus' dedication to his friends and the resurrection of the crucified may be viewed as counter-narratives of a traumatized group of disciples who lived in the aftermath of Christ's violent crucifixion. After having their aspirations shattered and crushed, the stories of the Gospels opened up new ways of seeing. The authors of *Trauma und Trauer* propose to think of different Biblical characters as helpful figures that could be called into the inner shelter to serve as guides and companions to the inner observer of the counselee, giving witness that, despite devastating experiences, new opportunities for life are possible. Mary Magdalene may be taken as an example here. Overcome by grief and sorrow, she does not recognize Jesus at first. When he finally addresses her, though, she is able to recognize him and to let him go at the same time. Another example could be found in St. Peter, who, in a phase of traumatizing dissociation, denies Jesus – the one he pledged his life to –, but then he is transformed when faced with the crowing cock. After a phase of denial, Peter is able to grieve and finally face the terror without being consumed by it. He can renew his discipleship in a different way.

This perspective sheds a new and interesting light on many biblical stories, both from the Hebrew Bible and from the New Testament. They come to be seen as counter-narratives or transformative narratives to traumatizing experience of violence. The priestly narrative of creation can be understood as a confirmation of God the creator of heaven and earth, even in the face of the traumatizing experience of the destruction of the Temple and the city of Jerusalem and the hardships of deportation and the Babylonian exile. The story of the flood can be read as a narrative of the remorse of God, who, after first engaging in acts of violent reciprocity against his »ungrateful« creation,

---

(Stuttgart: Kreuz, 2000), 16; Kerstin Lammer, *Den Tod begreifen. Neue Wege der Trauerbegleitung* (Neukirchen: Neukirchner Verlag, 2004), 2.

[11]   See Ursula Gast, Elisabeth Christa Markert, Klaus Onnasch, and Thomas Schollas, *Trauma und Trauer.*

finally extends a new covenant to all living beings. Jacob finally faces the realities of his life in his nightly battle at the River Jabbok, after a long and destructive history of fraud and deceit. He wrestles with God, comes to realize his broken relationships, and obtains God's blessing eventually. Elijah, in a state of deep depression and despair, wants to escape guilt and shame after slaying all the prophets of Baal. God reveals himself to Elijah not in a strong wind or in an earthquake, but in a »still small voice«.

Many of these narratives are ambiguous, especially with regard to the fascination of violence: The liberation of God's people from Egyptian bondage is achieved by violent plagues, the striking of the firstborn, and defeat of the Egyptian forces at the Sea of Reeds. The Deuteronomistic re-reading and reinterpretation of Israel's history in the situation of exile does not lend itself easily to establishing non-violent and peaceful ways of interaction between differing religions and religious traditions (to put it mildly).

And yet: The whole Bible is full of useful narratives, vivid images, metaphors, and symbols to offset dreadful and traumatizing experiences and images. In psalms of lament, intense metaphors that hint at the topics of distance and shelter can be found. They can serve as borrowed language, helping individuals to release destructive images from their minds and bodies. Even the psalms of revenge can be useful in this way, insofar as God may be seen as a proxy to the inner observer, thus reducing the appeal of mimetically engaging in violent reciprocity.

In assisting and counseling victims of traumatizing violence in the aftermath of violent events, mutual religious commitment as evoked in Biblical narratives can be a powerful resource. However, this resource of shared commitment should not inhibit people's ability to assess the issue of violence comprehensively, for example in noticing instances of social exclusion, injustice, or structural violence. Communicating the Gospel strives to embrace hope for social change and the commitment to living conditions that allow people to care for each other.

LITERATURE

Ahrens, Theodor. »Ungeschuldetes Geben.« In *Gegebenheiten. Missionswissenschaftliche Studien*, 192–203. Frankfurt a. M.: Lembeck Verlag.

Canacakis, Jorgos. *Ich sehe deine Tränen. Trauern, Klagen, Leben können*. Stuttgart: Kreuz, 2000.

Derrida, Jacques. *Ethik der Gabe*. Berlin: Akademie Verlag 1993.

Frettlöh, Magdalene L. »Der Charme der gerechten Gabe.« In ›*Leget Anmut in das Geben*.‹ *Zum Verhältnis von Ökonomie und Theologie*, Jabboq, vol. 1, edited by Jürgen Ebach, Magdalene Frettlöh, Hans-Martin Gutmann and Michael Weinrich, 105–161. Gütersloh: Gütersloher Verlagshaus.

Gast, Ursula , Elisabeth Christa Markert, Klaus Onnasch, and Thomas Schollas. *Trauma und Trauer. Impulse aus christlicher Spiritualität und Neurobiologie*. Stuttgart: Klett-Cotta, 2009.

Girard, René. *Das Heilige und die Gewalt*. Munich: Benzinger, 1972.

Gutmann, Hans-Martin. *Gewaltunterbrechung. Warum Religion Gewalt nicht hervorbringt, sondern bindet. Ein Einspruch*. Gütersloh: Gütersloher Verlagshaus, 2009.

Juergensmeyer, Mark. *Die Globalisierung religiöser Gewalt. Von christlichen Milizen bis al-Qaida*. Hamburg: Hamburger Edition, 2009.

Kippenberg, Hans G. *Gewalt als Gottesdienst. Religionskriege im Zeitalter der Globalisierung*. Munich: C. H. Beck, 2008.

Lammer, Kerstin. *Den Tod begreifen. Neue Wege der Trauerbegleitung*. Neukirchen: Neukirchner Verlag, 2004.

Mauss, Marcel. »Die Gabe. Form und Funktion des Austauschs in archaischen Gesellschaften.« In *Soziologie und Anthropologie*, vol. 2, edited by Wolf Lepenies and Henning Ritter. Berlin: Verlag Ullstein, 1978.

Mitscherlich, Alexander and Margarete. *Die Unfähigkeit zu trauern. Grundlagen kollektiven Verhaltens*. Munich: Piper, 1967.

Reddemann, Luise. *Imagination als heilsame Kraft. Zur Behandlung von Traumafolgen mit ressourcenorientierten Verfahren*. Stuttgart: Klett-Cotta, 2010.

Ricoeur, Paul. *Das Rätsel der Vergangenheit. Erinnern – Vergessen – Verzeihen*. Göttingen: Wallstein Verlag 2002, 3rd. ed.

Sofsky, Wolfgang. *Traktat über die Gewalt*. Frankfurt a. M.: Fischer, 1996.

Spiegel, Yorick. *Der Prozess des Trauerns. Analyse und Beratung*. Munich: Kaiser, 1989.

Stewart, Pamela J. and Andrew Strathern. *Violence: Theory and Ethnography*. London: Continuum Publishing for Athlone Press, 2002.

Waldenfels, Bernhard. »Das Un-Ding der Gabe.« In *Einsätze des Denkens. Zur Philosophie von Jacques Derrida*, edited by Bernhard Waldenfels and Dieter Gondek, 385–409. Frankfurt a. M.: Suhrkamp, 1997.

Spiritual Violence »In the Name of Jesus« The case of Neo-Pentecostal Ministries from West-Africa in Germany: A New Testament Perspective

Werner Kahl

Introduction

In 1993, a Ghanaian migrant church approached the head pastor and me with the request of using the church premises of the parish where I served as a pastor in training. Our church elders welcomed the Ghanaian congregation, and for many years I joined their services which took place on Sunday afternoons, functioning as co-pastor, band member of the music group, and as translator. This was one of the very first encounters between the Protestant Church of Germany and an African migrant church in the region of the Ruhr Valley. In the following years, as more and more migrant churches approached other German congregations with similar requests, I was regarded by a number of my colleagues as a resource person whom they contacted for advice in this respect.

During the worship services and Bible studies, I realized that the Christians from West Africa understood the Bible and faith in ways quite different from what I was used to in the Protestant Church. This raised my interest as a New Testament scholar, and in 1999 I got funding from the German Research Foundation (DFG) for a research project in intercultural Biblical hermeneutics, enabling me to conduct field work and research in Ghana for three years. In Ghana, there was a vacancy for New Testament at the University of Ghana, Legon, and I was employed there as full time lecturer. Ever since, Ghana has become my »second home«. Back in Germany, I have been serving as a cultural translator and mediator between the Protestant Church and West-African migrant churches.

The following reflections are situated in the context of ecumenical encounters in Hamburg between members of the *Missionsakademie* (Academy of Mission) and migrant Christians from the global South. At times, these encounters are challenged by irritations on all sides. One such irritation is the subject of this essay.

In Hamburg there are at present approximately eighty African migrant churches which have originated within the past two decades. Most of these churches are Neo-Pentecostal in orientation. A few months ago, I visited, together with a student group, a Neo-Pentecostal migrant church with a West-African leader and membership. We attended a regular Bible study on a Wednesday evening. When we arrived at the meeting place of the congregation – a large room in an office building in an industrial area –, we learned that the Bible study was replaced by a service due to the presence of a visiting preacher from Ghana. The sermon was delivered in the Ghanaian language Twi, and it was rendered into English by a translator. The topic was the experience of failures in everyday life due to spiritual attacks from home and the power of the believer to overcome such problems. The sermon was based on Matthew 18:18: »Truly I say to you, whatever you bind on earth shall be bound in heaven, and whatever you loose on earth shall be loosed in heaven.«

After the sermon the preacher led the thirty or so participants of the service in prayer. Everyone was supposed to pray aloud for Jesus' intervention to save them from *spiritual missiles* sent by family members in Ghana and to return the *missiles* to the senders resulting in their death.[1] The African members all engaged in such prayers for about fifteen minutes, many shouting and running up and down the room while making slashing movements with their arms as to act out the cutting down of their enemies »in the name of Jesus.« Following the procedure, the visiting preacher announced that the participants should be prepared to receive phone calls from home within the next couple of days communicating the premature death of their father, their mother, an uncle or aunt, or their child. By implication, he meant that such a person was the witch causing the misfortune of a relative in Germany.

Such belief in the reality of witchcraft is common knowledge among people of all walks of life and social status in and from West Africa, even though there are various degrees of readiness with which people might attribute a misfortune to the activity of a witch. At times, the wish to spiritually kill a witch translates into the physical killing of an accused person. A recent case in point was an incident reported from Ghana by the English speaking world-

---

[1]   Interestingly and typically, only the de-contextualization of Matthew 18:18 made it possible to use the verse as proof-text for spiritual killing: In the immediate context, *reconciliation* is emphasized.

wide media at the end of November 2010: An elderly woman, who was accused to be a witch by a Neo-Pentecostal pastor, was burnt alive by a group of his followers in the large industrial town of Tema.[2]

EXPERIENCES AND INTERPRETATIONS OF ENORMOUS STRESS IN MIGRATION

Many of those who have arrived in Germany from West Africa within the past two decades interpret their journey spiritually. They have left their home countries »to look for greener pastures« abroad, and they rely on the protection of God or of local gods to make it to their destined countries. As for Germany, Hamburg has the largest population of people with a sub-Saharan origin. The majority of these first-generation migrants are Christians from Ghana and Nigeria, many of whom represent, by Western European standards, the semi-educated stratum of society in West Africa. To many, life back home was an unbearable struggle to survive, marked by violence. This not only applies to situations of civil war, as is the case in some sub-regions, but oftentimes to everyday life experiences. Widespread communal, societal, and economic predicaments, which cause hardships on a personal level, are often fundamentally interpreted in terms of an underlying antagonistic *spiritual* war. Coming to Europe is connected with the wish not only to succeed in life in economic terms, but also to leave behind the destructive influence of evil spirits causing misfortune and suffering. The well-known West-African saying, »Poverty is a curse«, from an insider perspective actually indicates the widespread belief that poverty is being caused by evil spirits, local gods, ancestors, or witches. The causes for poverty are not attributed to structural conditions, as would be typical from Western European perspectives, but they are both spiritualized and personalized.[3]

This spiritual knowledge of the world among most migrants from West Africa marks a fundamental difference in world-view from most Western Europeans. The spiritual interpretation of life is grounded in *traditional* con-

---

[2]   See http://www.guardian.co.uk/world/2010/nov/29/ghanaian-woman-burned-death-witch (accessed on May 30, 2011).

[3]   See Chris Oshun, »Spirits and Healing in a Depressed Economy: The Case of Nigeria,« in *Mission Studies* 15/1. 29 (1998): 32–52. The author attributes the economic predicament of Nigeria to the continuing veneration of local gods in his country, i.e. to the space given these spirits to unfold their evil schemes.

ceptualizations of reality. For most, if not all ethnic groups in Sub-Saharan Africa, it can be presupposed that the material, visible world is *embedded* in the wider context of the invisible spiritual world, whose agents are regarded *as more powerful* than the ordinary human being. What happens within the visible world might have been caused by a spirit, be it an ancestor or a local divinity. These spiritual forces of traditional Africa are often identified, from a charismatic Christian perspective, with demons or Satan. In fact, from this perspective, it is essential that human beings act in accordance with the plans of these powers or be protected against their influence by a stronger power in order to avoid hardship in life.

Spiritual worldview in Sub-Saharan Africa

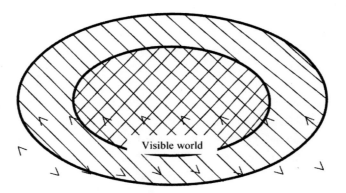

Invisible sphere

People in general understand themselves not as being independent subjects but rather as subject to wider communities, spiritually and socially (extended family, ethnic group). It is important to recognize that this self-understanding of many Africans in general, and of African Christians in particular, *contradicts* the self-understanding of a majority of Western Europeans who have been brought up by the notion that the human being is, or rather should be, the master of his or her own destiny, without any recourse to the activity of supernatural beings. In fact, the belief in spirits is generally despised. This understanding, of course, is an expression of a powerful myth of Western civilization since enlightenment.

West-African migrants in Europe in general and in Germany in particular have not only brought their »religious beliefs« along; in the country of arrival, they continue to view the world in familiar terms, i.e. spiritually. Many live and work in Germany at the margins of society, often without any legal papers or health insurance coverage. As in West Africa, life in the migrant situation all too often *continues* to be experienced as a war-zone, and many attribute such difficulties to the activity of adverse spiritual powers. This interpretation is being *reinforced* by Neo-Pentecostal preachers who offer spiritual solutions for the problems facing their flock, often for a fee.

Migrants from West Africa tend to experience an enormous amount of psychic pressure and mental stress, not only because they now live in a foreign and at times outright hostile environment but also because of demands from home. Their families in West Africa expect and often emphatically request financial assistance, and to meet this demand is often not within the range of possibilities for the expatriates abroad. Failure to comply with these requests from family members, however, might invite spiritual attacks from home. The misfortunes experienced abroad and the lack of success might be interpreted as the result of spiritual agents engaged by envious family members left behind. The prayers aimed at shooting back *spiritual missiles* »in the name of Jesus«, as might be encountered in some African Neo-Pentecostal ministries in Germany, are expressions of an enormous amount of pressure – on material, mental, and spiritual levels. These prayers are attempts to overcome this kind of stress. In fact, to many immigrants this is a question of life and death, of survival in a foreign place, of making it in life, of fulfilling one's divinely bestowed destiny or of missing it. Against this background, it becomes plausible that some West-African migrants resort to the act of spiritual killing to solve their problems, even though, from a Western European interpretation of the New Testament and also from a legal perspective of the host country, this seems unacceptable.

In this paper, I will try to make transparent first the plausibility of Neo-Pentecostal responses to the issue of evil before turning to the evidence concerning strategies of how to deal with evil and violence in the New Testament – in the perspective of Western exegesis.

The conceptualisation of Christ in West-African Neo-Pentecostalism

In contemporary West-African charismatic and Neo-Pentecostal Christianity, Jesus Christ is conceptualised predominantly as carrier of utmost spiritual power. As such, he functions as savior who makes life in its fullness a reality. Only by his power, one is able to overcome adverse evil spirits which are threatening the life, health, and success of individuals. Accordingly, »savior« in many West-African languages is literally rendered as »life-savior«, as in the Ghanaian language Twi: *agyenkwa*.[4] This interpretation of Christ, which seems plausible and relevant to many in and from West Africa, is brought to expression by popular songs, like the following:

Jesus Power
Jesus power, super power (2x)
Satan power, powerless power.
Mami Water power, powerless power
Mmoatia power, powerless power
Sasabonsam power, powerless power.

The Neo-Pentecostal version of Christianity in and from West-Africa is predominantly involved in »spiritual warfare«, a term used by Neo-Pentecostals in reference to Ephesians 6:10–17. In the revised translation by Martin Luther, this chapter is given the heading »Die geistliche Waffenrüstung« (The Spiritual Armor). Since Ephesians is in critical historical scholarship not regarded as an authentic Pauline epistle, and since it lacks the Lutheran teaching of righteousness by faith, this epistle is in general not held in high esteem in the Lutheran church. However, amongst Neo-Pentecostals in and from West Africa, this epistle is right at the heart of the concerns of many believers. The passage in Ephesians 6 connects especially well with the religious aspirations and expectations of the people.

Regarding the prayers for the return of the spiritual missiles to the senders, as described in the beginning of my essay, it is remarkable to realize that an interpretation is at work here which seems to move beyond the – semantically and syntactically suggested – legitimate range of meaning of Ephesians 6:16: »always carrying the shield of faith with whom you quench the burning arrows of the Evil One« ἐν πᾶσιν ἀναλαβόντες τὸν θυρεόν τῆς πίστεως, ἐν ᾧ δυνήσεσθε πάντα τὰ βέλη τοῦ πονηροῦ πεπυρωμένα σβέσαι. The preacher was not satisfied with just quenching the burning arrows. He was concerned with shooting back those missiles, not only to destroy an evil spirit but also to literally kill actual persons involved, in the name of Jesus.

---

4   See Werner Kahl, *Jesus als Lebensretter. Westafrikanische Bibelinterpretationen und ihre Relevanz für die neutestamentliche Wissenschaft,* vol. 2 of *New Testament Studies in Contextual Exegesis* (Frankfurt a. M.: Peter Lang Publishers, 2007).

NEO-PROPHETISM AS NEW WAVE IN WEST-AFRICAN NEO-PENTECOSTALISM

My colleagues Cephas Oemnyo and Abamfo Atiemo of the University of Ghana at Legon have described this rather recent trend in West-African Christianity in an article published in 2006 in the Ghana Bulletin of Theology: »Claiming Religious Space: The Case of Neo-Prophetism in Ghana.« In this article, they maintain a continuity of this type of prayer with African traditional religion (ATR). For example, Akan

> libations always include imprecations pronounced on (so-called) enemies (within the community) – that they should become impotent or barren; that they should come to shame and not live.[5]

From a traditional perspective, the enemies are those who have the spiritual power and wish to destroy one's divinely bestowed spirit, the *sunsum*, resulting in failure of all kinds of endeavours and eventually leading to sickness and sometimes untimely death. Omenyo and Atiemo observe that in mainstream Pentecostalism, a distinction is drawn between actual persons and spirits, i. e. the »enemy« is perceived as *spirit* not to be identified with the human vessel it employs. The attempt within mainstream Pentecostalism is »to balance the traditional view with the New Testament. In this sense, alleged witches ought to be shown love and considered as victims who need deliverance.«[6]

Neo-Prophetism as a new wave of Neo-Pentecostalism, however, presents an unbroken continuation of conceptions and practices within African Traditional Religions. This continuation is – from a New Testament perspective in general and from the perspective of the Gospel in particular – indeed problematic, since it is the result of an uncritical appropriation of a Biblical passage. Below are some examples of prayers against human beings within this latest version of Neo-Pentecostalism in Ghana:

> Lord,
> when I clap my hands and pray,
> may the enemies who work against me
> be struck by thunder;

---

[5] Cephas N. Omenyo and Abamfo O. Atiemo, »Claiming Religious Space: The Case of Neo-Prophetism in Ghana,« in *Ghana Bulletin of Theology* 1,1 (2006): 63.

[6] Omenyo and Atiemo, *Claiming Religious Space*, 63.

may they get hit and killed
by a car;
whether it is my father,
whether it is my mother
or whoever it is that is my enemy
let them all fall.

In Jesus' name
you enemy who does not
want me to prosper
I cane you.
I destroy you
in Jesus' name.
I destroy all your works
against me in the name of Jesus.

The enemy or enemies
that are harassing me
and work against my prosperity
I shoot them in Jesus' name – pee![7]

It is no coincidence that these prayers were expressed in the Ghanaian language Twi, and the Hamburg experience supports this view: The visiting preacher in the Hamburg congregation was not able to communicate fluently in English. According to Omenyo and Atiemo, what comes to expression here is the fact that this type of Neo-Pentecostalism thrives predominantly among those with a low level of formal education. At the same time and in contrast, classical Pentecostalism and mainstream Neo-Pentecostalism in general just recently discovered the value and need of theological education in seminaries and at universities:

> When the Pentecostal/charismatic-type churches become routinised, they tend to de-emphasise spiritual power and charisma and, in the process, develop Church cultures that leave virtually no space for people with low educational level to participate in leadership and general church life. (…) This development also creates room for a kind of spirituality that met the desires of ordinary Africans who do not find fulfilment in existing Christian traditions.[8]

---

[7]   Omenyo and Atiemo, *Claiming Religious Space*, 64–65. I have adjusted the capitalization.

[8]   Omenyo and Atiemo, *Claiming Religious Space*, 68.

In other words, in an upward-moving society where the Pentecostal/charismatic movement has »become the religion for the new educated urban middle class«[9], Neo-Prophetism expresses the fears, struggles, and wishes of those left behind.

It has been observed by sociologists of religion and by cultural anthropologists with respect to cultures permeated by primal religion that eruptions of spiritual violence have occurred in times of rapid societal change marked by extreme economic imbalances. Such was the case, for example, in the first half of the twentieth century with respect to the growth of the cocoa industry in the former Gold Coast, which made some Ghanaian businessmen very rich. At the same time, due to the attraction of a modern lifestyle marked by urbanisation and individualism, ties to the extended families in the villages weakened, resulting in the accumulation of wealth within the hands of a few. This put the extended family at a disadvantage in many cases when wealthy individuals refused to take responsibility for the needs of those in the village.[10] From the perspective of a communal organisation of life[11] and a spiritually informed conception of reality, this anti-communal behaviour raised suspicions. Within this framework of knowledge, success in life had always signified the involvement of spiritual forces, not only divine but also demonic. Anti-witchcraft cults became popular as a means to ward off adverse spirits which would hinder success.[12] But shrines were also consulted to find

---

[9] Omenyo and Atiemo, *Claiming Religious Space*, 67.

[10] The same dynamics have been described recently regarding Papua New Guinea. See Theodor Ahrens, »Hexereibeschuldigungen und Hinrichtungsbündnisse im Kontext: Pastoraltheologische Überlegungen,« (unpublished paper, 2011), 9: »Wenn die Erwartungen der Menschen an den Vorteilen wirtschaftlicher Entwicklung beteiligt zu werden, enttäuscht werden, wenn gleichzeitig die alten Verpflichtungsverhältnisse nicht mehr recht funktionieren, wenn soziale Abstände sich vergrößern, dann wird dies moralische Debatten freisetzen, die entweder in der traditionellen Sprache des Okkulten oder im Kontext einer modernen Ideologie ausgetragen werden können. Traditionelle Plausibilitätsannahmen werden neu ins Spiel gebracht. Hexereianklagen und Sündenbockmechanismen greifen auch darum um sich, weil soziale und wirtschaftliche Diskrepanzen den Eindruck nähren, dass die Dinge auseinander fallen. Die Revitalisierung des Hexenwahns hat politische Dimensionen. Und die Bekämpfung des Hexenunwesens schließt die Aufgabe ein, die sozialen und politischen Ursachen der Ängste, die Menschen erfahren, zu benennen und zu beheben.«

[11] See Kwame Gyekye, *African Cultural Values: An Introduction* (Accra: Sankofa Press, 1996).

[12] Max Assimeng, *Salvation, Social Crisis and the Human Condition* (Accra: Legon Press,

out the – demonic – powers behind the business success of a competitor, an enemy, or a rich family member who would refuse to share his wealth in terms expected, in order to employ spiritual weapons »to bring him down«. In contemporary West-African societies, this suspicion is very much alive. Popular movies produced in »Nollywood«, i. e. the Nigerian film industry, give ample evidence to this spiritual conception of reality and corresponding strategies to deal with economic imbalances. The acquisition of wealth creates ambivalence. It is both attractive and yet engenders suspicion of the possible involvement of Juju. West-African Neo-Pentecostalism in general, and Neo-Prophetism in particular, draw on concerns and strategies of African traditional religion in caring for the material and spiritual needs of people, in societal processes of transformation caused by the impact of modernity in a globalized economy.[13]

In the prayers quoted above, the urgent need for »prosperity«, i.e. literally »well-being« (Twi: *yie*), becomes transparent. The lack of »well-being« is attributed to spiritual enemies, especially witches disguised as family members. Jesus is invoked as the ultimate spiritual power to overcome these enemies by physically hurting or killing them. It is evident that in this scenario actual persons are not being distinguished from evil spirits possessing them for the enemies are conceptualised as witches that need to be destroyed both physically and spiritually. What becomes apparent here are both the conviction that poverty and hardship are attributed to the activity of evil spirits and witches and the desire to surpass this predicament, overcoming all obstacles to make it in life. Poverty, from a West-African Neo-Pentecostal perspective, has been typically described as a curse in the literal sense, and to be complacent with this situation means to give in to the works of the devil. For many in West Africa, »Life is war« (a popular bumper sticker in Ghana). Within knowledge-systems grounded in primal religion, this »war« connotes not only the difficulties in the organisation of daily life, but first and foremost the spiritual war caused by life-threatening spiritual powers, whose activities can become

---

1995); Meyer Fortes, »The Ashanti Social Survey: A Preliminary Report,« in *Rhodes-Livingston Journal* 6 (1948), 1–36; Jack Goody, »Anomie in Asante,« in *Africa* 27 (1957): 356–363; Birgit Meyer, »›Delivered from the Powers of Darkness.‹ Confessions of Satanic Riches in Christian Ghana,« in *Africa* 65 (1995): 236–255; Barbara E. Ward, »Some Observations on Religious Cults in Asante,« in *Africa* 26 (1956): 47–61.

[13] Kwabena Asamoah-Gyadu, »*Taking Territories & Raising Champions*«: *Contemporary Pentecostalism and the Changing Face of Christianity in Africa 1980–2010* (Accra: Trinity Press, 2010), 36–41.

manifest in actual situations. In order to make it in life, one is supposed to engage in »spiritual warfare«, a dominant concern of Neo-Pentecostal ministries in the sub-Saharan region. As such, spiritual violence, rampant in some versions of West-African Christianity, makes transparent the constant struggle of many to survive on a day-to-day basis. This is true not only for people in West Africa but also for many West-African migrants abroad.

SUFFERING AGGRESSION AND STRATEGIES TO DEAL WITH VIOLENCE IN EARLY CHRISTIANITY

Early Christians placed at the centre of their faith the conviction that the result of a cruel act of violence by the Jewish and Roman authorities in Jerusalem was reversed by divine intervention: God resurrected Jesus, who had been put to death by crucifixion.[14] The time and the personal history of Jesus were generally marked by oppression and violence due to the Roman occupation of Judea. Against this background, it can be claimed that Jesus just shared the plight of thousands of Jews who lost their lives on the cross in that period. In memory of those, however, who regarded him as the ultimate revelation of God, Jesus' life and death were of particular significance. At the core of the Christian faith resides the belief that God had undermined the plans of the authorities of this world by reversing the outcome of the death sentence they passed on Jesus. Seen in the context of ancient belief-systems, two aspects strike us as remarkable: (1) Those responsible for Jesus' death *are not struck dead* in an act of vengeance by God nor by the resurrected and risen Christ; (2) In the accounts of his activities as they are presented in the four Gospels, Jesus is portrayed as someone who was fundamentally *committed to non-violent action* and *self-sacrificial love* even though he was believed to have had divine power at his disposal.

A case in point is the story of how Jesus was taken captive, described in several passages. In the oldest account, in Mark 14:43–52, we are told that one of those present at the scene tried to defend Jesus, drawing his sword and severing the ear of the servant of the high priest without any further comment. According to the parallel in Matthew 26:47–56, it is one of the disciples of Jesus who attacks the servant. In this account, however, Jesus admonishes his disciple by saying, »Put your sword back, for all who draw the sword will

---

[14]   See Mark 16:1–8; Romans 1:2–4; 1Corinthians 15:3–4; Acts 2:23–24.

die by the sword. Or do you think that I cannot appeal to my father, who would promptly send more than twelve legions of angels to my defense?« (vv. 52–53). An interpretation of the incident of his capture is added, according to which it took place by necessity due to a prophecy in the Jewish Holy Scriptures (vv. 54–55). The account in the Gospel of John shares this admonition (John 18: 11) while Luke in his version (Luke 22: 47–53) adds a miraculous act of healing: »And after Jesus had touched the ear, he healed him.« (v. 51) This healing of the soldier who takes Jesus captive expresses a feature which figures prominently in Luke's portrayal of Jesus, namely *forgiveness* (see Jesus' words on the cross in Luke 23:34).

Jesus' advice to resist the usage of arms in Matthew 26:52 is in line with his teachings as presented programmatically in Matthew 5–7, the so-called *Sermon on the Mount* which has served as a main point of reference for those opting for *non-violent resistance* to acts of violence and aggression. The Sermon on the Mount is a composition of sayings of Jesus created by Matthew, drawing on material which in part goes back to Jesus. It reflects the situation of the addressees of this Gospel narrative in the last quarter of the first century, a time marked by the experience of the separation of the Christ-believers from the synagogue and by occasional violent persecutions on the local level. As such, the situation was typical of the experience of many Christians at that time.[15]

It is remarkable that the New Testament writings – in spite of their general variability – express more or less the same attitude towards violence. It is regarded as unjust but, nevertheless, it has to be *endured*. Retaliation or violent resistance are not propagated. The early Christians were, however, convinced that injustice and violence would be overcome and its perpetrators would eventually be punished *by God* in the final judgment, which was expected to be imminent.[16] The image of the Kingdom of God stands for the expectation of a new world designed according to God's standards. Divine justice, love, joy, and the absence of suffering mark that world order (Revelation 21:1–7; Matthew 11:28–30).

In the meantime, the Christ-believers are expected to live up to the standards of the Kingdom of God; they should not retaliate. Their suffering is in-

---

[15] See the respective accounts and references in Luke-Acts, the Gospel of John, the letters of Paul, and in Revelation.

[16] See Matthew 25:31–46; Luke 6:23–26; Romans 12:9–21; Revelation 13–20. See also Stefan Alkier, *Neues Testament,* UTB basics 3404 (Tübingen: Francke Verlag, 2010), 292–298.

terpreted in light of the violence suffered by Jesus. Enduring persecution could thus be understood as *following Christ* by taking one's cross upon oneself.[17] At the same time, they are encouraged »to seek the Kingdom of God and divine justice« (Matthew 6:33), i.e. they should try to live up to the values of the Kingdom of God by implementing strategies which aim at overcoming violence and which eventually aim at breaking the vicious circle of violence. Therefore, in the *beatitudes,* those who work for peace are declared blessed: »Blessed are the peacemakers for they will be called sons of God.« (Matthew 5:9) Similarly, the blessing of God is declared for those who suffer violence, persecution, pain and injustice (Matthew 5:3-13). Luke, in his version of the beatitudes, adds a condemnation of those who are responsible for the painful experience of those suffering from injustice (Luke 6:24-26), i.e. the rich and the satisfied. But again, the final judgment is left to God alone, who will retribute each and everyone according to his or her deeds, »at that day« (Luke 6:23).

The Christ-believers should *not judge* (Matthew 7:1-5) *or retaliate* (Matthew 5:38), but they should even go to the extreme of offering themselves freely to unjust treatment as Matthew has Jesus proclaim: »But I say to you not to offer resistance to the wicked. On the contrary, if anyone hits you on the right cheek, offer him the other as well« (Matthew 5:39). It should be noted that the action of hitting someone in the face is negatively marked as the activity of a wicked person. Again, this commandment is to be understood in the context of the expectation that God will retribute good and evil at the time of the final judgment. Until that time, the Christ-believers are advised to engage in actions by means of which opportunities are opened for the perpetrators of evil acts to repent and change their life and attitude. In this vein, New Testament writers as different as Paul and Matthew agree that the common human disposition of loving one's neighbors or friends (Leviticus 19:18) has been modified in light of the Christ-event and should therefore be extended to *loving even one's enemies* and to praising ones persecutors:

> Praise your persecutors; never curse them, praise them … Never pay back evil with evil … As much as possible and to the utmost of your ability, be at peace with everyone. Never try to get revenge; leave that, my dear friends, to the retribution. As Scripture says: ›Retribution is mine. I will pay them back,‹ the LORD promises. And more: ›If your enemy is hungry, give him something to eat; if thirsty,

---

[17]   See Mark 8: 34; Matthew 10: 38; 16: 24; Luke 9: 23; 2 Corinthians 1: 3-7; 4: 7-15; Philippians 1: 12-30.

something to drink. By this, you will be heaping red-hot coals on his head.‹ Do not be mastered by evil, but master evil with good (Romans 12:14-21).

And, similarly:

> You have heard how it was said: ›Love your neighbour and hate your enemy.‹ But I say this to you: Love your enemies and pray for those who persecute you, so that you may be children of your Father in heaven, for he causes his sun to rise on the bad as well as the good, and sends down rain to fall on the upright and the wicked alike. For if you love those who love you, what reward will you get? Do not the tax collectors do as much? And if you save your greetings for your brothers, are you doing anything exceptional? Do not even the gentiles do as much? You must therefore set no bounds to your love, just as your heavenly Father sets none to his (Matthew 5:43-48).

The New Testament accounts of the teachings and the actions of Jesus with respect to violence are in line with the understanding of his death and resurrection on the one hand and with the experience and ethics of the Christbelievers in the first century on the other hand. The latter interpreted their experiences of suffering violence in light of the teachings of Jesus and of the meaning of his death and resurrection. The category of *reconciliation* helped them to make sense not only of the Christ-event but also of their own experience. According to this understanding, everyone is in need of God's loving attention, and the love of God has its fullest expression in the Christ-event. In interpreting the Christ-event and in emulating the experience of Jesus, early Christians tried to reflect the values of the Kingdom of God in their daily life. They could do so (and some even went to the extreme of giving up their lives for the Gospel) due to their conviction that they were eternally grounded in the ultimate reality of God who is revealed in and through the historical person of Jesus of Nazareth, the Christ.

CONCLUSION

What Jesus Christ or the Gospel may mean in particular situations of violence – or after violence – today is open to careful debate. The New Testament writings can serve as an *orientation*, never as blueprint for today's actions. Some *tendencies* which are shared by all New Testament witnesses can however be identified as parameters within which Christian positions towards violence should be actualised: to be less concerned about one's own well-being but more about the *well-being of others*, in particular of the weak; overcoming hatred with *love for the enemy* as someone who has the potential to change – thus overcoming the *vicious circle of violence*; wrath is of the LORD only and *it is up to God to judge* with divine justice; the Gospel implies *forgiveness and reconciliation,* which the Christian believer is encouraged to give witness to in his or her life.

A responsible Christian decision on the use, the rejection, or the overcoming of violence in distinct situations should be informed by a *contextually* aware reading of relevant Biblical passages, by also considering their history of interpretation, supplemented by a careful analysis of the present situation and – this can be learned from Pentecostals – by prayers asking God for guidance.

With respect to the experience and interpretation of past and present experiences of violence among West-African migrants, it seems essential to create spaces for interaction between various generations of immigrants. Such encounters might help in finding ways for a better life after violence by employing common strategies, which might serve more effectively in attaining goals than spiritual strategies, which might be plausible in West Africa but which do not seem to be helpful in the Western world.

Christians of Western Europe and also of Neo-Pentecostal traditions from West Africa share the belief that the Gospel implies the announcement and creation of just living conditions in present times. The reception of the Good News is relevant to shaping society here and now, with the prospect that the fullness of life be tasted by each and everyone. The Gospel is not to be reduced to implying only the salvation of souls after death.

Upon arriving in Europe, many West Africans seem not to have escaped violence and suffering. In addition to experiencing difficult living conditions in a foreign country, many feel haunted by spiritual attacks. Neo-Pentecostal ministries do answer to the material and the spiritual misery of their flock, but it seems to me that oftentimes the belief in the power of evil spirits is being reinforced, and not overcome, aggravating the spiritual bondage of the people rather than liberating them.

In my view, things will only change with the upcoming second generation. The young people are being educated in the schools of the host country and they share the dominant non-spiritual worldview, i. e. many of them believe it is not plausible anymore to employ spiritual strategies to attain goals in Western European society, and they feel free from any demands or spiritual threats from extended family members in Africa. This disposition of the children of first generation migrants from West Africa might provide a good basis for finding a home in Western European society.

Literature

Ahrens, Theodor. »Hexereibeschuldigungen und Hinrichtungsbündnisse im Kontext: Pastoraltheologische Überlegungen.« Unpublished paper, 2011.

Alkier, Stefan. *Neues Testament*. UTB basics 3404. Tübingen: Francke Verlag, 2010.

Asamoah-Gyadu, Kwabena. »*Taking Territories & Raising Champions*«: *Contemporary Pentecostalism and the Changing Face of Christianity in Africa 1980–2010*. Accra: Trinity Press, 2010.

Assimeng, Max. *Salvation, Social Crisis and the Human Condition*. Accra: Legon Press, 1995.

Fortes, Meyer. »The Ashanti Social Survey: A Preliminary Report.« *Rhodes-Livingston Journal* 6 (1948): 1–36.

Goody, Jack. »Anomie in Ashanti?« *Africa* 27 (1957): 356–363.

Gyekye, Kwame. *African Cultural Values. An Introduction*. Accra: Sankofa Press, 1996.

Kahl, Werner. *Jesus als Lebensretter. Westafrikanische Bibelinterpretationen und ihre Relevanz für die neutestamentliche Wissenschaft*. New Testament Studies in Contextual Exegesis. Vol. 2. Frankfurt a. M.: Peter Lang Publishers, 2007.

Meyer, Birgit. »›Delivered from the Powers of Darkness.‹ Confessions of Satanic Riches in Christian Ghana.« *Africa* 65 (1995): 236–255.

Omenyo, Cephas N. and Abamfo O. Atiemo. »Claiming Religious Space: The Case of Neo-Prophetism in Ghana.« *Ghana Bulletin of Theology* 1, no. 1 (2006): 55–68.

Oshun, Chris O. »Spirits and Healing in a Depressed Economy: The Case of Nigeria.« *Mission Studies* 15/1, no. 29 (1998): 32–52.

Ward, Barbara E. »Some Observations on Religious Cults in Ashanti.« *Africa* 26 (1956): 47–61.

III
INTERRUPTING VIOLENCE:
THE FRAGILE PATH TOWARDS
RECONCILIATION

Forgetting Without Forgiving: the State of the Peace in Ireland, North and South

Siobhán Garrigan

By kind permission of Equinox Publishing, the following essay reproduces material previously published in Siobhán Garrigan, *The Real Peace Process: Worship, Politics and the End of Sectarianism* (London: Equinox, 2010).

For those of us who grew up in England or Ireland, the phrase »forgive and forget« was like a universal ethical principle, a basic human rule. Whether in school or at home, the way children were socialized to resolve conflict went like this: First, one or both parties is told to say sorry; then the teacher, parent or other grown-up says to all concerned: »forgive and forget.«

Of course, neither forgiving nor forgetting is a simple matter. The complicated and difficult nature of both, including habitual human resistance to them, was regularly explored in both classroom and playground. We came to understand that »forgiving« was usually a process rather than a magic word, and that »forgetting« was more a matter of *how* you remembered than some sort of mental erasure. As children we were helped to understand the importance of »forgiving and forgetting« by being taught that, just like us in our schoolroom scuffles, whole peoples were also having to learn to forgive and forget in places like India, Germany, Vietnam, or Zimbabwe.

Our own nations of England and Ireland were not mentioned as a case in point when I was in school, but they could be nowadays. Notwithstanding the recent outbreaks of serious violence in Northern Ireland, there has been a real past tense emerging to »the Troubles«, thanks to the efforts of so many to create and then implement »the peace process«. This process is dated as having had its turning point on Good Friday, 1998, when all the political constituencies signed the Belfast Agreement. Since then, Northern Ireland has encountered phenomenal change: shared government, devolved government, a new police force, new human rights laws and protections, massive urban development (including restaurants and tourist attractions), and, of course, the release of prisoners, the decommissioning of weapons and the maintenance of cease-fires.

However, under the veneer of the nice shops and despite the protections of a non-military police force, old attitudes and habits persist. These are noticeable in subtle and symbolic forms and ways, as will be discussed in a moment, but they are also evidenced in concrete sociological facts: Housing is more segregated than ever before; fewer children than ever are attending interdenominational schools;[2] and there has been a stark rise in explicitly sectarian crimes, such as intimidation.[3]

The Good Friday Agreement (GFA) brokered a political peace for an ethno-nationalist conflict. But it was not designed to address a vitally important factor that also had constituted, in part, the ethno-nationalisms that were in conflict: religion. And religion is one place where the old attitudes and habits can be seen to persist, but also where they may possibly be altered.

Although we may be living »after violence«, there will not be anything other than a »cold« peace[4] in Northern Ireland until religion, too, undergoes a peace process; and this will not happen until we see the problem as being an all-Ireland one, not confined solely to the six counties that make up Northern Ireland. This is because of the fact that, when it comes to religion, »the problem« is not just an argument about territory or civil rights; the problem is sectarianism: a historically island-wide problem consisting of an entrenched and all-pervading attitude of opposition to the religious other. Joe Liechty and Celia Clegg, in their long-term study of sectarianism in Ireland, argue that it is not best defined as its visibly violent events, but rather as »the

---

[1]   In 1999, The Northern Ireland Housing Executive (NIHE) classed 71 percent of housing estates in Northern Ireland as segregated; by 2006 the figure was 95 percent (www.nihe.gov.uk). Belfast city is more segregated than the rest of Northern Ireland, and, since the Good Friday Agreement, has become increasingly so. Shirlow and Murtagh assess that, unlike any previous point in the city's history, now »the majority of persons from a Catholic or Protestant community background live in places that are at least 81 per cent Catholic or Protestant.« Peter Shirlow and Brendan Murtagh, *Belfast: Segregation, Violence and the City* (London: Macmillan, 2006), 59.

[2]   See Tony Gallagher, Alan Smith and Alison Montgomery, *Integrated Education in Northern Ireland: Participation, Profile and Performance* (University of Ulster: UNESCO Centre, 2003).

[3]   See Shirlow and Murtagh, *Belfast: Segregation, Violence and the City,* 52–56; see also Rupert Taylor, *Consociational Theory: McGarry and O'Leary and the Northern Ireland Conflict* (Oxon: Routledge, 2009), 325.

[4]   »The Northern Ireland peace process has transformed a violent conflict into a cold peace.« Jonathan Tonge, *The New Northern Irish Politics?* (New York: Palgrave Macmillan, 2005), 1.

destructive patterns of relating« that create and reinforce divisions between groups. They insist upon the primacy of small, interpersonal interactions and judgments in the creation and maintenance of this sectarian system, saying that, »Sectarianism is a *complex* of problems – including dividing, demonising, and dominating.«[5]

My research has shown that sectarianism remains apparent in churches, in the worship practices of ordinary people, Protestant and Catholic, north and south. For example, through observation of worship practices in 26 churches (Protestant and Catholic, in Northern Ireland and in the Republic), I found that

- Vetting mechanisms sifting Protestant from Catholic masqueraded as ›greeting‹ or ›welcoming‹ rituals;
- The sign of peace was hardly ever passed in Roman Catholic churches, unlike in other countries, which would be notable at any time, but particularly so given that the country was undergoing a ›peace-process‹ at the time of the study;
- The cross was used in symbolically *triumphalist* ways;
- The singing was weaker in church than anywhere else in society, suggesting a possible ›withholding‹ of participation in music which is enmeshed in colonial and sectarian histories;
- There were nationalist flags in even the most anti-iconographic sanctuaries.

And each of these phenomena has a potential sectarian interpretation,[6] creating an expression of or negotiation of sectarian norms and values right at the heart of Christian worship. However, my research also argues that the things people do in church (particularly those that are non-verbal) could be set in the service of imagining and enacting a move beyond sectarianism, a move into a real peace, and the remainder of this essay will consider three specific examples in more depth.

---

[5]   Joseph Liechty and Cecilia Clegg, *Moving Beyond Sectarianism: Religion, Conflict and Reconciliation in Northern Ireland* (Dublin: Columba Press, 2001), 37 (italics mine). For a fuller discussion of the everyday interactions that comprise sectarianism's »destructive patterns of relating«, see 103–106.

[6]   For a more detailed assessment, please see: Siobhán Garrigan, *The Real Peace Process: Worship, Politics and the End of Sectarianism* (London: Equinox, 2010).

Forgetting Ireland: The Words of the Prayers

»Father, we ask you to look after the people of Zimbabwe, the poor Blacks who were held down for so very long, but now also the Whites who are being turfed off their farms. May peace come to that turbulent land and may the current violence stop.«

Roman Catholic (RC) Church in the Midlands, Irish Republic (IR)

»And we pray especially today for the people of Indonesia and everyone down there near the Indian Ocean. They're still struggling to recover from the tsunami and all they lost in it.«

Methodist Church in Northern Ireland (NI)

»Lord, in your mercy, hear our prayers for those who gather this week at the G-8 summit in Germany. Instill these our leaders with humility as well as courage, and guide them to construct policies that will protect this earth, our island home, from further abuse or catastrophe.«

Church of Ireland (CofI), NI

Throughout the Republic and Northern Ireland every Sunday morning, prayers are said for the lands and peoples of the whole world. The three prayers quoted above date themselves easily by the specificity of the concerns they express: anyone could go to a search engine, tap in the people and places named in the prayers and identify the year, if not the exact week, I recorded these words spoken in a church in Ireland. And yet, in all my research, from 2001–2008, I never heard the word »Ireland« (nor »Northern Ireland«, obviously) used in the prayer speech of any of the churches I visited.

In Ireland, I was very surprised to discover, Ireland is rarely mentioned in church. Sermons would use the phrases »at home«, »around here«, and »our leaders« but never named the locality, or the country, or the government. Prayers would be made for »justice« and »peace«, but never for any specific issue, person or place. On just three occasions (in three different churches across the spectrum in the sample) prayers included mention of »the peace process« in »the North« but nothing more detailed about it than that mere moniker.

When it came to the naming of Irish needs, concerns, and fears in worship, across the island and in all denominations, the language became vague or generalized, or both. This is in stark comparison to non-scripted prayer in Christian worship services in other countries, where the needs of the native region or nation are usually mentioned directly and frequently. Moreover, it is also in stark contrast to the ways in which Northern Irish and Irish people pray for the very specific needs of people and events in *other* very specific places, as seen in the three examples above.

Irish concerns, when mentioned, are emphasized as being in common with many others around the world. It is almost unanimously agreed that without its connections to the much bigger world, the peace that exists in Ireland would not have been gained. Significant international pressure promoted the actions of the respective governments, and substantial international investment created the economic conditions in which political conversation might stand a chance of practical application; so perhaps this habit of not naming Irish matters is a habit of deferral, placing the authority to create peace in Ireland in a context of much larger world constituencies. (Or, bluntly, just becoming as American as possible, due to the USA's economic and cultural power.)

However, more may be at stake here. In addition to the undoubted importance of its international connections in its recent history and self-perception, there is a self-abnegation about Ireland and Irishness that is also worthy of remark. Writing about the film *The Commitments* and the way the characters immerse themselves in popular (North American) culture, Luke Gibbons remarks that, »The absence of the Catholic Church, the lack of ›picturesque‹ local colour and, for Alan Parker, the indifference to the Northern conflict, all add to the universalism of the film, to the likelihood that it could have been set anywhere (the highest form of praise, it would seem, for an Irish film in recent years.)«[7]

Analogically, the highest aspiration of »good worship« in Ireland and Northern Ireland in recent years seems to be an avoidance of self-reference and a universalizing of a sense of belonging. It is a sort of self-erasure, the product perhaps of a certain desperation that was at play for so very long; desperation that knew that a specifically Irish, or Northern-Irish, notion of belonging could only be self-defeating in the long run, and which therefore cut out all specific self-reference in the hopes of salvation in universalism.

This points to the possibility that there may also be some fundamental insecurities about geography as well as culture being displayed in Irish ways of praying. Perhaps people in Ireland do not know who to pray for as »ourselves.« The four denominations that constituted my study were all-island in their governance, but the political and social lines of allegiance in the

---

7   Luke Gibbons, »The Global Cure? History, Therapy and the Celtic Tiger,« in *Reinventing Ireland: Culture, Society and the Global Economy,* eds. Peadar Kirby, Luke Gibbons and Michael Cronin (London: Pluto Press, 2002), 92–93.

country are divided. One might expect that their solution, when praying for their native location would be to say »Ireland, North and South« or »Northern Ireland and the Republic of Ireland«, but the fact that this seemingly obvious naming never happened points to a probable (and widespread) discomfort with it.

By not naming Ireland or Northern Ireland in worship, I would like to suggest that Irish Christians in fact might be performing accurately the reality that they are caught in, which is an un-nameable (or at least un-named) situation. The church in which they are worshipping is all-Ireland in its self-identity. The country in which they are living is most definitely not. Without the ability to name their geo-political location in ways that line up with their ecclesiology, they have become adept not only at evasion, but at naming the alternative reality thus formed. Irish prayers for »this place«, »here on earth«, and »this island home« locate Irish congregations in a place that is at once both non-parochial and universal.

On the other hand, however, repressing the conflict inherent in not knowing quite where their limits lie seems only to add to the conflict that so conditions the place where they live. Sectarianism thrives most, as Liechty and Clegg have demonstrated, where it is least acknowledged, and this problem of not knowing how to name one's place, and so not naming it, cannot be separated from the sectarianism in society at large.

Forgetting our Neighbour:
When the Other becomes the Opposite

»Lord, in this week when we break up for the summer holidays, look after all our schoolchildren and keep them safe over the summer. And the children from the other schools, keep them safe too.«

Prayers of the People, RC, Cavan, IR

»Help us to stay open to your grace in our lives, even when we are faced with disappointment, illness or other hurdles. Help us to be loving parents, good neighbours, and help us to be decent to those who are opposite to us.«

Time of Prayer, Presbyterian, Ballymena, NI

»It is you who hold us up. It is you who keep up going. It is you who shows the way. You are all we need. Whatever religion we were from before, take us now into your truth.«

Call to Worship, Evangelical CofI, Dublin, IR

»This week finds us in the international week of prayer for Christian Unity and so on Wednesday night we'll be gathering in the church hall for a bible study with the folks from St. Mary's, followed by tea and biscuits, of course. Please make an effort to come out for this very important night and show our warm welcome to our brothers and sisters from the other religion.«

Announcement, RC, Armagh, NI

It was my impression, hearing these four statements, that each was meant with the kindest, most sincere, and most charitable of intentions. The evangelical mission was trying to say the following: We may have an Anglican foundation, but even if you were raised Catholic, you have an absolutely equal right to be here this morning because there is only true authority, Jesus Christ. The other three remarks were, as I encountered them, not only significant statements of considerateness for their fellows in faith, but they also seemed to stem from a deep commitment to reconciliation in those congregations. They were among the most moving prayers and announcements I encountered in all of my research. They were saying a new thing. They were reaching for new words. They were creating new models of relationship and imagining a new world, being made new by God, in which previous divisions were healed. Each was said with a tone of earnestness, warmth, and profound hope.

And yet, the way in which Catholics referred to Protestants and *vice versa* was as »the other religion«, and this is a profoundly inaccurate term of reference, a term whose inaccuracy stems from and reinforces the sectarian landscape all around it. It is not just in worship that one commonly hears Catholics refer to Protestants as »the other religion« (and *vice versa*); this naming is also frequently encountered in the media and in politicians' remarks on both sides of the border.

Referring to Protestantism and Catholicism as »religions« is just how Christians in Ireland speak. Moreover, not only are fellow Christians referred to as belonging to a different religion, they are sometimes referred to as »the *opposite* religion«, as can be seen in the prayers and announcement above. Indeed, even where »opposite« was not explicitly said, it is an *oppositional* sort of otherness that defines »the other religion« in Ireland. It is not an *additional* sort of otherness, or a *strange* sort of otherness, or a *different-but-related* sort of otherness, or an *unknown entity* sort of otherness; it is very specifically an *opposite* sort of otherness. In common parlance, there are two main religions in Ireland, and one is conceived as being in direct, and oppositional, relation to the other.

While the context in which these words (»other religion« / »opposite religion«) were used in the examples above was one of hospitality and a desire for relationship, the words and phrases themselves nevertheless carried a certain antagonism in their very meaning. B. K. Lambkin confirms that such »split-thinking« is commonplace in Irish speech, and concludes that it is the result of Irish and Northern Irish people making the transition from the »Reformation paradigm« to the »Ecumenical paradigm« of Christian self-understanding without doing the thinking that the rest of Western Europe has engaged in; and why should they, he asks: »Why forsake the status quo, which is in effect a finely attuned mixture of sharing and separation, for the uncertainties of any radical change?«[8]

No doubt there are a raft of issues in political life that warrant a »modulation« between notions of separation and sharing among opposite entities; but when it comes to Christianity in the twenty-first century, such language must be examined for its patent inaccuracies. Protestants and Catholics may disagree on a range of matters, but they hold a very great deal in common in terms of beliefs, values, and practices, and the principal churches across the world, even those with profound historical schisms from one another, acknowledge that they are part of the *same* religion, sharing, on balance, more than they disagree upon. Liechty and Clegg remark that the phrase »opposite religions«, far from being a quirk of colloquial Irish naming habits, is, in fact, »a striking and chilling sign of a culture's customary mindset becoming infested by sectarianism, which typically seeks to magnify difference as far as possible.«[9]

With the best will in the world, one cannot, therefore, refer to one's fellow Christian as »opposite« or as being from an »other religion« and not, in fact, disown them in the process. Creating distance rather than promoting mutual understanding, such naming is in fact self-sabotaging. It keeps the neighbour with whom one seeks to connect in a place that is in fact *other*, or even *opposite*: ultimately different and perennially separated.

But even more than that, because of the meaning of *opposite*, such naming makes the other into the *enemy*. For most of the Christian world, the opposite of God is Satan, the opposite of believers are atheists, the opposite of the faithful are detractors, the opposite of salvation is damnation, the opposite of love is hate, and so on. Moreover, down the years Christians have turned these vocabularies on all manner of people with considerable vitriol,

---

[8] Brian K. Lambkin, *Opposite Religions Still? Interpreting Northern Ireland after the Conflict* (Aldershot: Averbury, 1996), 62.

[9] Liechty and Clegg, *Moving Beyond Sectarianism*, 37.

so that the Jews became Satan, the Protestants atheists, and the Catholics antichrists. The one who is not part of »us« is thus habitually damned: Abstract oppositionality is re-inscribed on the worldly enemy, falsely making that enemy a fierce opponent of God (who is surely on *our* side) – and not just a neighbour from whom one differs.

If in Ireland the *opposite* of Protestant is Catholic and *vice versa*, then the other is being set up as an enemy. Never mind the extreme inaccuracy of such a move theologically (both sets of believers being technically, in fact, Christian), it ensures that any notion of relationship between these entities is construed only along antagonist lines, no matter how subtle. Thinking about how this operates at the level of identity formation, Claire Mitchell concludes that when it comes to theological reflection in Ireland, »conflict and power struggles encourage not the unity of all Christians, but oppositional notions of community.«[10]

There is a powerful forgetting at work in this language. In seemingly »moving on«, by praying for »the other«, by being all friendly now, it actually re-inscribes an incorrect understanding of difference, while at the same time it perpetuates a non-relational mode of engagement.

What is required, I would like to suggest, is the forgiving that the forgetfulness of language has overlooked. The process of naming one another accurately would require us to think about ourselves *in relation* – to forego our old words, our old thoughts about the other. The process of interrogating our forgetfulness, noting what we have brushed under the carpet by glossing over its words, the very process of changing our language could, potentially, help to bring about the forgiveness.

defining/clarifying vs. exposing, illuminating

FORGETTING OUR PAST: ANNIVERSARIES

Anniversaries are a vital and permanent presence in the Irish social landscape. But we have, literally, forgotten them in church and, so, we miss the opportunity to forgive the realities to which they bear witness.

As a culture, anniversaries are of great significance to Irish and Northern Irish people. On the one-month marker of a loved one's death in the Roman Catholic community, the family, friends, and parish usually gather for

---

[10]   Claire Mitchell, *Religion, Identity and Politics in Northern Ireland: Boundaries of Belonging and Belief* (Abingdon: Ashgate, 2006), 73.

the month's mind Mass. Mass is said for them again at the one-year anniversary (often followed by a meal for family, friends, and neighbours), and then usually again for many subsequent anniversaries. This means that on any day in a Roman Catholic parish, there is a good chance that Mass will be said for somebody's anniversary. Anniversaries are thus intricately woven into the fabric of daily life for Roman Catholics.

Protestants also honor an intricate web of rituals that run the gamut of domestic-civic-ecclesial anniversaries. For example, Orange Order marches (and other public actions such as bonfire making) happen on many significant historic anniversaries (the most notable of which is the commemoration of the Battle of the Boyne on 12 July), or other ceremonies of civic commemoration, such as that on the anniversary of the armistice on 11 November each year.

However, when it comes to anniversaries related to recent Irish experiences, they were not mentioned in worship in any of the churches studied. The sole exception to this was one mention of 12 July, on 1 July 2001 in a large Presbyterian Church in Belfast during prayers for a peaceful parade the next weekend, and for an avoidance of a repeat of the problems at Drumcree.[11]

Most strikingly, on 20 August 2006, I went to two churches on the same morning in Donegal (one Catholic, the other Methodist) both of which prayed hard for the coming anniversary of Katrina (which happened in the USA in September of the previous year) but neglected to mention at all the anniversary of the bombing of Omagh, which had passed that very week and had happened just up the road in 1998.[12]

It is simply not the case that Irish memories only run to one year's length, so this lack of mention of important regional or national anniversaries in church must be about something else. The reference to anniversaries of American rather than Irish events may stem from the same desire to be part of American history that can be witnessed in many other aspects of media and cultural life. But I suspect the pattern of not naming anniversaries to do with the life of the nation/s has more to do with just not wanting to deal with ourselves or, rather, not knowing how to and so not doing it.

reluctance to re-open old wounds?

---

[11] »Drumcree« refers to the parade in Portadown, Co. Armagh, which, from 1995–1998 was undertaken in a particularly contentious (and ultimately deadly) manner, resulting in the march not being allowed to pass through nationalist areas in subsequent years.

[12] Omagh is a major town in Co. Tyrone, which suffered a terrible car bomb attack by the »Real IRA« on 15 August, 1998, killing 29 people and injuring at least 220 more.

It seems to me that honouring significant anniversaries in recent (as well as ancient) Irish history needs to become a vital part of the liturgical year in Ireland. To »forget« to do so is to fail to root our worship in our own culture, because anniversaries constitute such an important aspect of our particular society and its social and temporal norms.

Moreover, if it also became a common practice for *cross-community* anniversaries to be honoured in all the churches in Ireland and Northern Ireland, significant gains in moving beyond sectarianism could be made. Worship that marks anniversaries such as Omagh (15 August) are a potentially powerful ecumenical bridge because of their very cross-community nature, due to the fact that members of *all* communities lost people at the same time and still mourn it at the same time.

Worship that marks anniversaries such as New Year's Day are also a potentially powerful ecumenical bridge because they unite the community-at-large in a day of celebration and new beginnings. By knowing that people from all sides care about, remember, celebrate, and pray for the same specific things, at the same specific times, great strides can be taken in realizing that people hold far more *in common* than they do in opposition. Taking a cue from common experiences in those aspects of life that are common to both sides of the sectarian divide, churches can use anniversaries as a moment for noting their common experience, shared concerns, and mutual prayer, across denominations.

By literally remembering, instead of casually forgetting, we have the opportunity to confront, to investigate, to consider, to demand justice if such is needed, and then to let it go, to actually forgive.

The Good Friday Agreement (GFA) brokered a consociational sort of peace. It sought to identify key differences and patrol the borders between them. It protected – and stereotyped – cultural practices, but gave little other attention to religious activity. What this did was to »archive« the pre-existing cultural landscape, as Colin Graham has shown in his studies of photography in Northern Ireland. Prior to the GFA, he says, there had been a widespread hope that »the cultural complexities of Northern Ireland would figure in, and maybe even dictate, the shape of the future. But, by the time of the Agreement, a different« political imperative had taken hold« and »this switch in strategy gambled on consigning the past to the rubbish-bin of history.«[13]

---

[13] Colin Graham, »›Every Passer-by a Culprit?‹ Archive Fever, Photography and the Peace in Belfast.« *Third Text* 19, no. 5 (September 2005): 567–80, 567.

[handwritten annotations: "(similar to Rwanda & B.H) → clean the historical slate, & start over" and in the left margin "justice was reversed?"]

In a way, this is exactly what the GFA required because it called simply, for »A Fresh Start«.[14] It did not call for a truth and reconciliation commission. It did not even call for any apology, on any side. And whereas in other countries people who had participated in atrocities went to jail, in Ireland there were wide-scale releases of those in prison for committing the violence that had constituted the Troubles.

This ethic of asserting »a fresh start« is, then, very different to the ethic in which most Irish and British children are trained in school. Asserting a fresh start means moving on without forgiving. It means moving on without even interrogating, without even questioning, never mind finding answers to those questions or, ideally, forgiving the injustices one uncovers in such a process of gaining understanding.

If we were to pause for a minute in our worship, think how to name one another accurately, remember Ireland and Northern Ireland and their problems and pray for them, and remember the anniversaries that unite us as well as those that divide us, we might get to the point of actually forgiving, and not merely archiving, our suddenly forgotten past. And we must because history tells us that an archived past is a future war. Forgetting without forgiving creates temporary relief, but it is a very fragile peace. Until our worship remembers our truths and those of our neighbours, we are not living »after violence« but on top of it.

Literature

The Agreement: Agreement Reached in the Multi-Party Negotiations, »Declaration of Support.«, paragraph 2.

Gallagher, Tony, Alan Smith and Alison Montgomery. *Integrated Education in Northern Ireland: Participation, Profile and Performance.* University of Ulster: UNESCO Centre, 2003.

Garrigan, Siobhán. *The Real Peace Process: Worship, Politics and the End of Sectarianism.* London: Equinox, 2010.

Gibbons, Luke. »The Global Cure? History, Therapy and the Celtic Tiger« in *Reinventing Ireland: Culture, Society and the Global Economy,* edited by Peadar Kirby, Luke Gibbons and Michael Cronin. London: Pluto Press, 2002.

Graham, Colin. »›Every Passer-by a Culprit?‹ Archive Fever, Photography and the Peace in Belfast.« *Third Text* 19, no. 5 (September 2005).

---

[14]   *The Agreement: Agreement Reached in the Multi-Party Negotiations* (Good Friday Agreement), »Declaration of Support.«, paragraph 2.

Lambkin, Brian K. *Opposite Religions Still? Interpreting Northern Ireland after the Conflict.* Aldershot: Averbury, 1996.

Liechty, Joseph and Cecilia Clegg. *Moving Beyond Sectarianism: Religion, Conflict and Reconciliation in Northern Ireland.* Dublin: Columba Press, 2001.

Mitchell, Claire. *Religion, Identity and Politics in Northern Ireland: Boundaries of Belonging and Belief.* Abingdon: Ashgate, 2006.

Shirlow, Peter and Brendan Murtagh. *Belfast: Segregation, Violence and the City.* London: Macmillan, 2006.

Taylor, Rupert. *Consociational Theory: McGarry and O'Leary and the Northern Ireland Conflict.* Oxon: Routledge, 2009.

Tonge, Jonathan. *The New Northern Irish Politics?* New York: Palgrave Macmillan, 2005.

Interrupting Violence in a Postcolonial Society: A Case Study from Papua New Guinea

Theodor Ahrens

Dedicated to Paul-Gerhardt Buttler on the occasion of his 80th birthday

The Logic of Reciprocity

While Old Testament wisdom as quoted in the Sermon on the Mount limits violent retribution, suggesting that retaliation for the loss of a tooth should amount to not more than one tooth etc. (Matthew 5:23; Exodus 21:23-25), Jesus recommends to counteract violence with a non-violent response. Jesus' advice is to reciprocate not in kind, but in a different currency – in non-violent action.[1] The *logic of reciprocity* as such is not abandoned.

Hans-Martin Gutmann, in his recent monograph *Gewaltunterbrechung* submits that religions in general and Christianity in particular provide patterns of communication, resources, and social space all suited to transform negative reciprocity towards positive reciprocity. Notwithstanding the capability of a state to reduce levels of violence effectively under the rule of law, the state's institutions will not be in a position to definitively overcome violence. However, a deeply rooted desire for violence will only be uprooted after an emotionally deep, symbolically mediated experience of the fullness of life.[2] Such encounters are created in contexts and social networks which cultivate a sense of religious belonging, not least in the experience of common worship. Worship offers a time and a place where narratives, memories, and cultural practices are nurtured, which gives birth to the experience of one's life as gift. Hence, along with a distinction between good and bad reciprocity,

---

[1] See Tim Schramm, »›Pay-Back‹-Gesellschaft und der Verzicht auf Gewalt.«, in *Zwischen Regionalität und Globalisierung*, ed. Theodor Ahrens (Ammersbek: Verlag an der Lottbek, 1997), 417–418.

[2] See Hans-Martin Gutmann, *Gewaltunterbrechung. Warum Religion Gewalt nicht hervorbringt, sondern bindet. Ein Einspruch* (Gütersloh: Gütersloher Verlagshaus, 2009), 11.

the gift is advanced as the key metaphor signifying an abundance of divine goodness in one's own life-world. Gutmann admits that the symbolic world as rooted in Christian worship has a limited range; concurrently, he assumes that there is a capacity in all human beings to transform inimical and destructive behavior towards cooperation and fellowship.[3] Religious belonging shaped by Christian narrative and ritual will contribute to containing violence by supporting a practice of sharing, and, in fact, of spontaneous and free giving. If I am reading Gutmann correctly, he claims relevancy of his hypothesis primarily for limited contexts.

In a methodological perspective, Gutmann first establishes his key metaphors and terminology – religious belonging, reciprocity, and gift – then, in a second step, brings them to the arenas of social interaction. In this paper, I look at a situation where people actually relate to each other, giving, taking, and reciprocating; and then uncover the narratives, metaphors, and rituals people actually draw upon as they sort out their relationships.

In what follows, I present a case study from the Western Highlands in Papua New Guinea, a conglomeration of interrelated Melpa-speaking clans living within the framework of a post-colonial state. The focus is on conflict management, past and present. While tradition legitimises that a life should be given for a life taken, that is, the right to retaliate in kind, it also provides avenues to »repay« in a different currency other than violence. Ritualised forms of conflict management rival the legal system of the nation-state. Indeed, they weaken the legal jurisdiction of the courts. At the same time, they maintain space to experiment with traditional means to limit violence in contexts which remain beyond an effective control by the legal system of the nation-state. (≈ Gacaca trials)

My hunch is that we may not be faced with the two mutually exclusive alternatives, either to opt for the logic of the gift *or* the logic of reciprocity. Rather we have to develop and cultivate patterns of social interaction and audiences within which we can reasonably argue *to what degree* the logic of reciprocity and/or the logic of the gift should prevail.[4]

During the 1930s, when gold prospectors, missionaries, and Australian officials reached the Central Highlands of the then United Nations-mandated territory of Papua New Guinea, they found large populations which had been

---

[3]   See Gutmann, *Gewaltunterbrechung*, 115–116, 123.

[4]   See Hans Joas, »Die Logik der Gabe und das Postulat der Menschenwürde.«, in *Von der Ursprünglichkeit der Gabe. Jean-Luc Marions Phänomenologie in der Diskussion,* ed. Michael Gabel et al. (Freiburg: Verlag Karl Alber, 2007), 157.

living there for thousands of years and had developed a fairly sophisticated horticulture. Since the 1930s, the people have been affected by far-reaching economic, political, cultural, and religious changes. Consequently, traditional systems which cultivated mutual obligations have been weakened. Groups and individuals struggle to maintain traditional claims and to reposition themselves within the nation-state, which effectively widened the arena for political manoeuvring. There are winners and losers as people rival for access to government »development« funds.

Many people do their best to cultivate sustainable forms of communal living. Yet, time and again it happens that such efforts are frustrated. Scars left by old conflicts break open again. Population growth and migration sharpen disputes over land rights. New conflicts are added. For instance, widespread vote-buying during electoral campaigns gives rise to inter-group tensions and cause for violent conflicts. These conflicts result in loss of human lives and destruction of houses, gardens, and public buildings. A spiral of violence is unleashed, cools down for a while, only to regain momentum in a later stage.

DISPUTED LEGITIMACY OF VIOLENCE

The problem of violence is fundamentally related to the problem of legitimacy. A constitutional democracy based on the rule of law forbids any unlawful physical violence. What constitutes the legitimacy of violence? In modern society it is considered irrational, destructive, and meaningless if people take retaliation (revenge) into their own hands, outside the legal system of the state. However, in small-scale societies, such as we find in the Highlands of Papua New Guinea, retaliation has traditionally been considered normal, meaningful and, under given circumstances, even mandatory.[5] Revenge was *one* aspect of a comprehensive ideology of reciprocity, downside of a ritual system within which goods and valuables were periodically exchanged between clans to keep their relationships stable and flexible. Ceremonial retaliation as practised in traditional societies does not unleash potentially limitless violence; it is usually a mode to limit violence.[6]

The moral assessment of violence is dependent on the index of criteria for political legitimacy. In a modern state, based on a system of democratical-

---

[5]   See Pamela J. Stewart and Andrew Strathern, *Violence: Theory and Ethnography* (London: Continuum, 2002), 159.

[6]   See Marcel Hénaff, *Der Preis der Wahrheit. Gabe, Geld und Philosophie,* trans. Eva Moldenhauer (Frankfurt a. M.: Suhrkamp, 2009), 331.

ly legitimised rule of law, violence is also, in fact, fundamental. The imagined pre-legal condition of violence remains present in constitutional law of the state.[7] Concurrently, tribal warfare and traditional modes of conflict management continue. For weak states,[8] such as Papua New Guinea, this may cause problems, indeed affect their stability. As a matter of fact, the government of Papua New Guinea has lost its monopoly on the use of force, at least in parts of the country. Frequently, the legal system is not successful in defusing violent conflicts between rival *groups*. Various factors are at work. For instance, while a court will hold *individuals* responsible and accountable for their acts, factors working in the background on a *communal* level, such as gossip or hate stored in communal memory, are difficult to objectify to such a degree that a particular group could be held accountable for them in a court. It is unlikely that a court would set out to determine the share that a particular group may have in a violent outburst, other than in the most general terms. Group involvement remains a side issue. Also, it happens at times that politicians, businesspeople, and even the police are part of a conflict feeding the spiral of violence, while in public they advocate law and order. In the perception of the people involved in a conflict, such background factors undermine the legitimacy of the state's legal system.

It is against this background that groups involved in violent conflicts turn back to traditional practices of conflict management. In fact, they claim legitimacy for their means of conflict management which take place beyond the legal system of the state. After Papua New Guinea's Independence, such procedures to settle conflicts out of court spread rapidly.

If, in weak states, key government institutions do not function well and rival groups gain greater weight and more space for action as a consequence, such traditional modes of settling disputes based on the ideology of strict reciprocity may produce constructive as well as destructive results. We are

---

[7]   See Michael Moxter, »Gewalt als Phänomen und Grenze der Kulturtheologie,« in *Religion, Politik und Gewalt. Kongressband des XII. europäischen Kongresses für Theologie in Berlin 18.–22. September 2005* (Gütersloh: Gütersloher Verlagshaus, 2005), 630.

[8]   Weak states is a technical term in use since the 1980s in political science and development studies, particularly with regard to a great number of former colonies in Africa and Oceania that attained nationhood. A weak state is differentiated from strong states and from failing or failed states. It refers to the fragility of key institutions of a nation-state, such as education, police, and judiciary. Weak states are unable to deliver political goods such as security, effective political participation, and law and order.

[handwritten marginalia: How does ideology further complex reconciliation?]

looking at two ways of conflict management which are not simply complementary; their underlying ideologies are not easily reconciled.[9]

Cultural Background: Exchange, Retaliation, Evening Out, Cooling Down Hot Conflicts

Up to the 1990s, exchange rituals between neighbouring groups created mutual obligations that helped to establish relatively stable relationships without completely eliminating violence, killings, or sorcery. Groups had to invest continuously in such networks to keep them alive. Any human interaction takes into consideration one's own commitments and in addition creates new obligations on the side of an exchange partner. The ideology of reciprocity covers all dimensions of life, including relationships with unseen powers. At the heart of such relationships lies the idea of exchanging – positively or negatively – the power of life (life-power). Any social act, whether strengthening life or threatening an exchange partner, sooner or later demands an answer, which may be given either in the same currency – ›wealth for wealth, blood for blood, damage to life-power for damage to life-power‹ – or in a different medium (goods, wealth – formerly shells, pigs, cassowaries or other wealth, now also money) for a human life. A transfer of wealth (valuables), the gift, so to speak, is the medium to change social relationships. It is in this perspective that Marcel Mauss, in his seminal essay, discusses exchange rituals.[10]

Gift exchange cannot, as Stewart and Strathern have pointed out, coexist with open hostility. Exchange relationships are possible only where and when rivalries and open hostilities have been transformed into alliances.[11] While Berking, following M. Sahlins, maintains that exchange achieves for small-scale societies what the state does for modern societies, namely guaranteeing peace,[12] Mauss is a bit more careful, reminding us

[handwritten marginalia in left margin: equivocation of objects to human life? how do you change your relationship w/ those who have wronged you so deeply, w/o compromising yourself?]

---

[9]   See Andrew Strathern, »Compensation: ›Should There Be A New Law?‹«, in *Homicide Compensation in Papua New Guinea: Problems and Prospects,* ed. Richard Scaglion, Law Reform Commission of Papua New Guinea, Monograph No. 1, (Port Moresby: Office of Information for the Law Reform Commission, 1981), 5–24.

[10]   See Marcel Mauss, »Die Gabe. Form und Funktion des Austauschs in archaischen Gesellschaften.«, trans. Eva Moldenhauer et al. in *Soziologie und Anthropologie,* vol. 2 (Frankfurt a. M.: Fischer Taschenbuch Verlag, 1989).

[11]   See Stewart and Strathern, *Violence,* 175.

[12]   See Helmuth Berking, *Schenken. Zur Anthropologie des Gebens* (Frankfurt: Campus Verlag,1996), 67, 72–75.

how close feasting and fighting lie together. Exchange establishes a delicate balance between rival groups. Once the idea spreads that obligations have not been adequately honoured, exchange relationships are liable to break down. Positive reciprocity turns back to negative reciprocity and – in short – violence. *Can reconciliation foment violence?*

A customary group vouches for the life of any of its members. This applies both ways – to perpetrators as well as to victims. A life taken shall never be unrecompensed.[13] Both sides acknowledge the legitimacy of retaliation regardless of what state law may stipulate. The spirits of the departed oblige the living to take revenge against those who are believed to have caused the death/killing of a clan member. It is at this juncture that religion comes to bear on a conflict. The demand for revenge attributed to the spirits of the dead entails a symbolic power which comes to bear both on their descendants as well as on their partners in conflict.

Instead of retaliating in identical currency (in kind) – blood for blood, a life for a life – compensation may be given. Valuables may stand for a person's life and be accepted by the kin on behalf of the person who was killed. The principle of reciprocity is being maintained, though in a medium other than blood.[14]

In this way, traditional modes of exchange continue to be a building block of conflict management.[15] To label the outcome of such procedures as reconciliation would load too much meaning on the process; however, a relationship of physical conflict may be turned into an exchange relationship. A way is found to ward off physical retaliation. Hostile relationships are – for the time being – transformed into non-violent co-existence. This is an option. However, there is no guarantee that any violent conflict could be turned into a non-violent settlement.[16] Ideas of remorse, expiation, or punishment are, as far as I am aware, of no significance in this context. Such procedures, locally managed outside the courts, meet a sense of justice as held by the people in-

---

[13] See Henaff, *Wahrheit*, 331.

[14] See Hermann Strauss, *Die Mi-Kultur der Hagenberg-Stämme im östlichen Zentral-Neuguinea. Eine religionssoziologische Studie* (Hamburg: Kommissionsverlag Cram, de Gruyter & Co., 1962), 249–255, 238–242. Published in English as *The Mi-Culture of the Mount Hagen People*, Ethnology Monographs, no. 13, trans. Brian Shields, ed. G. Stürzenhofecker and Andrew Strathern (Pittsburgh: Department of Anthropology, University of Pittsburg, n. d.), 172–175, 180–183 see also Strathern, »Compensation.«

[15] See Stewart and Strathern, *Violence*, 175.

[16] See Strathern, »Compensation,« 11.

volved.[17] Compensation practiced in conflicts of a *limited scale* may be viewed as a primordial system of justice. While it keeps its distance from the legal system of the state, it need not necessarily lead to anarchy.[18] Justice, as a result of such efforts, is then a relative term. Its content is determined by a sense for meaning and values, which is contextually conditioned.

In a transitional society, such as Papua New Guinea, compensation payments as part of locally based conflict management carry some obvious advantages. Many people are involved. The process will show who actually has to settle a dispute with whom. Many individuals contribute to raise a compensation payment. Hence, within that group, obligations and alliances are also reshaped.[19]

Mauss views exchange rituals historically, as an early stage in the evolution of civil society. Eventually, he suggests, reason will prevail, and people will replace irrational explosions of violence by forming alliances, signing contracts and maintaining a practice of giving as an integral part of the *contract sociale.*[20]

In that perspective, the state as the sovereign power may tolerate such out-of-court practices of conflict management for a limited period of time. In the long run, a state based on a democratically controlled rule of law will not be able to tolerate such procedures, not least because in such out-of-court settlements, the individual perpetrators who have taken the life of another person are, as a matter of fact, granted amnesty.

Traditional Forms of Conflict Settlement in Present Day Papua New Guinea

How do traditional forms of conflict settlement function in present day Papua New Guinea? In brief, not too well! Postcolonial society has opened new areas for political maneuvering and rivalries. It has also, as was pointed out already, increased social tensions. Tribal fighting, as it is called, tends to cover larger areas, at times even bordering on civil war (Southern Highlands, Bougainville). Also, the system of compensation payments has seen an inflationary rise. At times, quite dubious compensation claims are raised and

---

[17] See Stewart and Strathern, *Violence,* 9, 109.

[18] See Stewart and Strathern, *Violence,* 12, a claim which does not apply to the Papua New Guinea Highlands only. See Elmar Klinger, »Revenge and Retribution.«, in *The Encyclopedia of Religion,* vol. 12, 1987, 363.

[19] See Strathern, »Compensation.«, 12.

[20] See Mauss, »Die Gabe.«, 141.

settled, involving huge payments quite out of proportion to the damage claimed. Examples are plentiful.[21] At times, even the government has taken up the practice of paying compensation, sometimes for quite questionable claims.

I do not want to suggest that conflict management through compensation payments should be seen as a solely negative heritage of tradition, increasingly irrelevant today. However, traditional systems of conflict management face a much more complex situation: As violence spreads over much larger areas, it involves larger numbers of groups while at the same time causing greater damage to private as well as to public property, not least being the cost to human life. These extended conflicts destabilize society at large. Attempts to employ compensation payments in a large-scale conflict undermine the legal system of the state. There will always be groups and individuals who claim to have been left out of the settlement while others take advantage, which then gives cause for renewed violence. Thus, the practice of compensation loses the function, effectiveness, and moral credibility which it originally possessed.

We noted already that the parties that try to settle a violent conflict by negotiating compensation payments do not acknowledge the authority and legitimacy of the legal system of the state. The fundamental problem is a lack of *voluntary* self-engagement committed to the idea of a democratically controlled rule of law. A state based on the rule of law protects *and* limits the freedom of individuals, as it enforces and shapes patterns of mutual acknowledgement, binding its citizens just as much as itself to the authority and rule of law. In that way, the state minimizes violence, if need be, by threatening the use of force. It is still a long way off before the idea of the state, based on a democratically controlled system of law and its legal institutions, will find unquestioned acceptance and support in Papua New Guinea's society at large.

Churches and non-governmental organizations (NGOs) are faced with a task here.[22] Space and opportunity for churches and NGOs to attend to this

---

21 For early developments see T.C. MacIndoe, »Tribal Fighting and Compensation in the Simbu Province.«, in *Homicide Compensation in Papua New Guinea: Problems and Prospects,* ed. Richard Scaglion, Law Reform Commission, Monograph, no. 1 (Port Moresby: Office of Information for the Law Reform Commission, 1981), 25-29.

22 See Volker Böge, »Friedenskonsolidierung in Nachkriegszeiten. Der Fall Bougainville.«, in *Arbeitspapier,* Nr. 3, ed. Forschungsstelle Kriege, Rüstung und Entwicklung, (Hamburg: Universität Hamburg, 1999); Volker Böge, »Konfliktpotentiale und Gewaltkonflikte im

problem have as yet been taken up only by a few agencies. Two levels of action offer themselves. Firstly, the National Council of Churches (NCC) engages with and supports public debate about use and abuse of human rights. However, the NCC is weak, the energy of its member churches often absorbed by internal problems. The National Catholic Bishops' Conference appears to be more effective in this regard. However, it is largely dominated by clergy of foreign origin. Secondly, because churches – perhaps even more than other NGOs – are in many cases well connected at the grass-roots level. They have special opportunities to take a stance if communal violence erupts among their parishioners. There are examples past and present that such opportunities have been used.

CHURCHES' CONTRIBUTIONS TO LIMIT VIOLENCE: ENCOURAGING THE EMERGENCE OF CIVIL SOCIETY

A BRIEF HISTORICAL NOTE

Christian missions coming to the highlands during the 1930s, in the early stages of colonization, recommended themselves as a peacemaking agency. In a context where traditional warfare, new conflicts with gold prospectors, and confrontations with officers of the Australian Mandated Territory caused people to be worried about their social and cultural survival, Christianity was adopted as a power that offered a religious rationale to end warfare.[23] For a while, the peace issue claimed center-stage in missionary preaching. As the Australian administration took responsibility to establish the *Pax Australiana*, law and order were installed, if need be by the threat of a gun, and illegal violence by gold prospectors as well as tribal warfare were brought under control to a fairly large degree. Churches turned to more conventional catechetical instructions. The peace message was sidelined in the work of the

---

Südpazifik. Optionen für den Zivilen Friedensdienst.«, in *Arbeitspapier*, Nr. 1, (Hamburg: Universität Hamburg Forschungsstelle Kriege, Rüstung und Entwicklung, 2001), Theodor Ahrens, »Chancen und Grenzen der Kirchen im Umgang mit Gewalt,« *Lernort Gemeinde*, 1 (2006): 9–12.

[23] Robin Radford, »Burning the Spears: A ›Peace Movement‹ in the Eastern Highlands of New Guinea 1936–37.« *The Journal of Pacific History* 12 (1977): 40–54 and Theodor Ahrens, »Die Verstoßung der alten Götter. Zur Frühgeschichte lutherischer Mission im östlichen Hochland von Papua Neuguinea.«, in *Der neue Mensch im kolonialen Zwielicht. Studien zum religiösen Wandel in Ozeanien* (Hamburg: LitVerlag, 1993), 45–63.

churches. Christian missions certainly had hoped to eradicate tribal fighting, sorcery' and witchcraft; however, all these phenomena do still exist, in spite of more than 80 percent of the population claiming membership in a church. Churches have tried to address these problems in various ways. In what follows, I present a sketch of such an engagement.

THE MELPA LUTHERAN CHURCH

A particularly impressive example has been given by the Melpa Lutheran Church in Papua New Guinea, mainly based in the Western Highlands around Mt. Hagen. For more than thirty years, the Bishop of this church, Sanangke Dole, has made peace work a major focus of his activities. In more than 20 cases of tribal fighting, he has mediated successfully. Such mediation work sometimes took months to achieve its ends.[24] This work usually has three distinct phases. First, a retreat for the mediating team to prepare itself, then a phase of mediation styled along the lines of local politics, and, finally, a public worship service.

Before the bishop travels to the field where armed conflict is actually being waged, he gathers a team of 8-10 pastors and elders for a retreat. They engage in Bible studies, confessions of one's own shortcomings in dealing with conflicts, and extended sessions of intensive prayer to build up a sphere of positive power to protect the team members as they enter a field ridden by destructive powers that will come up against them. Thus, »they prepare their lives for the spiritual battles as well as physical battles.«[25] It is supposed that the visible world and any human actions are surrounded by and potentially affected by powers based and hidden in the unseen world. It is believed that the God of the Bible, as well as the powers of traditional religion, not least the departed, may at any time directly intervene in the course of events.

With that done, the team moves out to make camp somewhere along the borderline between the territories of the fighting parties. At times they camp

---

[24] See Melpa Lutheran Church in Papua New Guinea, *Reconciliation: A Paradigm of Mission* (Mt. Hagen: Melpa Lutheran Church, 2006), 11-15. For the genesis of the Melpa Lutheran Church see Theodor Ahrens, »›Geistliche Säuberungen‹ als Strategie kirchlicher Identitätssicherung?« in *Gegebenheiten, Missionswissenschaftliche Studien* (Frankfurt a. M.: Lembeck Verlag, 2005), 258-291; for transformation of traditional means to straighten things out see Theodor Ahrens, »Verfahren des In-Ordnung-Bringens. Seelsorge und Kontrolle in der Verbundenheit der Gruppe. Eine interkulturelle Perspektive,« in *Vom Charme der Gabe. Theologie interkulturell* (Frankfurt: Lembeck Verlag, 2008), 215-237.

[25] Melpa Lutheran Church, *Reconciliation*, 12.

on the battlefield itself. The bishop is known by the people, a well-respected person in the region. He remains with his team on the spot. His time contingent is unlimited. He resumes traditional patterns of conflict management. Together with his team, he moves back and forth between the quarters of the warring parties looking for considerate people (for people who possibly have second thoughts about what is going on). Usually such people can be found. Then, though he is dealing with a conflict between groups, he needs to evoke a readiness to talk in individuals, opinion leaders, and decision makers. Particularly the instigators, those who were responsible to push the conflict, must not be allowed to stay back. The aim of this time-consuming going back and forth is to bring both parties (including the instigators) together to talk and face the real issues at stake.

At this stage narratives begin to play a role. The two groups do not have at their disposal a shared narrative, acceptable to both sides, which would tell why and how the conflict emerged and illuminate the real issues at stake.[26] Each side has its own story to tell. On decisive points they are not agreeable. These competing stories do have complex effects. They reinforce differing group identities and they describe the contribution that individuals and groups had in the explosion of violence. Both parties view themselves as victims of an aggression, and this, as a matter of fact, tends to be the case not only in Papua New Guinea. Further, one's own narrative legitimizes violence against each and everyone who is considered to be a member of the opposite group. Hence, the narrative of each side turns into a dangerous weapon. (This is even more so in case of hidden violence, such as sorcery/witchcraft). Last but not least, such stories function as a bridge, tying an element of religion into the social and political dimension of a violent conflict. The narratives legitimize revenge, because supposedly, the spirits of the departed (victims) demand it. Violence needs symbols to intimidate others and to claim dominance.[27] Both sides feel and act out of the immediately available plausibility of their narrative.[28]

What about the efficacy of counter-stories which Hans-Martin Gutmann[29] discusses? For the time being, the bishop does not explicitly draw on the Christian meta-narrative as a counter-story. He first tries to get down to the

---

[26] See Theodor Ahrens, »Versöhnung als Horizont christlicher Mission.«, in *Vom Charme der Gabe. Theologie interkulturell* (Frankfurt: Lembeck Verlag, 2008), 263–282, 277–282.

[27] See Stewart and Strathern, *Violence*, 170–171.

[28] See Stewart and Strathern, *Violence*, 17–20, 37, 152, 170.

[29] See Gutmann, *Gewaltunterbrechung*, 68.

facts, to bring into the open what really happened, the root causes which are hidden in and behind the particular group narratives. These facts, including conflicting interests of the warring groups, need to be put on the table. Incidents which caused an outbreak of violence rarely are the root causes of conflict. The vicious circle of violence cannot be interrupted unless the people involved have squarely faced these and begun to work on them. Having worked through these facts, the parties concerned are not likely to arrive at a mutually shared meta-story accommodating everything the two parties had to tell. However, being confronted with the facts, including a square look at the destruction the conflict caused, they may finally be willing to mutually tolerate the version of the other side.[30]

The Melpa Lutheran Church has taken up the tradition of compensation payments, formerly called »blood payment«, as part of what they call their peace work.[31] The relatives of those who killed member(s) of the enemy group will give a »down-payment« to the family of the victim(s) to cool down the heat of their resentment, before the main transfer of valuables and money agreed to from group to group takes place.[32] It is in this way that bishop Sanangke's work is geared to achieve an agreement. The conflicting parties are introduced to the idea of law in the widest sense of the word – law as a guardian of an agreed-upon order which must be honoured.

The result then is a state of co-existence, which, for the time being is free of violence. The transfer of valuables symbolizes mutual acknowledgement. Negative reciprocity was transformed into an exchange relationship of the two groups. It would perhaps, depending on the criteria applied, be too much to talk about reconciliation. I do not think it is useful to approach such processes with a pre-set collection of criteria, such as repentance, airing the issue of guilt, remorse, and forgiveness. Instead of loading such processes with a maximum of theological concerns, it may be more useful to leave it to the freedom of the people involved to negotiate a relationship of mutual recognition free of violence. Co-existence of formerly warring parties as such is a major achievement, even though it remains a delicate relationship. Yet, it holds potential for further positive developments. Mutual acknowledgement entails the notion of a gift, an offer, so to speak.[33]

---

30   See Stephanie van de Loo, *Versöhnungsarbeit. Kriterien – theologischer Rahmen – Praxisperspektiven* (Stuttgart: Kohlhammer, 2009) quoting Susan Dwyer, 296–297.

31   See Melpa Lutheran Church, *Reconciliation*, 13.

32   See Melpa Lutheran Church, *Reconciliation*, 13.

33   See Henaff, *Der Preis der Wahrheit*, 179.

The »peace agreement« is celebrated in an open-air service, sometimes a communion service. This concluding service is important because many people, including representatives of the provincial government and the police forces, hear and see that this bloody conflict came to an end, not because people were compelled to do so by outside forces or because they were threatened and had no other choice, but as a result of voluntary negotiations. Both parties exchange a Bible while promising to each other that henceforth they will refrain from physical violence as they relate to each other. A large wooden cross is erected as a memorial at the place where the agreement was negotiated.

The notion of exchange/reciprocity is not nullified. Transfer payments have been made. Bibles were exchanged. In this way, the concept of a voluntarily agreed-upon relationship free of violence is rooted within the ritual of a Christian service. At this particular occasion, the Christian counter-narrative is placed at centre-stage. For the participants, it opens a horizon beyond the rationale of strict reciprocity.

CONCLUSIONS

The peace work of the Melpa Lutheran Church is a paradigm under the following restrictions: (1) The conflict involved two groups and was of limited scope; (2) legal authorities of the state were unable to achieve positive results because the conflict took place in an area too remote for police and courts to exercise effective control and too far away from the political centre for the government to be bothered; and (3) in some cases, police and politicians had compromised their authority anyway by being part of the conflict while publicly advocating law and order. Under such circumstances, church leaders who have built up trust and respect in the area and understand the rules and tricks of local politics can possibly play a constructive role; that is, if they find considerate people who are prepared to work with them towards a peaceful settlement of a dispute which got out of hand.

The conflicting parties and the churches' mediators both presuppose that the desire for revenge may be satisfied by transactions in a medium other than taking a life for a life. This is taken up by the mediating team from the church. The churches' representatives, do not, of course, own the competency to negotiate peace. But they help to clarify conflicting interests and to sort out the facts relevant in the genesis of a conflict. It is clear what the team stands for – relationships free of violence as the greater common good. The church people have their own reasons and motivations to engage in that kind of work. But they do not bring along a set of prescriptions as they try to get

Rx for cure = useless

people to talk with each other. The liberty of the conflicting groups is respected. Under the conditions prevailing in a modern society, peace in the public sphere can ultimately not be enforced from outside or from top to bottom. It is the people involved who either identify with that ideal, support it, or reject it.[34] The idea of collective responsibility directs the ritual of negotiation. Yet, the instigators of violence, opinion leaders, and decision makers, are brought to the negotiation table. Thus the principle of individual responsibility is taken seriously.

In traditional society, religion and the rules which patterned communal life were indistinguishably bound together by the principle of reciprocity. However, religion and law separate their ways and a free space emerges,[35] as the state of Papua New Guinea enshrined in its constitution the notion of a society based on the rule of law, by which both citizens and government are held accountable. It is in this free space that the public worship service concluding the negotiations is placed. The concluding service presents portions of the Christian narrative and offers a broader framework of understanding, which relativises the ultimate meaning of strictly reciprocal relationships. Signs are placed and a story is tapped into, suggesting that, beyond the obvious need to find pragmatic solutions to interrupt circles of violence, each and any social relationship depends on that unknown resource. That unknown resource is placed beyond any normal social togetherness, from which human interaction has made withdrawals and will continue to make them. We are citizens of a universe which lives by forgiveness. As far as God is concerned, no one will be reduced to the sum of his or her deeds or misdeeds. This insight of faith places fellow human beings beyond the reach of strict reciprocity. A society based on an ideology of strict reciprocity would run hot and come to a halt, like a gearbox without oil. Each transfer of goods to compensate for a misdeed entails more than the agreed upon equivalent of previous damage – a word is given, a handshake is offered, initial trust granted, an invitation that opens further possibilities to relate to each other.

Politicians and representatives of the legal institutions attending that service need to pick up at this point. They will have to tackle the problem of how to balance contextual notions of justice (as they guide compensation practices) with the necessity to protect the rule of law. This is not an easy task in

---

[34] See Traugott Koch, »Der Friede in der Politik.« *Zeitschrift für evangelische Ethik* 47 (2003): 184.

[35] Giorgio Agamben, *Die Zeit, die bleibt. Ein Kommentar zum Römerbrief* (Frankfurt a. M.: Edition Suhrkamp, 2006), 134.

a society with a democratic façade, yet severely impacted by shadowy and confusing constellations of power. While the revival of traditional conflict management via compensation payments outside the state's court system is driven by the conviction that government institutions have no business whatsoever to interfere in what the people involved consider to be their own affairs, the representatives of the judiciary must insist that the state's constitution provides a new frame of reference, transcending the level of local group politics. Within this frame of reference, the state as the sovereign has to shoulder the task to establish a generally acceptable social order and, thus, institutions and procedures to foster peace ad intra. The major common good is to protect relationships based on mutual acknowledgement of the right that each individual life is inviolable.

These days, in some areas, tribal fighting has taken the form of proxy wars. Groups which are in conflict now hire semi-professional gangs who fight on their behalf with automatic weapons. Traditional forms of mediation which produced good results in a number of cases can hardly function under such circumstances. The bishop has become quite discouraged.[36] This turn of events confronts the custodians of public order with the option either to withdraw from particular areas or to decide for armed conflict with their own citizens. If that happens, society is threatened by a state of emergency as a permanent structure.[37] The only other strategy would be to choose a long and cumbersome path back to the restitution of law and order. However, as long as the political elite behave as if they are accountable only to their own small constituency, this will be a difficult road to travel.

A further impediment shall be noted: as long as the people concerned are unable to distance themselves from a realm of myths which legitimises, even demands, retaliation, and as long as they claim that it is no one else's business but their own to settle a dispute, they will not be willing to acknowledge the principle of separate (legislative, executive, and juridical) powers. What the churches could do in this respect is, first, to discover or re-discover the Old Testament's prophetic critique of religion; and, secondly, to seriously engage in adult education focusing on human rights issues. The competency of local churches to contribute to a generally acceptable social order will depend on whether or not they can identify such needs and motivate their constituency to address them.

---

[36] Sanangke Dole, interview by author, June 2009.

[37] See Giorgio Agamben, *Homo sacer. Die souveräne Macht und das nackte Leben* (Frankfurt a. M.: Edition Suhrkamp, 2002), 49.

A subtle contribution of Christianity regarding the legitimacy of reciprocal violence may be drawn from the Apostle's Creed. Common sense has it that the spirits of the departed are calling for vengeance. Two things need to be done: (1) Churches need to create time and space to remember the dead, and (2) there is need to demythologise the hate projected onto the world of the spirits which in turn falls back on the living. The Apostle's Creed reminds us that each and everyone, including the dead, remains answerable to a Last Judgment, thus alleviating the living from passing final judgment on each other.

A final point also concerns the world of religious imagination. Do Christians believe that God, to be able to forgive, had first to be satisfied by the sacrifice of his son? If so, the principle of reciprocity would be sanctioned by the highest possible authority. The passion story may be read otherwise, namely that Christ was an innocent victim of human violence. This opens the page for another paper.

Literature

Agamben, Giorgio. *Homo sacer. Die souveräne Macht und das nackte Leben.* Frankfurt a. M.: Edition Suhrkamp, 2002.

Agamben, Giorgio. *Die Zeit, die bleibt. Ein Kommentar zum Römerbrief.* Frankfurt a.M.: Edition Suhrkamp, 2006.

Ahrens, Theodor. »Die Verstoßung der alten Götter. Zur Frühgeschichte lutherischer Mission im östlichen Hochland von Papua Neuguinea.« In *Der neue Mensch im kolonialen Zwielicht, Studien zum religiösen Wandel in Ozeanien,* 45–63. Hamburg: LitVerlag, 1993.

Ahrens, Theodor. »›Geistliche Säuberungen‹ als Strategie kirchlicher Identitätssicherung?« In *Gegebenheiten, Missionswissenschaftliche Studien,* 258-291. Frankfurt a. M.: Lembeck Verlag, 2005.

Ahrens, Theodor. »Chancen und Grenzen der Kirchen im Umgang mit Gewalt.« *Lernort Gemeinde* 1 (2006): 9–12.

Ahrens, Theodor. »Verfahren des In-Ordnung-Bringens. Seelsorge und Kontrolle in der Verbundenheit der Gruppe. Eine interkulturelle Perspektive.« In *Vom Charme der Gabe. Theologie interkulturell,* 215-237. Frankfurt a. M.: Lembeck Verlag, 2008.

Ahrens, Theodor. »Versöhnung als Horizont christlicher Mission.« In *Vom Charme der Gabe. Theologie interkulturell,* 263-282. Frankfurt a. M.: Lembeck Verlag, 2008.

Berking, Helmuth. *Schenken. Zur Anthropologie des Gebens.* Frankfurt: Campus Verlag, 1996.

Böge, Volker. »Friedenskonsolidierung in Nachkriegszeiten. Der Fall Bougainville.« In *Arbeitspapier,* Nr. 3, edited by Forschungsstelle Kriege, Rüstung und Entwicklung. Hamburg: Universität Hamburg, 1999.

Böge, Volker. »Konfliktpotentiale und Gewaltkonflikte im Südpazifik. Optionen für den Zivilen Friedensdienst.« In *Arbeitspapier*, Nr. 1, edited by Forschungsstelle Kriege, Rüstung und Entwicklung. Hamburg: Universität Hamburg, 2001.

Gutmann, Hans-Martin. *Gewaltunterbrechung. Warum Religion Gewalt nicht hervorbringt, sondern bindet. Ein Einspruch*. Gütersloh: Gütersloher Verlagshaus, 2009.

Hénaff, Marcel. *Der Preis der Wahrheit. Gabe, Geld und Philosophie*. Frankfurt a. M: Suhrkamp, 2009.

Joas, Hans. »Die Logik der Gabe und das Postulat der Menschenwürde.« In *Von der Ursprünglichkeit der Gabe. Jean-Luc Marions Phänomenologie in der Diskussion*, edited by Michael Gabel and Hans Joas, 143–158. Freiburg: Verlag Karl Alber, 2007.

Klinger, Elmar. »Revenge and Retribution.« *The Encyclopedia of Religion*. Vol. 12, 362–369. 1987.

Koch, Traugott. »Der Friede in der Politik.« *Zeitschrift für evangelische Ethik* 47 (2003): 181–192.

Loo, Stephanie van de. *Versöhnungsarbeit. Kriterien – theologischer Rahmen – Praxisperspektiven*. Stuttgart: Kohlhammer, 2009.

MacIndoe, T. C. »Tribal Fighting and Compensation in the Simbu Province.« In *Homicide Compensation in Papua New Guinea: Problems and Prospects*, edited by Richard Scaglion, Law Reform Commission, Monograph, no. 1, 25–29. Port Moresby: Office of Information for the Law Reform Commission, 1981.

Mauss, Marcel: »Die Gabe. Form und Funktion des Austauschs in archaischen Gesellschaften.« In *Soziologie und Anthropologie*. Vol 2. Frankfurt a. M.: Fischer Taschenbuch, 1989.

Melpa Lutheran Church in Papua New Guinea, ed. *Reconciliation. A Paradigm of Mission*. Mt. Hagen: Melpa Lutheran Church, 2006.

Moxter, Michael. »Gewalt als Phänomen und Grenze der Kulturtheologie.« In *Religion, Politik und Gewalt. Kongressband des XII europäischen Kongresses für Theologie 18.–22. September 2005 in Berlin*, 626–641. Gütersloh: Gütersloher Verlagshaus, 2005.

Radford, Robin. »Burning the Spears. A ›Peace Movement‹ in the Eastern Highlands of New Guinea 1936-37.« *The Journal of Pacific History* 12 (1977): 40–54.

Sahlins, Marshall. *Stone Age Economics*. Chicago: Aldine Transaction, 1974.

Schramm, Tim. »›Pay-Back‹-Gesellschaft und der Verzicht auf Gewalt.« In *Zwischen Regionalität und Globalisierung*, edited by Theodor Ahrens, 409–422. Ammersbek: Verlag an der Lottbek, 1997.

Strathern, Andrew. »Compensation: Should There Be A New Law?« In *Homicide Compensation in Papua New Guinea. Problems and Prospects*, Monograph no. 1, 5–24, edited by Richard Scaglion. Port Moresby: Office of Information for the Law Reform Commission of Papua New Guinea, 1981.

Stewart, Pamela J. and Andrew Strathern. *Violence: Theory and Ethnography*. London: Continuum, 2002.

Strauss, Hermann. *Die Mi-Kultur der Hagenberg-Stämme im östlichen Zentral-Neuguinea. Eine religionssoziologische Studie*. Hamburg: Kommissionsverlag Cram. De Gruyter & Co., 1962. (engl. *The Mi-Culture of the Mount Hagen People*, translated by Brian Shields, edited by G. Stürzenhofecker and Andrew Strathern. Ethnology Monographs No. 13. Pittsburgh: Department of Anthropology, Pittsburgh, n.y.

Walzer, Michael. *Sphären der Gerechtigkeit. Ein Plädoyer für Pluralität und Gleichheit.* Translated by Hanne Herkommer. Frankfurt: Campus Verlag, 1992.

Towards an Ecumenical Theology of Just Peace at the Conclusion of the »Decade to Overcome Violence«: Churches Seeking Reconciliation and Peace, 2001-2010

Fernando Enns

Introduction

In 1932, at the International Youth Peace Conference at Ciernohorské (Czechoslovakia), Dietrich Bonhoeffer issued a call to develop a theological foundation for the World Alliance for Promoting International Friendship through the Churches.[1] He made a plea that is both simple and convincing. When the churches actually begin to develop a fresh ecumenical self-understanding, this must and will find expression in a new theology. Bonhoeffer was certain that only a theology that reflected and affirmed a fresh direction in church life could demonstrate that a radical change was taking place from what were hitherto nationally minded churches to a true catholicity of the Church:

> As often as the church of Christ has reached a new understanding of its nature it has produced a new theology, appropriate to this self-understanding. A change in a church's understanding of itself is proved genuine by the production of theology. For theology is the church's self-understanding of its own nature on the basis of its understanding of the revelation of God in Christ, and this self-under-

---

[1]   After initial contacts between some Christian social movements and peace organizations from various churches and nations at the beginning of the 20th century, the World Alliance for Promoting International Friendship through the Churches was founded on August 2, 1914, at the same time as the outbreak of the First World War, and with it began organized ecumenical endeavors for peace. See Ans J. van der Bent, »World Alliance for Promoting International Friendship through the Churches.«, in *A Dictionary of the Ecumenical Movement*, eds. Nicholas Lossky et al. (Geneva: WCC Publications, 1991), 1216-1217. See Harmjam Dam, *Der Weltbund für Freundschaftsarbeit der Kirchen 1914-1948: Eine ökumenische Friedensorganisation* (Frankfurt a. M.: Lembeck, 2001).

standing of necessity always begins where there is a new trend in the church's understanding of itself.[2]

The International Peace Convocation 2011 at the Conclusion of the Decade to Overcome Violence

Many proponents of the ecumenical movement look forward with great hopes and expectations to the International Ecumenical Peace Convocation 2011 in Kingston, Jamaica. This Peace Convocation is a significant event in a series of milestones in the long succession of ecumenical activity and thinking on the possibilities of non-violent conflict resolution and commitment to justice for all.[3] Its immediate inspiration comes from the ecumenical Decade to Overcome Violence: Churches Seeking Reconciliation and Peace 2001–2010, and it will bring this decade to its official conclusion. For the past ten years, churches throughout the world – often with partners from other religions and from the secular realm – have begun fresh peace initiatives, setting up organizations for non-violent conflict resolution, strengthening existing programs to prevent violence, intensifying initiatives in demand of just relationships, and engaging in theological and ethical reflection on what it means to be churches of just peace. National and regional councils of churches as well as the World Council of Churches (WCC) have served as forums for sharing and mutual support and encouragement. This has led to experiences being shared, creative upsurges in activities for peace and justice, people working closely together in nearly insoluble complicated situations of violence, and processes of healing and reconciliation being initiated. We

---

[2]   Dietrich Bonhoeffer, »A Theological Basis for the World Alliance?«, in *No Rusty Swords: Letters, Lectures and Notes 1928–1936*, ed. Edwin H. Robertson (New York: Harper & Row, 1965), 157–158.

[3]   See the detailed description of these developments in Fernando Enns and Stephan von Twardowski, »Glory to God and Peace on Earth: The Struggle of the Fellowship of Churches for Ethical Peace Positions.«, in *Paths of Hope: Pioneering Initiatives by the World Council of Churches Over Six Decades*, eds. Hans-Georg Link and Geiko Müller-Fahrenholz (Frankfurt a. M.: Lembeck, 2008), 348–377. See also Fernando Enns, »Ehre sei Gott – und Friede auf Erden: Der lange Weg zu einer ökumenischen Friedenskonvokation.«, in *Mache Dich auf und werde Licht!: Ökumenische Visionen in Zeiten des Umbruchs / Arise, Shine!: Ecumenical Visions in Times of Change. Festschrift für Konrad Raiser*, eds. Dagmar Heller et al. (Frankfurt a. M.: Lembeck, 2008), 322–333.

have often summed up all these activities as ›developing cultures of peace‹.[4]

It was in Harare, Zimbabwe, 1998, at the 8th Assembly of the WCC, when delegates from the churches of the world assembled and tried to identify the shape of a calling for the future programmatic work. We had been very much inspired by the previous Decade »Churches in Solidarity with Women«, which had left the wide-spread phenomenon of ongoing violence against women as a continuous challenge to the churches, as well as the WCC campaign »Peace to the City«, which allowed most of us to see what churches – together with others – can in fact do: overcome violence in a concrete situation! We were encouraged by the fascinating examples of people in seven cities from around the world who proved what it really meant to become ambassadors of reconciliation, once a congregation decides to dedicate itself to the violent context in which it is located.

»PEACE TO THE CITY«–CONTEXTUAL EXPERIENCES AS A STARTING POINT

Seven cities in different parts of the world were chosen as examples of places where successful attempts to overcome violence had been launched: Belfast, Northern Ireland; Boston, USA; Colombo, Sri Lanka; Durban, South Africa; Kingston, Jamaica; Rio de Janeiro, Brazil; and Suva, Fiji.[5] Consideration of these creative and successful initiatives for reconciliation prompted a re-examination of the contexts of violence and mechanisms for overcoming it, and on this basis, fresh theological reflection also began on familiar themes. An in-depth study of this kind obviously had to be organized along interdisciplinary lines, drawing on the knowledge available in history and political science, sociology and economics, behavioral research, psychology, and law. In this sense, too, the Decade called for an »ecumenical« approach.

Experiences in the cities showed that the cycle of violence is a self-perpetuating phenomenon, constantly generating new violence from within itself. Examples from countless places of conflict around the world confirm the theory that violence is self-perpetuating: Israel/Palestine, Afghanistan, the Balkans, Sudan, Indonesia, etc. The motor that keeps these cycles turning is

---

[4]   For a definition of the concept of a ›culture of peace‹ see reflections by György Konrád, »Culture of Peace?« in *Culture of peace*, ed. Horst-Eberhard Richter (Giessen: Psychosozial-Verlag, 2001), 39–49: »What is a culture of peace? Perhaps something that inevitably cannot be named: what we do daily without being aware of it« (49).

[5]   See Dafne Plou, *Peace in Troubled Cities: Creative Models of Building Community Amidst Violence* (Geneva: WCC, 1998). Additional cities joined the network later.

injustice (social, economic, political, and other) which is reinforced and per-petuated by violence, so that it becomes entrenched. No conspiracy theories are needed to confirm this mechanism. The insight is as old as human life in community itself; the Biblical traditions reflect this fundamental truth. It is also true of violence that it is often used with the most honorable intentions. It does not make any difference whether we are talking about direct/personal, indirect/structural, or even cultural violence.[6] In fact, there is a far deeper connection between these different forms of violence than the theoretical dis-tinction might suggest. The picture becomes yet more complicated and dif-ficult to understand when other levels are taken into account: the inter-re-latedness of the personal, collective, national, and global levels.[7] In what follows, we concentrate on the experiences of injustice from some of the seven selected cities.

Rio de Janeiro, Brazil, is one of the places in the world where injustice is visible to the naked eye. Anyone who has visited this city with its idyllic set-ting is bound to have been struck by the wealth and poverty existing there side by side. Perhaps the visitor may even have been the victim of crime be-cause anyone who can afford to travel to Rio is likely to have more money than most of the local population. The wealthy protect themselves behind barbed-wire fences and walls, aided by private, armed »security forces«, which do not, however, create a sense of security. The social inequality and the unfair dis-tribution of goods have turned the city into a hotbed of crime. Young people growing up in the *favelas* basically have no chance of ever crossing the divide and being able to lead a regular family and working life. They feel marginal-ized and see no point in going to school when all that awaits them at the end of it is unemployment. Young people can earn more money through drug-deal-ing and theft than by any other effort they might make. So the two »sides« are armed and ready, scraping along from day to day, and the city lives in a gen-

---

[6] We speak of direct violence when people kill or injure other people and of indirect vi-olence when people are subjected to influences which prevent them from developing as they could, e.g. unequal opportunities or balance of power; cultural violence designates any feature in a culture which may serve to legitimate direct or indirect violence, e.g. an extreme right-wing ideology postulating inequality. See the distinctions drawn by Johan Galtung, »Gewalt, Frieden und Friedensforschung.«, in *Friedensforschung, Entscheidungs-shilfe gegen Gewalt*, ed. Manfred Funke (Bonn: German Federal Office of Political Forma-tion, 1975), 99–132.

[7] See Jennifer Turpin and Lester R. Kurtz, *The Web of Violence: From Interpersonal to Global* (Urbana: University of Illinois Press, 1997).

eral climate of mutual distrust. State agencies, above all the police, have at best given up, but in most cases have actually become part of the cycle of violence and try to make what money they can from it. No laws are going to rescue a city where the authorities are no longer in control of violence and where all confidence in the executive has disappeared – and rightly so. It is bound to end in chaos for injustice fosters violence and vice versa, and so it goes on.

In **Belfast, Northern Ireland,** the reasons for violence are different. Here, the equation of denominational affiliation and national identity (Unionist/ Protestant – Republican/Catholic) has unleashed a spiral of hatred. The population has been trapped for decades in sectarian violence, backed by old traditions and symbols. Mutual ignorance and physical separation make it almost impossible for prejudices ever to be called in question, and they constantly rekindle the flames of intolerance, mistrust, and discrimination. Walls – ironically known as »peace walls« – physically mark these divisions and have even helped to reinforce them. The emotional state of the people who live in this situation is reflected in their sense of frustration at the hopelessness of the conflict, depression, or, again, a resurgence of anger at the injustice of it all. Many people suffer from recurring nightmares and from problems such as insomnia as a result of the violence they have experienced. Some suffer breakdowns due to the permanent threat and experience of being at the mercy of others. In addition, one needs to add the inability to cope with the desire for revenge and one's own anger. In more than a few cases these constant tensions lead to domestic violence. In some families, the situation is compounded by the harsh reality of long-term unemployment. Against this background, young people in particular are naturally drawn towards paramilitary groups which give them a sense of belonging and being needed. Nobody seems to be able to break the cycle.

Colombo, the capital of Sri Lanka, illustrates how the reasons for violence can vary, although the dynamics remain the same. Civil war has been raging here for more than two decades, fueled by a mixture of ethnic, religious, and political interests. Some of the tensions stem from events of the colonial era: First came the Portuguese, bringing Catholicism, then the Dutch, bringing Protestantism, followed by the British, bringing Anglicanism and Methodism. Although Sri Lanka is actually a multifaith, multiethnic and multicultural country, the proportions speak for themselves: 74 percent Singhalese (Buddhist), 18 percent Tamils (Hindus, migrants from India brought here by the British to work on the tea plantations), 7 percent Muslims (who arrived later as traders), and 1 percent Burghers (descendants of the former colonial rulers). Around 7.5 percent of the population is Christian, and the Christian religion is the only one which is not directly linked with a particular ethnic group. The different ethnic groups have also retained their own languages.

The struggle for power in the country began very soon after independence in 1948, when the Singhalese denied the Tamils citizenship. An unjust situation developed within the country, and tensions mounted. The Tamils demanded the right to self-determination and the right to call Sri Lanka their home. The government allowed the Muslim and Singhalese »home guards« to arm. In 1987, the Indian army tried to settle the conflict by military intervention but left the country two years later without succeeding. On the contrary, violations of human rights increased, divisions deepened, and prejudices, hatred, and the desire for revenge redoubled. Now, society is heavily militarized, and women, children, and young people are recruited as a matter of course. Young people were particularly sought after because they were ready to be trained for the much-feared suicide commandos, the »Baby Tigers«. Here again, the police forces are guilty of abuse and discrimination. Economically and socially, the tensions are a disaster for the whole country, causing unemployment, poverty, and displacement, as the »cost of war report«[8] testifies. All communication between the opposing sides broke down long ago. Religious fundamentalism also plays a part in these conflicts, especially among the Buddhist monks, who do not want to lose their positions of privilege. In many cases, it is the clergy who rekindle the torch of violence. There are of course others, who urge that Buddhism should return to its roots, i.e. »the practice of non-violence, peace-building, respect for life and the belief that all people are equal, rejecting caste and racial superiority.«[9]

Despite the diversity of these contexts, common features can be noted. Cycles of violence are vicious circles, in the truest sense of the word, as the examples from the cities show. The cycles are not only perpetuated by injustice within the city itself, but are reinforced by injustice from outside, be it the unfair global market economy, which further marginalizes the countries of the South and gives only an elite a share of the profits; or the international arms trade, which makes profits out of military conflicts but also out of societies with high levels of criminality, where people are prepared to invest huge amounts in private weaponry; or the political refusal to develop international

---

[8]   See http://www.ices.lk/sl_database/ethnic_conflict/cost_of_war.shtml (accessed on March 28, 2011).

[9]   Plou, *Peace in Troubled Cities*, 56.

law to allow human-rights violations to be prosecuted across national boundaries. The global is reflected in the local and vice-versa.

Whenever one begins to probe the causes of violence, one inevitably comes up against injustice which leads to unhealthy relations, or the denial of any relations, relations which are wholly concerned with the exercise of power and dependence, where one side always intends to fulfill its own needs at the cost of others, where fear of losing power leads to oppression of others. Traditions and religions are sometimes used for this purpose, but sometimes they are themselves part of a pattern of behavior based, roughly speaking, on the principle of »I'm fine so long as they're not.« In such situations, fears are not unfounded for the oppressors' awareness of their own ruthlessness makes them deeply distrustful of those they hold in subjection. Consequently, they cultivate stereotyped images of the enemy in defense of their own misdeeds, which are to some extent acknowledged as such and ultimately used to justify a »war against evil«.[10] The mere fact of difference is then in itself sufficient reason to argue for separation and isolation. This does not, however, bring security, because any relaxation of the pressure on the other is seized upon as a sign of weakness, and retaliation can be expected.

These are simply observations reflecting the real-life experience of people directly affected, and are not intended as a comprehensive theory. Since violence is such a basic but destructive human experience, it seemed obvious that the ecumenical community needs to focus on it in order to strengthen those who take up the challenge, to learn from each other, to walk in solidarity, and to heal wherever it is possible. Is this not the gist of the ecumenical task *par excellence*?

Community-Building, Presence, and »Sanctuaries« as Means of Overcoming Violence

None of the seven cities started with a clear strategy for overcoming violence, but rather with the problems affecting them. Thus it was clear from the outset that the important issues were concrete human needs, and that those directly affected should be brought into a position to take matters into their own hands. In each case, the development began by building on these experiences and the wisdom gained from them, which led to visible, tangible changes. Only in retrospect can common, recurring patterns be identified. This

---

[10] »It is very difficult for a Tamil to understand the official discourse of a ›war for peace‹. It is as if they are being told, ›We are killing you to help you‹.« Plou, *Peace in Troubled Cities*, 54.

emerged from the cities' networking among themselves. Again, we look at some examples of what has been done, in the hope of deriving more general lessons in the search for effective means of overcoming violence.

What initially sparked off the program to overcome violence in the city of Boston (the »Ten Point Coalition«) was the insight of one local congregation that they were not able to affect the surrounding cycles of violence unless they were to develop a meaningful presence in the neighborhood. The members of the congregation learned the simple yet decisive philosophy from a drug dealer: »You can't do anything if you're not out there.« They began by leaving the safety of their church premises, going out into the streets to meet people. Thus began a movement that has actually reduced violence and saved lives.

Experiences in the seven cities have shown clearly that opening up spaces is essential if cycles of violence are to be broken. This is meant in a practical sense: rooms, sheltered spaces where community-building can happen without any danger of slipping back into the old familiar patterns of behavior. Can local churches become this kind of sanctuary? In most cities we visited, projects began with individuals getting together with others. Before long, someone's house became the center (like the Baker-House in Dorchester, near Boston), serving as an open, hospitable space for building community. Opening sanctuaries here is also meant in the metaphorical sense. Overcoming violence calls for a sheltered space where realities can be named without fear of reprisal; it calls for spaces where injustices of all kinds can be articulated. Without such spaces, people cannot begin to work through what has happened; there can be no steps towards reconciliation.

Sometimes the media took notice and gave their support to the attempts to find alternatives to counter the culture of violence. Many volunteers were needed and were mostly given initial training on the ground as part of the program, so that they were drawn into the movement (for example the *agentes de futuro* involving more than 10,000 young adult volunteers in Rio, Agents of Peace in Belfast, and others). Contacts were sought in other organizations and government offices, specialists, or people exercising specific functions in society. Gradually, a trend was established in a local community, and a change of attitude began.[11] Things which once appeared to be impossible began to

---

[11]   »The new movement decided to take the name ›Viva Rio‹ as a way of affirming that it was possible to create a trend among citizens to overcome violence, promoting dignity and equal opportunities for all.« Plou, *Peace in Troubled Cities*, 8.

seem possible and mentalities changed. In this way, a culture of peace and non-violence can grow. In those cities, opportunities for participation and community-building seemed to be a key factor as people do not naturally want to be »urban nomads«.

All those involved confirm, however, that these are long and difficult processes, fragile and dependent upon the initiative and staying-power of individuals. They say it can only be done with others, in a community offering mutual encouragement and reassurance, where individuals can sometimes be weak because others are there with them.

Along with representatives of various organizations and peace initiatives, I was once invited to discuss the Decade to Overcome Violence in a medium-sized German working-class city. Violence is present there in all its many forms, but there is a well-established network of support involving the women's, youth and children welfare offices, the police, and the schools. Until recently, the churches had not been represented in this network. In the course of our discussion, the inevitable question was asked, »What would the churches' involvement in this network genuinely have to offer?« At the end of this first encounter it emerged that in joining the network, the church would above all bring with it a hopeful vision. The people engaged in this work are often worn out by their daily struggle with violence and the sometimes frustrating search for ways to break the cycle. Between the reality and the objective pressures; it is all too easy to lose sight of the hope and the goal of this difficult journey – let alone to have a vision.

The Mediation Network in Belfast, founded in 1991, is a good example.[12] Churches; public agencies and politicians; groups working for justice, peace and reconciliation; neighborhood groups; and local communities found points of contact because they were all affected by the violence. They drew strength from working together and building relations; their effectiveness increased. This collective work itself became a touchstone of their capacity for overcoming violence for here, too, there was always the danger that people might try to stake out territory for fear of losing power and becoming dependent. The willingness to invest a measure of mutual trust was the basis for a common undertaking, sustained by the understanding that ultimately it was to the benefit of all sides. In Belfast, the aim of education was to establish identity,

---

[12] »The network promotes the idea of working for peace while developing mutually respectful relations within and throughout a divided community. It is an open network, with the capacity to maintain liaisons with dozens of private and public groups and organizations.« Plou, *Peace in Troubled Cities*, 27.

tolerance and acceptance of political and cultural differences. Neighbors could not remain strangers, areas of encounter developed. Difference then ceased to be considered first and foremost as a danger, and was seen instead as an opportunity. Security was no longer based on establishing boundaries but on the resilience of the community. The goal was always the wellbeing of others as well as oneself because the idea had taken root that »I am fine if they're fine, too.«

The declared aim of the National Peace Council founded in Colombo in 1995 was likewise to break the cycle of violence. The initiative brought together people from all religious groups and representatives of a dozen organizations, all working for the common good. They chose three guiding principles: (1) to accept only a negotiated settlement of the conflict; (2) to seek dialogue among all the parties involved, and (3) to consider the hopes of all the people living in Sri Lanka. For the conflict in Sri Lanka had made it clear that (1) it cannot be left only to the governing parties to find a solution to a conflict of this kind; (2) the population must be the guarantors of a lasting peace, and everyone's democratic rights must be institutionally guaranteed; (3) genuine peace work must be independent of all political forces and must guarantee the basic rights of the oppressed.

It was not a case of starting from scratch. Each religion and culture had its own inherent conventions for structuring and regulating community life satisfactorily and for containing or overcoming violence: »We decided to begin the task by focusing actions on the long tradition of good relations that had existed before the conflict.«[13] The first step was to encourage mutual hospitality, which helped to develop respect for the other's dignity. In Colombo and in many villages, workshops picked up old traditions, and ancient myths were revived through popular dramas and plays offering the opportunity for people to participate and express their own feelings. Interreligious dialogues were organized, where the very fact that clergy were present had an enormous symbolic and exemplary force (»religious leaders must be the first to be educated for peace«).[14] Political decision-makers were also drawn in. For the churches in the cities, the most important thing was to make their presence felt, not to barricade themselves behind stout church walls but to be present in the places where violent conflicts were actually being conducted. This was not without repercussions in the life of local congregations.

---

[13] Plou, *Peace in Troubled Cities*, 51.
[14] Plou, *Peace in Troubled Cities*, 56.

AT THE END OF THIS DECADE–REVISITING THE ORIGINAL GOALS

A good number of churches are now engaged with determination in investigating and exploring non-violent methods of conflict prevention and resolution, civil forms of conflict management, training of civilian peacemakers and active work for reconciliation after recourse to violence. Churches are gradually becoming aware of their responsibility to set up non-violent alternatives if their call to overcome violence is to be credible. It is no longer enough – and never has been – to limit oneself to general demands to the world community for an internationally binding rule of law and respect for universal human rights.

The abovementioned initiatives will become visible and tangible during the Peace Convocation. We will celebrate with praise and thanksgiving the fact that churches have committed themselves to take this path. It will, however, also be an occasion for confession and repentance for all that has not been achieved – when churches have failed miserably, when they have remained implicated in violence and entrenched behind »thick church walls«. This metaphor can be quite appropriately applied to all situations where churches were timid and inward-looking and chose to be isolated from the real challenges facing society, supposedly for the sake of self-preservation or maintaining their privileges as churches or ecumenical organizations. The objectives set at the beginning of the Decade need to be critically revised in order to give an account of our credibility. These were some of the major goals:[15]

– Moving peace-building from the periphery to the centre of the life and witness of the church and building stronger alliances and understanding among churches, networks, and movements which are working toward a culture of peace;
– addressing holistically the wide varieties of violence, both direct and structural, in homes, communities, and in international arenas and learning from the local and regional analyses of violence and ways to overcome violence;
– challenging the churches to overcome the spirit, logic, and practice of violence; relinquishing any theological justification of violence; and affirming anew the spirituality of reconciliation and active nonviolence;

---

[15] See The World Council of Churches, »Call to Recommitment: Mid-Term of the Decade to Overcome Violence 2001–2010: Churches Seeking Reconciliation and Peace,« (paper presented as the preparatory background document in Programme Book, Ninth Assembly, Porto Alegre, Geneva, Switzerland, February, 2006), 116–118.

- creating a new understanding of security in terms of cooperation and community instead of domination and competition;
- learning from the spirituality and resources for peace-building of other religions and working with them in the pursuit of peace; challenging the churches to reflect on the misuse of religious and ethnic identity constructions;
- challenging the growing militarization of our world, especially the proliferation of small arms and light weapons.[16]

THE PEACE CONVOCATION IN THE RUN-UP TO THE WCC ASSEMBLY IN 2013

It would be, of course, one-sided to treat the Peace Convocation as simply the conclusion of the decade. The objectives set for it by the WCC also point to the future. The Convocation will take up the necessity to develop an »ecumenical theology of just peace that has central significance for the self-understanding of the Church and for Christian spirituality and action.«[17] The Peace Convocation is intended to set the course »for the work of the churches and the ecumenical movement for just peace in preparation for the WCC Assembly in 2013« in Pusan, South Korea. Indeed, it is to capture »a new vision of ecumenical unity for our time.« That amounts to what Bonhoeffer was looking for in 1932: developing a theology by means of which a new self-understanding of the Church as an ecumenical community becomes visible. The Decade to Overcome Violence thus serves as the long-term preparatory process leading to this new self-understanding of the Church and of its unity now finding expression in theological thought.

The mere fact that this process is actually taking place is the litmus test for this new self-understanding of the churches, the ecumenical movement as ambassador of reconciliation that has been recognized and accepted through the Decade to Overcome Violence. The past decade has made it abundantly clear that there are church communities throughout the world that seriously

---

[16] See The WCC Central Committee, »Decade to Overcome Violence – Message, Letter, Basic Framework« (the working document approved by the WCC Central Committee in World Council of Churches, Central Committee, Minutes of the Fiftieth Meeting, Geneva, Switzerland, August 26 – September 3, 1999), 185–195.

[17] See »International Ecumenical Peace Convocation,« http://www.overcomingviolence.org/en/peace-convocation.html (accessed February 5, 2010). See also the minutes of the WCC Executive Committee, »International Ecumenical Peace Convocation (IEPC): Methodology and Progress Report on Planning« (document no. 14a, presented at the meeting of the WCC Executive Committee, Bossey, Switzerland, February 23–26, 2010).

accept their calling to be reconcilers while suffering violence and experiencing injustice with great faith, immeasurable courage and unimaginable creativity. Ecumenical forums are accompanying the process in clear solidarity and are doing many things that hitherto only seemed impossibilities. Are we, in fact, prepared to take seriously the encouraging – and also sobering – experiences of the Decade as challenges to our church life, and our ecclesiology?

Preliminary Thoughts for an Ecumenical Theology of Just Peace

God's Shalom and Human Violence

In the course of the years, we, the churches of the ecumenical community, have learned, in regard to our common roots with our Jewish brothers and sisters, not to reduce peace to the absence of war. That would be a too narrow »negative concept of peace«.[18] Rather, *shalom* in the Old Testament means »›completeness, soundness, welfare, peace‹. Shalom is a broad concept, embracing justice (*mishpat*), mercy, rightness (*tsedeq*) or righteousness (*tsedeqah*), compassion (*hesed*), and truthfulness (*emet*).«[19] This integrity and

---

[18]   The negative concept of peace is defined as follows: »Such peace research has as its major concern international relations and nation states and international alliances as its subject matter. Concentration on the origins, development or prevention of military conflicts ignores the fact that in times without war the situation is by no means peaceful.« The Centre for Conflict Research, Philipps University, Marburg, in (in German) »Peace and Conflict Research. On the difficulties in defining such a specialist area.« see »Friedens- und Konfliktforschung – Über die Schwierigkeiten, ein Fach zu beschreiben.«, http://www.uni-marburg.de/konfliktforschung/studium/fachbeschreibung (last modified December 17, 2007). Areas of research need to be further developed for alongside »military violence, there also exist other various forms of violence that from another perspective at least demand the same attention, e.g. torture or enforced relocation. The discussion was expanded with the introduction of the concept of violence; it still continues to spark controversies. Besides direct forms of violence, social conditions come into view, characterized by various forms of oppression or exploitation in which direct physical violence is not used (structural violence).«

[19]   »International Ecumenical Declaration on Just Peace.« http://www.overcomingviolence.org/fileadmin/dov/files/iepc/peace_declarations/drafting_group/Initial_Statement_JustPeaceDeclaration_full.pdf (accessed January 29, 2011).

wholeness arise from justice: liberation from oppression, justice for victims of injustice, the poor and foreigners. In short, *shalom* means a full life, in life-enhancing relationships, relationships between God and humans, between humans, and within creation as a whole. *Shalom* is God's promised just peace. »*[t]sedaqah* is not in humans, but humans are in *[t]sedaqah*.«[20]

Violence is a denial of these relationships. During the Decade to Overcome Violence, we have learned together to understand violence, in a similar broad sense, as the opposite of *shalom*.[21] Such a broad definition has constantly been the object of criticism.[22] Wrongly so, as I see it, for the complexity of the existing situations of violence which we find ourselves in does not allow us to accept a more narrow definition. True to reality, to have a wide theological definition of violence allows it to be addressed holistically.

Violence (not *force* or *power*) includes:

- physical or psychological acts of denying, injuring, or destroying human persons – their freedom of choice, their integrity, their dignity, and thereby the fact that the human person is made in the image of God and is justified by God's grace
- denial of community, created, reconciled, and brought to completion by God, through which right relationships between people become possible
- damage to nature or its destruction, refusal to respect it as God's gift and to care for it as God's stewards.[23]

---

[20]   Klaus Koch, »SDQ in the Old Testament: An Historical Survey« (Dissertation: University of Heidelberg, 1953), 41.

[21]   In the course of the Decade, the WCC has constantly had recourse to the official definition of the World Health Organization (WHO) in order to be able to refer to an agreed and publically recognized definition. It is that violence is »the intentional use of physical force or power, threatened or actual, against oneself, another person, or against a group or community that either results in or has a high likelihood of resulting in injury, death, psychological harm, maldevelopment or deprivation.« See »World Report on Violence and Health 2002: Summary.«, World Health Organisation, http://www.who.int/violence_injury_prevention/violence/world_report/en/summary_ge.pdf (accessed January 29, 2011).

[22]   Among others see Wolfgang Lienemann, who pleads for a narrower definition of violence, in Wolfgang Lienemann, »A Critique of Violence.«, in *Perceptions of Violence: Rescuing from Violence: Theological and Religious Perspectives*, eds. Walter Dietrich and Wolfgang Lienemann (Stuttgart: Kohlhammer, 2004), 7–30.

[23]   I have proposed this definition earlier (in German) in Fernando Enns, »The Ecumenical Ecclesiology of the Peace Churches: A Trinitarian Theological Approach,« *Ökumenische Rundschau* 2 (2006): 131–148.

Such violence can find direct expression in violent acts, but also indirectly through unjust structures, such as economic discrimination, or in cultural forms, such as the disadvantaging and even oppression of women.

When violence is defined broadly in this way, then it also becomes clear to what extent dealing with violence and the concern for just peace (*shalom*) affects the foundations of our identity and our theology. This fact was a central concern for the group producing the first draft of the Declaration of Just Peace.[24] Hence, the Declaration is based on humankind as bearing God's image and it follows a Trinitarian approach, which has become the orienting concept for ecumenical ecclesiology.[25]

GOD IN RELATION: A TRINITARIAN APPROACH

The Trinitarian approach helps us to hold creation, reconciliation (or redemption), and consummation together in our reflections. It helps us to recognize that the God of Abraham and Sarah and the God who freed Israel from slavery is also the God who has become incarnate in Jesus Christ and thence indwells (*shekinah*) this violent world with divine life-giving Spirit. It is God who desires liberation from violence, including violence in the form of injustice, not only for Christians but also for followers of other religions, and not only for humankind but also for the whole of creation. Christian belief does not have a static but a dynamic understanding of that relating God characterized by the great bond of love within the fellowship of God's own relational self. From there flows the decisive belief that we *participate* in and through Christ in the (economic) fellowship of the Godhead. God's very self is fellowship, taking the form of relationships, in that God grants participation in this fellowship. That implies, inasmuch as it is legitimate, that the Church does not idly long for the promised just peace of God, but commits itself to make this reality part of human experience. That does not in fact lead to an understanding of self-made redemption, but it does prevent believers and the Church from falling into triumphalism. The consummation of the kingdom of God remains God's work. But in Christ, participation in the divine social fel-

---

[24]   See »Initial Statement Towards an Ecumenical Declaration on Just Peace,« http://www. overcomingviolence.org/en/resources/documents/declarations-on-just-peace/drafting-group/initial-statement.html (accessed February 5, 2010).

[25]   See the recent ecclesiological study The World Council of Churches, »The Nature and Mission of the Church: A Stage on the Way to a Common Statement,« (Faith and Order Paper 198, Geneva, Switzerland, 2005). See also The World Council of Churches, »The Nature and Purpose of the Church« (Faith and Order Paper 181, Geneva, Switzerland, 1998).

lowship of love becomes possible. Church and believers are drawn into the building of *shalom*, and it is only now that they *can* act liberated from violence.

The Self-Understanding of the Churches as Churches of Just Peace – Realistic Perspectives

From the place of shalom springs the self-understanding as a church of just peace as well as appropriate prospects in the face of the existing violence in the world. From there emerges the need and the possibility of redemption and reconciliation. Thus, the fragmentary and provisional nature of the kingdom of God does not lead to our coming to terms with violent and unjust relationships but, on the contrary, encourages us not to accept apparently insuperable circumstances as the last word. We do have a sense of what is unjust. We do know of a world according to God's purposes – and that we already have a share in it. That is what legitimizes the title of the Decade – the Decade to *Overcome* Violence. It was to take seriously Paul's challenge: »Do not be overcome by evil, but overcome evil with good« (Romans 12:21). That means taking seriously evil in all its horror as much as possible while not allowing ourselves to be possessed by it, but to see how limited its power is because another reality – God's just peace – is a permanent presence in the world through the *Christus praesens*, the Holy Spirit.

The Gift of Reconciliation in Christ – the Healing of Life

The gift of reconciliation and being servants of reconciliation must not be separated since both reflect Christ's act of reconciliation as well as God's entering and restoring of creation. The Church believes and confesses that God in Christ renews the relationship between God and us, has re-established it, once for all, irrevocably. We are justified and thus liberated to live a life of just relations. No human beings can thus be reduced to what they do, but they remain – even if their violent deeds are to be condemned – justified before God. This is the ultimate basis for the inalienability of the dignity of the human person. We thus regard life itself as sanctified, often still in broken ways, but with the conviction that God's good Spirit will bring this sanctification to completion. We are called to live lives conformed to this sanctification (1 Peter 1:15–16). Thus the commitment to peace and justice is not an optional extra, not a mere area of conduct in theological ethics. In its theological reflection on action for just peace, the Church focuses on its genuine ministry of reconciliation primarily and completely *in* the world (2 Corinthians 5:18).

At the beginning of the modern ecumenical movement, there was the deep insight that the divided state of the churches was an obstacle to their witness and mission. That, it was said, must not continue. Unity must be sought amid all the differences of approach between the churches in the Commission on Faith and Order, in the Life and Work movement, the International Missionary Council, or the World Alliance for Promoting International Friendship through the Churches. In each case, it came down ultimately to the credibility of the Christian witness and thus to the self-understanding of the churches in fellowship with other churches. The original ecumenical vision of unity – in reconciled diversity – is contemporaneous with the peace witness of the Church of Christ. Ecumenism is not an end in itself; the Church is not in the world for its own sake. The transmission of the gift of reconciliation in Christ is the deepest and ultimate motive for our striving for reconciliation between Christians and between the churches worldwide (*koinonia*). The awareness that they are reconciled in Christ creates the desired visibility of unity, because only in that way does the Church become sure of itself. In anticipation and celebration of God's peace (*leiturgia*), in witness (*martyria*), and in working for just peace (*diakonia*), it is the Church of Jesus Christ. It lives out »cultures of peace«, and thus participates in the *missio Dei* for just peace, for *shalom*. The ecumenical community changes things simply by what it *is* precisely because its members understand themselves as *simul iustus et peccator*, as both sinners and justified, and thus do not rely on their own actions for reconciliation but point – in what they are and do – to the gift of reconciliation given in Christ.

The mission statement of the Peace Convocation says, »The IEPC aims at witnessing to the Peace of God as a gift and responsibility of the *oikumene*. It seeks to assess and strengthen the church's position on peace, provide opportunities for networking and deepen our common commitment to processes of reconciliation and peace.«[26] It contains an invitation to the churches to engage in self-reflection as building blocks for a new ecumenical theology of just peace, not with a bang in Kingston in 2011 but through persistent advance by the churches of the world towards just peace in prayer, debate, advocacy, and in fresh common action, all of it accompanied by rigorous theological reflection.

The motto for the Peace Convocation points precisely to this programmatic approach: »Glory to God and Peace on Earth«. It begins with a confes-

---

[26] See »International Ecumenical Peace Convocation.«

sion of praise to the Triune God, who exists in relation and who offers and installs relationship as a condition that makes possible life-enhancing relationships – between individuals, men and women, young and old; in the smallest of communities, within nations and in the international community; among churches of very different traditions, in their relationships with believers of other faiths; in their relation with nature as the gift God lent us to be its accountable stewards. It is in that way that the ecumenical movement seeks to reach an appropriate assessment of situations of violence and injustice, in order, as persons and communities reconciled in Christ, to deplore, to heal, to overcome – and to strengthen one another.

Conclusion: The 2011 Peace Convocation as a Kairos in the Ecumenical Movement

From these perspectives, the Peace Convocation must read *the signs of the times.* It is more clearly recognized today that it is necessary to seek possibilities for reconciliation together with other faith communities. Just peace cannot be established or experienced apart from people of other faiths. It will not be possible to overcome violence without recognizing and welcoming the indispensible contributions made by the believers of »sister-religions« (Jayasiri T. Peiris). Reconciliation will hardly be able to take place without appreciation of the worth of those who are different, which also gives rise to uncertainty and questioning of one's own position. All theological reflection and concrete overcoming of violence now takes place in the context of today's plural societies. It must be reflected within the context of the increasing (primarily economic) globalization of all areas of life world-wide, which has become the dominant scourge of the majority of the world's population. Its violent effects are by no means limited to the human community but are now making more clearly evident than ever before to what extent the environment, climate, indeed, the whole of God's creation, is being affected and suffering violence.

It must not be allowed to be diverted into costly activism or, even worse, result in a flood of renewed well-meant declarations of intent and moral appeals by church leaders. In the longer term what is determinative is quite different: Will the churches of the world in fact make use of the Peace Convocation at the conclusion of the Decade to Overcome Violence to set up a process in which they will give a theologically well-thought out account of their own nature on the basis of their understanding of God's revelation in Christ? Only such a self-understanding would, in Bonhoeffer's words, give evidence of a »new trend in the church's understanding of itself« as an indication of a Church and an ecumenism of just peace. That is not yet a foregone conclusion. »If it does not succeed in this, that will be evidence that it is nothing but a new and up to date improvement in church organisation. No one requires a theology of such an organisation, but simply definite action in a concrete task.«[27] The International Ecumenical Peace Convocation in 2011 is the *kairos* when we shall find out!

> Compassionate God
> We speak of love and are accomplices in violence
> We cry for justice and are entangled in injustice
> We claim the truth and accept a lie
> We hope for peace and fail to live it
>
> Prince of Peace
> You have taken upon you the sin of the world
> You have suffered the violence of humankind
> You have confronted the injustice of the powers
> And faced the force of death
>
> Creator Spirit
> Give us the courage and strength
> To speak the truth in love
> To do justice with peace
> To be merciful as you are.[28]

---

[27]   Bonhoeffer, »A Theological Basis for the World Alliance?« 158.

[28]   A prayer from The World Council of Churches, »Telling the Truth about Ourselves and the World: A Study Guide for Individuals and Churches Together to Reflect and Act on While the 2001–2010 Decade to Overcome Violence: Churches Seeking Reconciliation and Peace is Being Celebrated at the International Ecumenical Peace Convocation.« (Geneva: WCC, 2010). See also »Telling the Truth About Ourselves and Our World.« World Council of Churches, http://www.overcomingviolence.org/fileadmin/dov/files/iepc/resources/TellingTheTruth_v100115.pdf (accessed October 15, 2010).

Literature

Bonhoeffer, Dietrich. »A Theological Basis for the World Alliance?« In *No Rusty Swords: Letters, Lectures and Notes 1928-1936*, edited by Edwin H. Robertson, 157-158. New York / Evanston: Harper & Row, 1965.

Centre for Conflict Research of the Philipps University Marburg. »Friedens- und Konfliktforschung – Über die Schwierigkeiten, ein Fach zu beschreiben.« Last modified December 17, 2007. http://www.uni-marburg.de/konfliktforschung/studium/fachbeschreibung.

Dam, Harmjam. *Der Weltbund für Freundschaftsarbeit der Kirchen, 1914-1948: Eine ökumenische Friedensorganisation.* Frankfurt a. M.: Lembeck, 2001.

Enns, Fernando and Stephan von Twardowski. »Glory to God and Peace on Earth: The Struggle of the Fellowship of Churches for Ethical Peace Positions.« In *Paths of Hope: Pioneering Initiatives by the World Council of Churches Over Six Decades*, edited by Hans-Georg Link and Geiko Müller-Fahrenholz, 348-377. Frankfurt a. M.: Lembeck, 2008.

Enns, Fernando. »Ehre sei Gott – und Friede auf Erden: Der lange Weg zu einer ökumenischen Friedenskonvokation.« In *Mache Dich auf und werde Licht!: Ökumenische Visionen in Zeiten des Umbruchs / Arise, Shine!: Ecumenical Visions in Times of Change: Festschrift für Konrad Raiser*, edited by Christina Kayales, Barbara Rudolph, Dagmar Heller, Gert Rüppell, and Heinrich Schäfer, 322-333. Frankfurt a. M.: Lembeck, 2008.

Enns, Fernando. »The Ecumenical Ecclesiology of the Peace Churches: A Trinitarian Theological Approach.« *Ökumenische Rundschau* 2/2006 (2006): 131-148.

Galtung, Johan. »Gewalt, Frieden und Friedensforschung.« In *Friedensforschung: Entscheidungshilfe gegen Gewalt*, edited by Manfred Funke, 99-132. Bonn: The German Federal Office of Political Formation, 1975.

Koch, Klaus. »SDQ in the Old Testament: An Historical Survey.« Dissertation: University of Heidelberg, 1953.

Konrád, György. »Culture of Peace?.« In *Culture of Peace*, edited by Horst-Eberhard Richter, 39-49. Giessen: Psychosozial-Verlag, 2001.

Lienemann, Wolfgang. »A Critique of Violence.« In *Perceptions of Violence: Rescuing from Violence: Theological and Religious Perspectives*, edited by Walter Dietrich and Wolfgang Lienemann, 7-30. Stuttgart: Kohlhammer, 2004.

Plou, Dafne. *Peace in Troubled Cities: Creative Models of Building Community Amidst Violence.* Geneva: WCC, 1998.

Turpin, Jennifer and Lester R. Kurtz. *The Web of Violence: From Interpersonal to Global.* Urbana and Chicago: University of Illinois Press, 1997.

Van der Bent, Ans J. »World Alliance for Promoting International Friendship Through the Churches.« In *A Dictionary of the Ecumenical Movement*, edited by Geoffrey Wainwright, John S. Pobee, José Miguez Bonino, Nicholas Lossky, Pauline Webb and Tom F. Stransky, 1216-1217. Geneva: WCC Publications, 1991.

WCC Central Committee. »Decade to Overcome Violence – Message, Letter, Basic Framework.« The working document approved by the WCC Central Committee in World Council of Churches, Central Committee, Minutes of the Fiftieth Meeting, Geneva, Switzerland, August 26 – September 3, 1999.

WCC Executive Committee. »International Ecumenical Peace Convocation (IEPC): Methodology and Progress Report on Planning.« Document no. 14a, presented at the meeting of the WCC Executive Committee, Bossey, Switzerland, February 23–26, 2010.

World Council of Churches. »Call to Recommitment. Mid-Term of the Decade to Overcome Violence 2001–2010: Churches Seeking Reconciliation and Peace.« Paper presented as the preparatory background document in Programme Book, Ninth Assembly, Porto Alegre, Geneva, Switzerland, February, 2006.

World Council of Churches. »Telling the Truth about Ourselves and the World: A Study Guide for Individuals and Churches Together to Reflect and Act on While the 2001–2010 Decade to Overcome Violence: Churches Seeking Reconciliation and Peace is Being Celebrated at the International Ecumenical Peace Convocation.« Geneva: WCC, 2010.

World Council of Churches. »The Nature and Mission of the Church: A Stage on the Way to a Common Statement.« Faith and Order Paper 198, Geneva, Switzerland, 2005.

World Council of Churches. »The Nature and Purpose of the Church.« Faith and Order Paper 181, Geneva, Switzerland, 1998.

World Council of Churches. »Initial Statement Towards an Ecumenical Declaration on Just Peace.« Accessed February 5, 2010. http://www.overcomingviolence.org/en/resources/documents/declarations-on-just-peace/drafting-group/initial-statement.html (accessed February 5, 2010).

World Council of Churches. »International Ecumenical Declaration on Just Peace.« Accessed January 29, 2011. http://www.overcomingviolence.org/fileadmin/dov/files/iepc/peace_declarations/drafting_group/Initial_Statement_JustPeaceDeclaration_full.pdf (accessed January 29, 2011).

World Council of Churches. »International Ecumenical Peace Convocation.« http://www.overcomingviolence.org/en/peace-convocation.html (accessed February 5, 2010).

World Council of Churches. »Telling the Truth About Ourselves and Our World.« http://www.overcomingviolence.org/fileadmin/dov/files/iepc/resources/TellingTheTruth_v10 0115.pdf (accessed October 15, 2010).

World Health Organisation. »World Report on Violence and Health 2002: Summary.« http://www.who.int/violence_injury_prevention/violence/world_report/en/summary_ge.pdf (accessed January 29, 2011).

Divine Reconciliation and Human Restitution in a Broken World: Revisiting Anselm's Satisfaction Theory

Ulrike Link-Wieczorek

Introduction

The Ecumenical Decade to Overcome Violence has forced us to concentrate on the unhealed realities caused by violence. In doing so, the decade has formulated the theological challenge that these realities need to be brought into dialogue with our God talk and our proclamation of the Gospel. No doubt, this can be understood as a key test for the theological reflection of the religion in whose centre stand the symbols of cross and resurrection. How may we speak of Christian hope in a plausible way as we seek to be attentive to experiences of violence?

There are two sets of questions concerning this issue which have been newly brought to our theme. First and foremost, the question is this: How should we understand the event of Jesus' coming as bringing about once-and-for-all salvation and forgiveness of sins for all humankind? Jürgen Moltmann has encouraged us in the context of a theology after Auschwitz to talk about the gift of reconciliation in light of the unredeemed state of the world.[1] But what is meant by the gift of reconciliation?[2] What exactly is this ›gift‹? And how is the connection of gift and task to be understood? Or in other words, how is the Christian work of reconciliation connected to the divine gift of reconciliation? Is it that God's gift of reconciliation becomes a gift only when people accept it as their task? How can we ensure that our talk of God's gift neither is too abstract nor becomes a deification of human action?

These questions are at the heart of the matter when churches of the

---

[1]   See for example Jürgen Moltmann, *The Way of Jesus Christ. Christology in Messianic Dimension* (Minneapolis: Fortress Press 1993), 28–37.

[2]   See Fernando Enns on the gift of reconciliation in this volume.

South accuse those of the North that their theology is moving as if in an abstract, academic glass-bead game. These questions arise as well when the churches of the North are skeptical about the theology of the churches of the South as to whether there might be too little distinction between divine and human activity. Proponents of both positions will hopefully be able to understand and communicate with each other in a stronger eschatological re-visioning of the once-and-for-all nature of the Christ story, in which redemption is understood more as a process than as an isolated event, a process which has its beginnings in creation.[3] In this vein, salvation does not simply refer to forgiveness, but is rather understood to enable fullness of life, the gift of life itself. In order to clarify this position further, the theological reception of sociological and philosophical theories of the gift will prove helpful.[4]

The second problem concerns the connection of reconciliation and justice. If theology confines its discussion to the doctrine of justification by grace alone, is not the relationship between reconciliation and justice too quickly elided? In a non-theological context, we know this problem under the name of amnesty. How can we avoid a concept of reconciliation which ignores the dignity of the victims of violence? Is that not what justice requires? During recent years, those doing theology have looked for concepts which offered a voice for victims, and this has led to a re-visioning of the traditional Christian image of the Last Judgment.[5] The theological work of the Ecumenical Decade to Overcome Violence has significantly inspired us to hermeneutically reconstruct this strong image through the model of restorative justice. This model is opposed to the dominant concept of retributive justice; God's justice does not aim at a devastating judgment of the perpetrators, but rather at enabling the common future of victims and perpetrators in a process of restoration. However, this does not exclude but rather includes the process of discovering truth. This is what is illustrated by the re-visioned image of the Last Judgment, which holds the potential to illuminate the process of separation of good and evil.

Both problems necessitate a dynamic concept of reconciliation in which the relationship between the apparent difficulties of interpersonal reconcili-

---

[3]   Fernando Enns suggests a similar approach with the image of *shalom* in this volume.

[4]   For the theological adoption of the gift-metaphoric see Veronika Hoffmann, ed., *Die Gabe. Ein »Urwort« der Theologie?* (Frankfurt: Lembeck Verlag, 2009).

[5]   See Heinrich Bedford-Strohm, ed. *»Und das Leben der zukünftigen Welt«: Von Auferstehung und Jüngstem Gericht* (Neukirchen-Vluyn: Neukirchener Verlag, 2007).

ation (including a concept of righteousness that takes into account the different perspectives of victims and perpetrators) and God's proclamation of salvation is clarified. In search of such a dynamic theology of reconciliation, one would also have to explore whether the theological tradition might have as yet undiscovered treasures in store. It is this part of the task which I would like to tackle in this contribution by taking a fresh look at a very traditional aspect of Christian soteriology which has been the focus of much criticism of late: the satisfaction theory by Anselm of Canterbury.[6] This might be surprising at first, because it is exactly Anselm's doctrine of the inevitable restoration of God's honor, having been damaged by sin, which would show little regard for God's mercy while suggesting an explicit connection between the mercy and the righteousness of God, generally taken as a plea for a rather rigid and retributive sense of God's righteousness. This impression appears to be reinforced by the fact that the death of Jesus as *God-man (Deus-homo)* should suffice for the demand for God's righteousness. And finally, Anselm's satisfaction theory has stood for a soteriology that – in its concentration on the relationship of God and humanity – offers a dual dramaturgy: God appears as the only victim of sin; other human victims of (sinful) violence fade away out of sight. In this sense, the doctrine became *the* determinative soteriological model in the Western Church. Even the Reformers did not reject it – although we ought to say that Martin Luther used it sparsely; he resorted to other models instead.[7] In Reformed theology as well as in Protestant Orthodoxy, it played a large role. Today Anselm's satisfaction theory is regarded as an expression of New Testament atonement theory in evangelical circles in Europe and even more so in the US. Admittedly, this does not help matters as we attempt to gain a new perspective on it.

This endeavor occurs by no means in isolation from the rest of theological research. Surprisingly, Anselm's concept has once more become subject

---

[6]   This contribution is partly a revision of my earlier publication, »Sündig vor Gott allein? Überlegungen zur Re-Interpretation der Satisfaktionstheorie Anselms von Canterbury in schöpfungsethischer Perspektive.«, in *Die Aktualität der Sünde. Ein umstrittenes Thema der Theologie in interkonfessioneller Perspektive,* ed. Rochus Leonhardt (Beiheft zur Ökumenischen Rundschau 86 – Texte des Interkonfessionellen Theologischen Arbeitskreises ITA) (Frankfurt: Lembeck Verlag, 2010), 121–143.

[7]   For Protestant adoption see Georg Plasger, *Die Not-Wendigkeit der Gerechtigkeit. Eine Interpretation zu »Cur Deus homo« von Anselm von Canterbury* (Beiträge zur Geschichte der Philosophie und Theologie des Mittelalters, Neue Folge, vol. 38) (Münster: Aschendorff, 1993), 17–33.

of serious academic consideration, in spite of concurrent critiques, particularly in British and European-American theology as well as in German theology and philosophy.[8] The main trend seems to be that Anselm is being protected against his reception, both against his critics as well as his evangelical defenders. It is recognized that his concept entails more references to Biblical testimony than has been acknowledged hitherto.[9] Especially his concept of *ordo* is now being perceived as a dimension of a theology of creation. Drawing on this insight, the traditional reception has been changed dramatically. Anselm is now considered as already operating with ideas comparable to the concept of *shalom* as an element of a theology of reconciliation. So, recent perceptions see Anselm not concentrating only on God and humanity in cold abstraction, but in the midst of strife in the first Investiture Controversy. A world that threatened to fall apart as a result of the sin of humankind comes into focus, a world desperately in need of being rescued through God's concern for salvation. As a consequence, the connection between the interpersonal reconciliation and the divine-human relationship is particularly important to him, which befits the first of the problems outlined above.

But the second problem, an interest in a concept of restorative justice, can also be brought to light in Anselm's work. I would like to engage the conversation with reference to the contested theory of restitution, which is included in the model of satisfaction. Traditionally, the restitution theory proceeds from the perception that sinful human acts have profoundly dam-

---

[8] Out of the many new publications see Hansjürgen Verweyen, *Anselm von Canterbury, 1033–1109. Denker, Beter, Erzbischof* (Regensburg: Verlag Friedrich Pustet, 2009); Jan-Olav Henriksen, *Desire, Gift, and Recognition: Christology and Postmodern Philosophy* (Grand Rapids: Eerdmans, 2009), 269–294; Giles E. M. Gasper and Helmut Kohlenberger, eds., *Anselm and Abaelard. Investigations and Juxtapositions* (Toronto: Pontifical Institute of Mediaeval Studies, 2006); Brian Davies and Brian Leftow, eds., *The Cambridge Companion to Anselm* (Cambridge: Cambridge University Press, 2005); Sandra Visser and Thomas Williams, *Anselm* (Oxford: Oxford University Press, 2009); David E. Luscombe and Gillian R. Evans, eds., *Anselm. Aosta, Bec and Canterbury: Papers in Commemoration of the Nine-Hundredth Anniversary of Anselm's Enthronement as Archbishop 25 September 1093* (Sheffield: Sheffield Academic Press, 1996); J. Denny Weaver, »The Defenders of Anselm.«, in *The Nonviolent Atonement* (Grand Rapids: Eerdmans, 2001), 180–188.
[9] See Martin Bieler, *Befreiung der Freiheit. Zur Theologie der stellvertretenden Sühne* (Freiburg: Herder 1996); Gerhard Gäde, *Eine andere Barmherzigkeit. Zum Verständnis der Erlösungslehre Anselms von Canterbury* (Würzburg: Echter, 1989); Helmut Steindl, *Genugtuung. Biblisches Versöhnungsdenken – eine Quelle für Anselms Satisfaktionstheorie?* (Freiburg: Universitätsverlag, 1998); Georg Plasger, *Not-Wendigkeit.*

aged God's honor in such a way that an effective restoration of the human-divine relationship appears to be impossible. Although humans are not able to pay God back, God seeks restitution for God's self as the basis of true reconciliation. The concept of restitution in reconciliation processes has been a contested issue not only with regard to Anselm's theory but also in contemporary debates. A variety of experiences of interpersonal reconciliation work as well as debates on reparation payments after historical conflicts foreground the issue of restitution. Can there be reconciliation without that wish of restitution at least being articulated? Is it so beyond our imagination that Anselm himself had possibly thought of interpersonal conflicts – drawing on his experiences from pastoral care and brotherly counsel in monastic life? In the following passages I wish to examine whether the essential aspect of Anselm's *satisfactio* (restitution) could be conceived in the meaning of restorative justice. Could it be considered as a necessary practice of reconciliation that enables a mutual future for both victims and perpetrators of violence?[10]

This question stands in the centre of this article. I proceed with awareness of the numerous critical objections Anselm's doctrine has received from the time he was living until today. These objections entail questions about whether the inner logic of this doctrine is comprehensible, whether it is based on too rigid an idea of God's sovereignty that conceals the love of God and dwarfs its possibilities, and whether Anselm actually lacks the awareness of the fact that the deed of restitution as explicated by him consists in the horrific death of a human being.[11]

Satisfaction for the Sake of the Victims: A Re-Interpretation

Catholic theologian Piet Schoonenberg writes about the fundamental intention of Anselm's doctrine:

> The intention, however, is expressed in a confusing way particularly through the usage of a juridical framework. It becomes however clearer as one reflects on the

---

[10]   Essential stimuli for this interpretation I found in Dorothea Sattler, »Erlösen durch Strafe? Zur Verwendung des Strafbegriffs im Kontext der christlichen Lehre von Heil und Erlösung,« in *Aufgebrochen. Theologische Beiträge* (Mainz: Grünewald, 2001), 11–35.

[11]   See for example Weaver, *The Nonviolent Atonement*, 179–224 and Jan-Olav Henriksen, *Desire*, 273–278.

question whom sin attacks. Not only God. The violation, the destructive power of sin above all attacks the creatures. It assaults God in so far as they are His creatures and His children.[12]

Through this explanation, a decisive change of perspective occurs. The interpersonal level comes into view and with it the »destructive power of sin« that can be felt *here,* that which »above all attacks the creatures.« Can this really be found in Anselm's work? Schoonenberg refers with his remark to Anselm's concept of *ordo* as it is presented in *Cur Deus Homo* I,15. Both in the violation of God's will and in the violation of his honor, the destruction of the world order is at stake.[13] In the words of Sandra Visser and Thomas Williams,

> Reflecting our purpose he suggests that rectitude of will consists in loving God for his own sake; reflecting on our place he suggests that rectitude of will consists in maintaining, so far as it lies within our power, the fitting order that God has established in the universe as a whole.[14]

Anselm regards the order as a guarantee for the beauty of creation as well, which for Visser and Williams is an argument for the interpretation that the command theory is not there merely for its own sake.[15] As a consequence, it means this: If God's will and God's glory stand for the order of the world, which makes life possible, the history of human sin does not concern any individual, isolated violation, and reconciliation with God. In Anselm's words,

---

[12] Piet Schoonenberg, »Tod des Menschen und Tod Christi.«, in *Auf Gott hin denken. Deutschsprachige Schriften zur Theologie,* ed. Wilhelm Zauner (Freiburg: Herder, 1986), 225–243, 223. (italics: U. L.-W.).

[13] Plasger, *Not-Wendigkeit,* 91; see also Gisbert Greshake, »Erlösung und Freiheit. Zur Neuinterpretation der Erlösungslehre Anselms von Canterbury,« *Theologische Quartalsschrift* 153 (1973): 323–345, here 328; Raymund Schwager, *Der wunderbare Tausch. Zur Geschichte und Deutung der Erlösungslehre* (Munich: Kösel, 1986), 168; Hödl, *Anselm,* 775.

[14] Visser and Williams, *Anselm,* 196.

[15] See also Verweyen, *Anselm von Canterbury,* 118. The philosophical »command-theory« states that, even in a post-Christian society, moral terms such as »should« and »ought« – which could be understood as remains of talking of God as the divine lawgiver – have a broader meaning than simply a legalistic derivation; see www.iep.utm.edu/divine-c/ (accessed on May 5, 2011).

When it [the creature] wills what it ought to will, it honors God – not because it bestows something on him, but because it willingly submits itself to God's will and direction, and keeps its own place in the universe of things, and maintains the beauty of that same universe, as far as in it lies. But when it does not will what it ought, it dishonors God, as far as it is concerned, since it does not readily submit itself to his direction, but disturbs the order and beauty of the universe, as far as lies in it ... (I,15; 124).[16]

In keeping with God's will, humankind respects nothing less than the preciousness of creation. This insight has significant consequences that constitute the cornerstone of the new Anselm research. It changes the impression of God from narcissistic to caring. It converts the interpretation of the process of reconciliation from one modeled as a commercial transaction into one of relationship.

It is true that the breadth of meaning of these words [*debere* and *debitum*, U. L.-W.] allows Anselm to switch back and forth between the language of commercial transactions and the language of justice and obligation, but we should not be tempted to think that Anselm regards justice as a kind of commercial exchange in which God acts as a rather obsessive auditor who insists that the books be balanced down to the last farthing. Rather ... it is better to say that for Anselm, debt is a species of obligation and can therefore serve as an illuminating analogy for our relationship to God.[17]

In the newly aroused attention to this issue, old questions are brought up again, namely whether in the case of Anselm – according to the Catholic theologian Gisbert Greshake – one should rather assume a conscious recourse to Germanic legal systems of thought. In this line of thought, the feudal system represents, in its emphasis on the prestige of the monarch, the maintenance of the societal »order of freedom, law and peace.«[18] What is at stake is not merely an insult against God but rather the order of

---

[16]   The English translation of Anselm's *Cur Deus Homo* is taken from »Why God Became Man.«, in *A Scholastic Miscellany: Anselm to Ockam*, ed. and trans. Eugene R. Fairweather (London: SCM Press, 1956), 100–183. Page numbers in brackets after the quotations refer to this edition.

[17]   Visser and Williams, *Anselm*, 224–225. See also Hendriksen, *Desire*, 270 about Anselm's relational understanding of sin.

[18]   Gisbert Greshake, »Erlösung und Freiheit. Zur Neuinterpretation der Erlösungslehre von Anselm von Canterbury,« in *Gottes Heil – Glück des Menschen. Theologische Perspektiven* (Freiburg: Herder, 1983), 89.

life represented by God. In this context, it is noteworthy that not only in Germanic law but in Roman law, too, this aspect can be found.[19] I suggest, however, that for Anselm as spiritual advisor of a monastery, an orientation on Biblical terminology would have been more probable than the traditional reception assumes. By revisiting the Biblical strands in Anselm's work, reflections on the Biblical terminus of the *Glory of God* (in Hebrew: *kavot*, in Greek: *doxa*) become pivotal.[20] All these concepts, *glory/kavot/doxa*, have a relational connotation. The bearer comes to stand in a representative function for the whole. The recent theological research on the Biblical concept of the Glory of God clearly shows how God's connectedness with his counterpart should be assumed. One could even suggest a relationship that entails a particular kind of interaction similar to the concepts of call and response or – recently receiving some attention in theology – giving and actively receiving. In the New Testament, a response character can be found in the understanding of the glorification of God.[21] Magdalene Frettlöh translates the corresponding Hebrew concept *kavod* as »giving God weight«, and »considering God seriously.«[22] In surveys of German theological works, she illustrates how the concept of the Glory of God reaches beyond aspects of ruling. Instead, it gives account of God's impressive, irresistible, but also courting and enticing, effect on the creatures, which seeks for an echo, an answer that is gracious and actively involved in promoting life.[23] Particularly monastic life might be considered to be inspired by this theology, and one would assume that this could have been Anselm's background when he talked of God's *honor.* Georg Plasger concurs in this vein: »But his *honor* radiates onto

---

[19]   See Plasger, *Not-Wendigkeit*, 85–98.

[20]   See Rainer Kampling, ed., *Herrlichkeit. Zur Deutung einer theologischen Kategorie* (Paderborn: Ferdinand Schöningh, 2008); Wolf Krötke, *Gottes Klarheiten. Eine Neuinterpretation der Lehre von Gottes »Eigenschaften«* (Tübingen: Mohr Siebeck, 2001); Magdalene L. Frettlöh, *Gott Gewicht geben. Bausteine einer geschlechtergerechten Gotteslehre* (Neukirchen-Vluyn: Neukirchener Verlag, 2006), 57–150; Victor H. Matthews, ed., *Honor and Shame in the World of the Bible*, Semeia 68, 1996; David Arthur DeSilva, *The Hope of Glory: Honour Discourse and New Testament Interpretation* (Collegeville, Minnesota: Liturgical Press 1999); Nicole Chibici-Revneanu, *Die Herrlichkeit des Verherrlichten. Das Verständnis der doxa im Johannes-Evangelium* (Tübingen: Mohr Siebeck, 2007).

[21]   See, for example, Marlis Gielen, »Von Herrlichkeit zu Herrlichkeit. Doxa bei Paulus zwischen den Polen protologischer und eschatologischer Gottebenbildlichkeit am Beispiel der Korintherkorrespondenz.«, in *Herrlichkeit*, ed. Kampling, 79–122.

[22]   Frettlöh, *Gott Gewicht geben*, 2.

[23]   Frettlöh, *Gott Gewicht geben*, 57–121.

creation and asks for humankind's answer, for the recognition of God as ruler.«[24] That in turn has consequences for the understanding of sin against God; it becomes transparent for those who, as creatures, have been *concretely damaged and violated.*[25] The violation of God through sin can, as it were, be understood in »substitutional« terms. I shall be returning to this aspect towards the end.

When one looks into Anselm's text, *Cur Deus Homo*, four observations stand out that often go unnoticed in the usual paraphrase of the satisfaction theory:

1. Repeatedly, Anselm states that it is »impossible for God to lose his honor« (I, 14, 123): »As far as God himself is concerned, nothing can be added to his honor or subtracted from it. For to himself, he himself is honor incorruptible and absolutely unchangeable.« (I, 15; 123) Ultimately, Anselm says that the violation of God's honor caused by humankind was »non actual«, meaning that it could not affect God in a way that would threaten God's »substance«. We may see here something like an apathy axiom.[26] However, the fact that Anselm so deliberately maintains that the violation of God's honor is »non actual«, is striking. Anselm is understood by many of his critics as insisting God is, in this case, an unbearable stickler for God's principles. But perhaps something else is at stake. Does Anselm point to the »non actual« violation of God in contrast to the »actual« destruction on the level of creation? Apparently, there is destruction of creation happening which calls for divine punishment for the sake of God's righteousness. Accordingly, Anselm's proposal reads like this: God won't lose God's honor because God would let it automatically be »regenerated« if it were violated. As a result, punishment is in turn defined to be related to the violation of creation. It consists of human beings not living up to their destiny as creatures, which is eternal sanctity (*beatitudo*) (I, 14).[27] This has to be prevented. Anselm's argumentation in the terminology of compensation-payments leads to the idea that it has to be prevented or else humanity forfeits its life:

> In this matter we should observe that, just as man in sinning seizes what belongs to God, so God in punishing takes away what belongs to man. For not only what

---

[24] Plasger, *Not-Wendigkeit*, 98.

[25] See Henriksen, *Desire*, 270: »Anselm implicitly points to how the compensation implied includes recognition of the violated ...«

[26] See Schwager, *Tausch*, 169.

[27] See for the following Gäde, *Barmherzigkeit*, 94.

a man already possesses is said to belong to him, but also what he has it in his power to possess. Thus, since man was so made that he could obtain blessedness if he did not sin, when he is deprived of blessedness and every good on account of sin, he pays from his own property, all unwillingly, what he stole. (I, 14, 123)

What is at stake is not a »retrieval« of God's honor, but instead the *rescue of humankind* facing the loss of its future in God's presence (= eternal holiness, *beatitudo).*

2. Notwithstanding, all this is somehow »hypothetical« as far as Anselm is concerned.[28] He himself says that God's decision for the sanctity of humankind is irrefutable. (I, 10; II, 1; II, 4). It is therefore an established fact that only Christ brings the rescuing alternative, which can be thought of as a voluntary deed of *satisfactio.* This line of argument that Christ's satisfaction is, indeed, an affirmation of the *Gospel,* has so far not been taken into account sufficiently in the attempts to interpret Anselm. In light of this retrospective knowledge of God's salvation-pledge and in the awareness of the death of Jesus, Anselm reconstructs the history of salvation hypothetically by seeking to offer a plausible theory.[29]

3. Another idea of Anselm is surprising. He maintains that, if God tried to forgive humans without a deed of *satisfactio,* that they would be thereby damaged since we would then stand as beggars (*indigens*) before God (I, 24; I, 11). Whether one should follow Anselm's reasoning here is a regular issue of ecumenical debate. However, it is clear that *satisfactio occurs to the advantage not of God, but of the sinner.*[30]

4. The concept of satisfaction, *satisfactio,* which in the paraphrase usually gets a formalistic and narrow accent, seems, as far as Anselm is concerned,

---

[28]   See for this interpretation also Ralf K. Wüstenberg, *The Political Dimension of Reconciliation. A Theological Analysis of Ways of Dealing with Guilt During the Transition to Democracy in South Africa and (East) Germany,* translated by Randi H. Lundell (Grand Rapids: Eerdmans 2009), 224, in German: *Die politische Dimension der Versöhnung. Eine theologische Studie zum Umgang mit Schuld nach den Systemumbrüchen in Südafrika und Deutschland* (Gütersloh: Gütersloher Verlagshaus, 2004), 454, Anm. 81; and Plasger, *Not-Wendigkeit,* 122. He refers to the point that the loss of *beatitudo* as consequence of sin in fact means mortality and death. So the punishment for sin would be death, which means it is a question of death or everlasting life, and in the end the liberation of humankind that is at stake.

[29]   See also Plasger, *Not-Wendigkeit,* 57–78.

[30]   I contend Anselm's emphasis on the dignity of the sinner in relation to God could fairly be compared with the »Treatise on Christian Liberty.«

to be a direct result and reflection of real-life situations of reconciliation. Though juridically imposed, it serves the purpose of ›setting right‹ whatever has been done wrong. As examples he refers to something like compensation payments, a »restitution« in case of humiliation or in case of theft, a settlement beyond merely returning the stolen item:

> For it is not enough for someone who has injured another's health to restore his health without making some recompense for the pain and injury suffered, and, similarly, it is not enough for someone who violates another's honor to restore the honor, unless he makes some kind of restitution that will please him who was dishonored … (I, 11; 119)

The issue at stake is the infringement of somebody else's personal sphere. »[I]n view of the insult committed, he must give back more than he took away.« (I, 11; 119) The »kind of restitution« should »please … the dishonored.« (I, 11; 119) It always must be *something more* than the simple reimbursement of the damage, a materially thinkable restoration of the former status, a restitution *ad integrum*. Why such petty stinginess? Obviously, there is a greater need for reimbursement because what is at stake is a relationship – saved by honor – destroyed through culpable infringement. If one understands this concept more in sync with the Biblical terminology of the *Glory of God*, as outlined above, the relational aspect becomes much clearer. Apparently, the additional value of the *satisfactio* demanded is grounded in the recognition of the right of the damaged – expressed within the divine-human dramaturgy in the picture of the violation of God's Glory.[31] Thereby the question arises if there is not more behind the juridical terminology than abstract equation thinking, and, correspondingly, if the asymmetry of *satisfactio* does not point to something other than a rigidly hierarchical image of God.[32]

---

[31] Schoonenberg contends that, according to Anselm, the extent of the restitution at stake is not held to be in relation to the extent of God's Glory, but to the extent of sin; of course, the »universal« size of sin as sin of universal humankind. Christ's death outshines »number and greatness of all sins« (II, 14; 163). Also, this equivalence-calculation is, of course, thinkable only under the condition that the problem is actually already solved by God.

[32] Quite often the definition of *satisfaction* as retaliation is not sufficiently differentiated in the reception. It is clearly a juridical term primarily for punishment or compensation with the intention of »restorative justice« in view of the future of the community concerned. This inaccuracy can already be observed in connection with the interpretation of the respective biblical references, see Steindl, *Genugtuung.*

One must therefore say that it is a reduction of Anselm's concept to only look at the »insult« leveled against God, and not at the same time to take into account the looming danger for the world as a whole, as well as focusing solely on the gravity of the insult by comparing its size to the greatness of God. To the contrary, Anselm sees a direct relevance of the non-acknowledgement of the will of God, the Creator, for the well-being of creation – even if he may postulate this rather tentatively and, as a child of the 11th century, sees the well-being in creation mainly as the conservation of the hierarchical order on which it is based. »There would arise a certain ugliness, derived from the violation of the beauty of the order« and »God would seem to fail in his direction of the world.« (I, 15; 124) In the historic context of the Investiture Controversy and the struggle for the rights of the church against the king, this admittedly has a very concrete context. Foremost, it becomes clear that the deed of satisfaction has to occur for the sake of the sinner. It serves nothing but the restoration of humanity's dignity before God: One should be able to pursue the destination of his or her life in accordance with the order of creation as dignified partner of God, with one's head held high.

One should realize what that means: Anselm does not say that the disturbance of the glory of God brought about by sin would merely have *consequences* on the interpersonal or the creational realm. The will of God stands here for all that which God »has in mind« with his creation in general and for humanity and human nature in particular: the *beatitudo*. Insolence for God's will is being shown whenever the goodness of creation is disregarded.

CONSEQUENCES FOR THE UNDERSTANDING OF RESTITUTION/RESTORATION

Considering God as advocate for creation, the damaging of God's honor occurs as a response to the damaging of creation. In this train of thought it is fruitful to remember Anselm's dialectic of »actual« and »non-actual« violation of the Glory of God. One could develop this dialectic further into an understanding of God's complex relational nature expressed in the terms of *intercession, substitution,* and *representation.* One may say that the damaged and threatened creation finds in its creator not only its mediating advocate, but also a prosecutor against its enemies as well as a just judge, who acts in the interest of righteousness. In this role, one can see God also demanding »restitution« from humanity in the sense of Anselm – with the degree of strictness necessary for the healing of wounds incurred by creation through the recurring demolition of what is life-giving. Anselm articulates this, arguing that, without *satisfactio*, something remains in disorder in God's sovereignty (I, 12; 120). Thereby, he is referring to the threateningly dangerous constellation that, through disregard of God, the life-giving structure of creation is put in disorder and, as a result, the world could be sailing towards destruction.

Following these considerations, I wonder whether this would not ultimately put Anselm's demand for restitution, *satisfactio*, into a new, as yet undiscovered perspective. Is it possible that Anselm heard God demanding *satisfactio* as an instrument of reconciliation in view *of the victims* of sin who require to be reinstated in their rights? It would clearly move beyond the original context of confession, in which it is generally understood as a process exclusively for the relief of the conscience of perpetrators. The demand for *satisfactio* as such could even be interpreted as a metaphor, which is gained from the experience of interpersonal reconciliation processes and has to be valued in that context. It reflects the fact that victims need to attain *satisfactio* while acknowledging at the same time that *satisfactio* cannot be achieved adequately. The concept would then be heard in a greater context of Biblical terms concerning the deed of reconciliation, finally as a visible sign of *metanoia*.[33]

But the drama of Anselmian reconciliation is even more complex. Above all, it culminates in God's deed of reconciliation in Jesus Christ who already has fulfilled the necessary *satisfactio*. Actually, the whole of humankind would be challenged to bring about this huge restitution. But as the damaged creation is represented by God as its advocate, who makes charges about the damage, Anselm also sees here the necessity of substitution. Humankind has to be represented by God, respectively by *God-man*, to bring forward restitution – otherwise adequate *satisfactio* is not possible for them. Brought forward by humanity, it could only be incomplete.

In this drama, one can therefore say God is at work in Christ – as a vindicator, who acquits the destroyer of creation (the sinner) as perpetrator. In the framework of Chalcedonian Two-Natures theory, Anselm's soteriology presents us with God as the incarnate Christ, the one bringing forward the *satisfactio* in our stead. Doubtless, he thus combines the Biblical atonement metaphoric with the juridical metaphor.

---

[33] See Raymund Schwager's ideas regarding the connection of *satisfactio* and repentance in his article, »Logik der Freiheit und des Natur-Wollens. Zur Erlösungslehre Anselms von Canterbury.« *Zeitschrift für Katholische Theologie* 105 (1983): 146-147.

SYMBOLIC »SATISFACTIO« IN RECONCILIATION PROCESSES

As a possible frame of reference for contemporary experiences of reconciliation, the process to which Anselm refers with the theory of satisfaction may lead one to recall the recent problematic German experience of reparation payments to the former forced laborers during the Nazi regime. Does it not lead to the realization that adequate reimbursement would *absolutely not* be brought forward? How on earth could a damages payment for forced labor ever manage to correspond to the wording of its title?

If restitution by reimbursement would obviously be inadequate, should one not totally refrain from it? Ralf Wüstenberg attended to this problem in his research on processes of dealing with guilt in South Africa and in Germany after the reunification.[34] He contends reimbursement as an attempt of reparation payments plays a minor role in a process of reconciliation – both materially as well as juridically, one soon reaches the limits of what could be settled by accurate calculations and weighing of charges and admissions of guilt. Wüstenberg maintains, therefore, that the concept of satisfaction could have relevance solely as a christological statement within a theological discourse on talking about God's reconciliation. More especially, it must not be understood as *prerequisite* to concrete reconciliation.[35]

If that was the only feasible interpretation of Wüstenberg's research, the metaphor of Anselm's *satisfactio* admittedly would be deprived of its empirical connection. The truly horrific forms of physical punishment in the Middle Ages and early modern times may serve as a negative case in point in this regard. Abhorrent pain and suffering were inflicted as a means of a retaliative measure of restitution.[36] On the other hand, as Joachim Zehner has recently shown, one can observe a renaissance of the concept of »atonement« in many non-theological disciplines. I would like to point to recent developments in the realm of criminal law, where forms of sanctions like the perpetrator-victim negotiations are discussed and put into practice.[37] In juvenile criminal law in particular, it has become a trend to try to confront the perpetrators with their victims, so that the perpetrators can realize the »hurtful

---

[34]   See Ralf K. Wüstenberg, *The Political Dimension.*

[35]   See Wüstenberg, *The Political Dimension,* 223-225.

[36]   See Joachim Zehner, »Sühne, Ethisch.«, in *Theologische Realenzyklopädie,* vol. 32, 356.

[37]   See Joachim Zehner, *Das Forum der Vergebung in der Kirche. Studien zum Verhältnis von Sündenvergebung und Recht* (Gütersloh: Gütersloher Verlagshaus, 1998), 64-75.

character of their conduct.«[38] It is noteworthy that attempts of atonement can also play a role in mitigating a sentence. In contemporary criminal law discussions in Germany, a terminological discrimination is being developed in order to differentiate between material reimbursement and symbolic restitution. It is also discussed how far it is possible to consider situations in which *satisfactio* beyond an individual level can be taken into account, for example concerning state or public institutions.[39] In German political science, Gesine Schwan hints at reimbursement as a means against »silencing the guilt« after historical political experiences with guilt.[40]

In view of these developments, one may conclude, although retribution/*satisfactio* can neither be produced nor imagined as an adequate balancing of the consequences of the deed, it does not seem possible to do without it either. Religiously, it belongs to the sphere which is talked about in the language of atonement, including notions of remorse and repentance.[41] This appears to be particularly necessary for the recognition of the victims. This is an aspect which the classical theory of atonement does not explicitly attend to, but which hopefully comes to bear implicitly in the application. Retribution should be understood in a wider sense, namely as proof of the indispensable recognition of the situation of the victims.[42] Unsurprisingly, Ralf Wüstenberg also arrives at the conclusion that it is an essential element in the process of reconciliation that an understanding is reached about »the basic needs of the victims concerning the recognition of their suffering.«[43] For political reconciliation, it is necessary that their suffering be made known publically as a mutually acknowledged »truth«. Wüstenberg calls this *moral restitution*. But also in the interpersonal or legal sphere, reconciliation processes cannot be successful if the suffering of the victims remains unheard. This can be seen in the South African Truth and Reconciliation Com-

---

[38]   Zehner, *Forum*, 65.

[39]   See Christian Laue, *Symbolische Wiedergutmachung* (Berlin: Dunker und Humblot, 1999).

[40]   Gesine Schwan, *Politik und Schuld. Die zerstörerische Macht des Schweigens* (Frankfurt: Fischer, 1997), 234.

[41]   See Schwan, *Politik*, 29–34 and 63–68, who finds a secularized emergence of religious wisdom of reconciliation in the insight that there is a salutary necessity of atonement and penance also in punitive measures in terms of criminal law.

[42]   One could sense this insight already even in Anselm's »more«.

[43]   Wüstenberg, *The Political Dimension*, 123 with regard to the situation in Germany, 48–50, 97–99, carefully in critical-constructive tone against romanticising interpretations with regard to the situation in South Africa.

mission, which is based on this principle.[44] Here, both the victims of the apartheid regime – fathers and husbands maimed through torture by police or women who had been raped and wounded – as well as perpetrators appeared and could speak. Perpetrators had to face the questions and verbal attacks by their victims. Even here, ambivalences should not go unmentioned. For example, the debate is ongoing whether the Commission's decision to grant amnesty to perpetrators who spoke publicly before the TRC about their misdeeds was an appropriate attempt to address South Africa's past.[45]

Nevertheless, through the work of the Truth Commission one can gain insights in personal reconciliation processes in the context of historical guilt. In this regard, I am concerned with the realization that recognition of the suffering of the victims should be articulated not only verbally but that it should happen, in our case, in the whole interrelationship of victims, perpetrators, commission members, and audience in which the outcome for the community could be felt. Recognition cannot only be declared; it needs to take place. Wüstenberg points out that this process inevitably remains fragmented and fragile as recognition of the suffering of the victims can never mean that their suffering is ever fully understood. This holds true even more if one realizes the different perspectives of the participants in reconciliation processes. There are the immediate perpetrators and their victims, or the even more complex situation of perpetrators who were also victims, as well as people indirectly involved like relatives a generation later. Torture, experiences of humiliation, participation in massacres, and social disintegration of the family with consequences for many generations – all this can only be comprehended and recognized in fragments. Hence, it must be noted that, even in a broader sense, comprehensive and exhaustive restitution as recognition of the sufferings of the victims remains humanly impossible, yet necessary. For the community as a whole, this could mean that to hope for reconciliation means to learn to live with fragmentary, incomplete forgiveness and with repentance which falls short. It is due to this fragmentary character that reconciliation depends on symbolic actions of restitution, which have to be accepted in their actual incompleteness. In social transformation processes beyond the individual level, one has therefore to develop sensitivity for the »impossible possibility« of reconciliation and for the function of symbolic restitution.[46]

---

44   Wüstenberg, *The Political Dimension* 133–136, 141–173 (lit.).

45   See Tinyiko S. Maluleke's essay in this volume.

46   Gesine Schwan terms it a »lively consensus … a *common sense* … a civic ethical prin-

The emphasis on the need for restitution instead of *punishment* in Anselm's thoughts is grounded in his interpersonal experience of *irreconcilability* and in the general »impossible possibility« of reconciliation. The interpretation of restitution is crucial at this point. Only from the outside does it appear like compensation for there cannot be a real balancing of the scales. Nevertheless, the form of the compensation is still not meaningless because the ways victims and perpetrators relate to it shapes the arduous and painful process of the recognition of wrongdoing. The fact that God alone can perform this compensation and that God desires it is at the heart of Anselm's Christocentric soteriology.

This dimension of the Christian creed is promised to us in the justification message as an encouragement to devote ourselves to the painful process of the compensation of justice in interpersonal reconciliation. It develops in such a way that a mutual future through restorative justice comes into view. The balancing is not final but rather a means towards the disclosure of truth, recognition, and thus eventually repentance/return/*metanoia*.

CONCLUSION

Anselm's staurocentric argument, according to which the only way for reconciliation with humankind to be brought about was that God had to become human and had to die, has one decisive fault: The *satisfactio* which is regarded as inevitable consists of the death of a human being. One may well regard his argument as having failed. The observations expressed here are not trying to give an interpretation of the death of Jesus in which he would have to be seen as a God-given sacrifice for restitution. Anselm himself tries everything in his argumentative powers to prevent that impression. He resorts to a line of formalistic reasoning that is complicated for us today, in which the voluntary giving-up of Jesus' human nature is presented in a model of an axiomatically constructed realistic Two-Natures Doctrine. In a post-medieval, modern ontology, this no longer suffices. Revisioning Anselm's theory of reconciliation needs to embrace a *practice* of reconciliation beyond this theory. And this is only possible if we interpret his dual dramaturgy of the event of God and

---

ciple«, that calls for »magnitude of heart on the side of the victims«, »which one may neither demand nor expect ... which one may plead for, which one may hope for.« *Politik*, 235.

humanity as a framework which depicts divine salvation in relation to all threatened creation.

If we read Anselm in this *socio-centric* way, an insight for a theology »after violence« may be gained. Accordingly, we are no longer to read it only as an event between God and Human, but as a dramaturgy of preservation and fulfillment of a threatened creation, which is suffering from the absence of reconciliation. The core concepts of Anselm's argumentation would then be *ordo*, the benevolent order of creation, as well as *kavod* and *doxa*, God's glory as preservation of God's magnificence in favor of creation. Following Anselm's implicit theology of representation, God could be depicted as the creation's counsel and vindicator. Representative restitution through Christ could be understood as reinstallation of those who are being victimized in the midst of sinfulness of humankind through injustice, senseless violence, or ignorance. Anselm's insisting on *satisfactio* in relation to God turns out to be a *satisfactio* which God demands for the un-reconciled life of creation. The fact that God is made available in Christ can then further be understood as a divine promise that God will also bring to completion our fragmented attempts of reconciliation. This hope can serve as an encouragement and challenge to keep on trying in the midst of the brokenness of creation.

LITERATURE

Link-Wieczorek, Ulrike. »Sündig vor Gott allein? Überlegungen zur Re-Interpretation der Satisfaktionstheorie Anselms von Canterbury in schöpfungsethischer Perspektive.« *Die Aktualität der Sünde. Ein umstrittenes Thema der Theologie in interkonfessioneller Perspektive,* (Beiheft zur Ökumenischen Rundschau 86 – Texte des Interkonfessionellen Theologischen Arbeitskreises ITA) edited by Rochus Leonhardt, 121–143. Frankfurt: Lembeck Verlag, 2010.

Bedford-Strohm, Heinrich, ed. »*Und das Leben der zukünftigen Welt:« Von Auferstehung und Jüngstem Gericht.* Neukirchen-Vluyn: Neukirchener Verlag, 2007.

Bieler, Martin. *Befreiung der Freiheit. Zur Theologie der stellvertretenden Sühne.* Freiburg: Herder, 1996.

Canterbury, Anselm of. »Why God Became Man.« *A Scholastic Miscellany: Anselm to Ockam,* edited and translated by Eugene R. Fairweather, 10–183. London: SCM Press, 1956.

Chibici-Revneanu, Nicole. *Die Herrlichkeit des Verherrlichten. Das Verständnis der doxa im Johannes-Evangelium.* Tübingen: Mohr Siebeck, 2007.

Davies, Brian and Brian Leftow, eds. *The Cambridge Companion to Anselm.* Cambridge: Cambridge University Press, 2005.

DeSilva, David Arthur. *The Hope of Glory: Honour Discourse and New Testament Interpretation.* Collegeville, Minnesota: Liturgical Press, 1999.

Frettlöh, Magdalene L. *Gott Gewicht geben. Bausteine einer geschlechtergerechten Gotteslehre.* Neukirchen-Vluyn: Neukirchener Verlag, 2006.

Gäde, Gerhard. *Eine andere Barmherzigkeit. Zum Verständnis der Erlösungslehre Anselms von Canterbury.* Würzburg: Echter, 1989.

Gasper, Giles E.M. and Helmut Kohlenberger, eds. *Anselm and Abaelard. Investigations and Juxtapositions.* Toronto: Pontifical Institute of Mediaeval Studies, 2006.

Gielen, Marlis. »Von Herrlichkeit zu Herrlichkeit. Doxa bei Paulus zwischen den Polen protologischer und eschatologischer Gottebenbildlichkeit am Beispiel der Korintherkorrespondenz.« *Herrlichkeit. Zur Deutung einer theologischen Kategorie,* edited by Raymung Kampling, 79–122. Paderborn: Ferdinand Schöningh, 2008.

Greshake, Gisbert. »Erlösung und Freiheit. Zur Neuinterpretation der Erlösungslehre von Anselm von Canterbury.«, in *Gottes Heil – Glück des Menschen. Theologische Perspektiven,* 80–104. Freiburg: Herder, 1983.

Henriksen, Jan-Olav. *Desire, Gift, and Recognition: Christology and Postmodern Philosophy.* Grand Rapids: Eerdmans, 2009.

Hoffmann, Veronika, ed. *Die Gabe. Ein »Urwort der Theologie?«* Frankfurt: Lembeck Verlag, 2009.

Kampling, Raymund, ed. *Herrlichkeit. Zur Deutung einer theologischen Kategorie.* Paderborn: Ferdinand Schöningh, 2008.

Krötke, Wolf. *Gottes Klarheiten. Eine Neuinterpretation der Lehre von Gottes »Eigenschaften«.* Tübingen: Mohr Siebeck, 2001.

Laue, Christian. *Symbolische Wiedergutmachung.* Berlin: Dunker und Humblot, 1999.

Luscombe, David E. and Gillian R. Evans, eds. *Anselm. Aosta, Bec and Canterbury: Papers in Commemoration of the Nine-Hundredth Anniversary of Anselm's Enthronement as Archbishop 25 September 1093.* Sheffield: Sheffield Academic Press, 1996.

Matthews, Victor H., ed. *Honor and Shame in the World of the Bible,* Semeia 68, 1996.

Moltmann, Jürgen. *The Way of Jesus Christ. Christology in Messianic Dimension.* Minneapolis: Fortress Press 1993.

Plasger, Georg. *Die Not-Wendigkeit der Gerechtigkeit. Eine Interpretation zu »Cur Deus Homo« von Anselm von Canterbury* (Beiträge zur Geschichte der Philosophie und Theologie des Mittelalters, Neue Folge. Vol. 38). Münster: Aschendorff, 1993.

Sattler, Dorothea. »Erlösen durch Strafe? Zur Verwendung des Strafbegriffs im Kontext der christlichen Lehre von Heil und Erlösung.« In *Aufgebrochen. Theologische Beiträge,* 11–35. Mainz: Grünewald, 2001.

Schoonenberg, Piet. »Tod des Menschen und Tod Christi.« *Auf Gott hin denken. Deutschsprachige Schriften zur Theologie,* edited by Wilhelm Zauner, 225–243. Freiburg: Herder, 1986.

Schwager, Raymund. »Logik der Freiheit und des Natur-Wollens. Zur Erlösungslehre Anselms von Canterbury.« *Zeitschrift für Katholische Theologie* 105 (1983): 125–155.

Schwager, Raymund. *Der wunderbare Tausch. Zur Geschichte und Deutung der Erlösungslehre.* Munich: Kösel, 1986.

Schwan, Gesine. *Politik und Schuld. Die zerstörerische Macht des Schweigens.* Frankfurt: Fischer, 1997.

Steindl, Helmut. *Genugtuung. Biblisches Versöhnungsdenken – eine Quelle für Anselms Satisfaktionstheorie?* Freiburg: Universitätsverlag, 1998.

Verweyen, Hansjürgen. *Anselm von Canterbury, 1033–1109. Denker, Beter, Erzbischof.* Regensburg: Verlag Friedrich Pustet, 2009.

Visser, Sandra and Thomas Williams. *Anselm.* Oxford: Oxford University Press, 2009.

Weaver, J. Denny. »The Defenders of Anselm.« In *The Nonviolent Atonement,* 180–188. Grand Rapids: Eerdmans, 2001.

Wüstenberg, Ralf K. *The Political Dimension of Reconciliation. A Theological Analysis of Ways of Dealing with Guilt During the Transition to Democracy in South Africa and (East) Germany,* translated by Randi H. Lundell. Grand Rapids: Eerdmans, 2004.

Zehner, Joachim. »Sühne. Ethisch.« *Theologische Realenzyklopädie.* Vol. 32, 355–360.

Zehner, Joachim. *Das Forum der Vergebung in der Kirche. Studien zum Verhältnis von Sündenvergebung und Recht.* Gütersloh: Gütersloher Verlagshaus, 1998.

Translation: Ben Khumalo-Seegelken

AFTER VIOLENCE: IMPRESSIONS OF STUDENT OBSERVERS

Anne Wehrmann and Laura Koch

This statement is not meant to be scientific. As students of Protestant Theology in Germany, we are not generally in a position to question the facts of the lectures given, and some topics of this conference were so new to us that, while they evoked curiosity and interest on our part, we have not yet arrived at a clear opinion on them. Consequently, we have looked back upon the conference focusing rather on our emotional reception of this disturbing topic.

It was a relief to hear the definition that trauma after violence is actually an appropriate reaction to an extreme situation as the psyche has to cope with highly distressing experiences. The causes of trauma are just as varied as the forms trauma may take, and it seems hardly possible to arrive at general assumptions or conclusions about it.

Observing this conference as students who are especially interested in the connections between individual and collective trauma, we were impressed by the shared understanding of and respect for the severity of the pain and despair people go through when they have been traumatized. Seeing how the individual trauma process can be transferred to processes of whole groups of people (e. g. in countries such as Rwanda) was interesting but quite shocking at the same time. When we heard about the apathetic reaction of the Rwandan church to the genocide by Jean-Pierre Karegeye, what surprised us most was that we actually *were* surprised. We were also deeply shocked when we heard what people are doing to each other even though, in an abstract manner, we already knew that violence is a reality for millions of people. It was a reminder that knowing of something is different from actually being aware of it, from feeling it.

Tinyiko S. Maluleke challenged the conference title »After Violence« as it might imply the final overcoming of violence. He pointed out that, in the case of South Africa, the country has been going through various waves of recurring violence after the end of apartheid.

It was striking to learn about the variety of forms violence can take as well as the resources people are able to mobilize in dealing with it. The most vivid examples were those given by Sabine Förster from Liberia. Violence like that in Liberia has reached dimensions that can hardly be imagined. And it led to very divergent ways of dealing with it. While the Women in White came together in a peaceful struggle for a life worth living under the motto, »Pray the devil back to hell!«, the women-fighters found a different way to address the violence directed against them. They took the war back to the men threatening them with rape and murder. Having grown up in a fairly wealthy and peaceful European country like Germany, it is hardly fathomable how existentially threatening a situation must be to make one defend oneself with a weapon. *recognition of privilege*

Solidarity with both forms of victimized groups seemed to be the first step in the process of re-thinking violence. But how can this be achieved? Theo Ahrens pointed at the necessity of communication, of getting to know the stories and interpretations maintained by the »other side«, which may then help in correcting one's own assumptions and prejudices. Not all violence is physical and easily visible. It is hidden in symbols, songs, and rumors, in avoidance, or non-greeting, as Siobhán Garrigan pointed out in her detailed account of the current situation in Ireland (North and South). Choosing what to remember – and what to forget – seems to be vital in coming to grips with the traumatic past. The forms such memory may take were fascinatingly illustrated in Brigitte Sion's contribution. Beyond the meaning each of the memorials has for the communities, relatives, or survivors of the respective horrors, they became symbols of caution and responsibility to us – encouragements to work towards the prevention and interruption of violence before new memorials need to be built.

The possibility of interrupting violent structures by using counter-narratives from indigenous traditions, the Hebrew Bible, and the New Testament in the appropriate context, breaking with a linear perception of time, seems a fruitful idea to respect the reality of the traumatized while at the same time not leaving the last word with violence, as Andrea Bieler pointed out. From the perspective of future pastors, it seems important to give time and space in liturgy and worship for mourning, memory, and fellowship, and to give people opportunity to experience moments of bliss, in which the gift of life is felt in its fullness. It seems not far-fetched to regard this as an appropriate expression of the Gospel today.

Envisioning a new heaven and a new earth (Isaiah 65:17) appears to be the major task for us as church members, not without rethinking and redefining ourselves in terms of social values, theological approaches, and institutional hierarchies. As mentioned earlier, we were surprised to actually be stunned about all the forms and the intensity of violence, and we felt a bit ashamed to have been so naïve. But after two days of reflection we come to the conclusion that being surprised about violence is not necessarily a bad thing. It includes the moment of *not being used* to violence and *refusing to get used* to it in the future. In the context of violence, we dearly hope to keep being shocked. Only by doing so we can envision a reality where violence actually *is* overcome.

CONTRIBUTORS AND EDITORS

Theodor Ahrens is Professor Emeritus of Missiology and Ecumenics and Director of the Institute for Missiology, Ecumenics and the Study of Religions at Hamburg Divinity School. Publications: *Grace and Reciprocity: Missiological Studies*, Point No. 26 (The Melanesian Institute: Goroka, 2002); *Vom Charme der Gabe. Theologie interkulturell* (Frankfurt a. M.: Lembeck, 2008); *Zur Zukunft des Christentums. Abbrüche und Neuanfänge* (Frankfurt a. M.: Lembeck 2009).

Andrea Bieler is Professor of Christian Worship at Pacific School of Religion and at the Graduate Theological Union in Berkeley, California. Publications: in cooperation with Hans-Martin Gutmann, *Embodying Grace: Proclaiming Justification in the Real World* (Minneapolis: Fortress Press, 2010); in cooperation with Luise Schottroff, *The Eucharist: Bodies, Bread and Resurrection* (Minneapolis: Fortress Press, 2007); *Gottesdienst interkulturell: Predigen und Gottesdienst feiern im Zwischenraum* (Stuttgart: Kohlhammer, 2007).

Christian Bingel is Research Assistant and Junior Lecturer at Hamburg Divinity School, completing his Doctorate on encounters of migrant and mainline churches in the Hamburg region.

Fernando Enns is Professor of Theology and Ethics in the Faculty of Theology at the Free University Amsterdam and Director of the Institute of Peace Church Theology at Hamburg University. He is a member of the Central Committee of the World Council of Churches. Publications: *Ökumene und Frieden. Theologische Anstöße aus der Friedenskirche*, Theologische Anstöße vol. 4 (Neukirchen-Vluyn: Neukirchener, 2012); *The Peace Church and the Ecumenical Community. Ecclesiology and the Ethics of Nonviolence* (Kitchener/Ontario: Pandora Press and Geneva: World Council of Churches, 2007); in cooperation with Scott Holland and Ann Riggs, eds., *Seeking Cultures of Peace: A Peace Church Conversation* (Telford/PA: Cascadia and Geneva: World Council of Churches, 2004).

Sabine Förster is Head of Studies at the Academy of Mission at the University of Hamburg. Her work focuses on the situation of refugees, especially women in Liberia, and on human rights.

Siobhán Garrigan is Senior Lecturer in Theology at the University of Exeter and Director of the Exeter Centre for Ecumenical and Practical Theology (EXCEPT). Publications: *The Real Peace Process: Worship, Politics and the End of Sectarianism* (London: Equinox Publishing, 2010); *Beyond Ritual: Sacramental Theology After Habermas* (Aldershot: Ashgate Publishing, 2004).

Hans-Martin Gutmann is Professor of Practical Theology at Hamburg Divinity School. Publications: *Gewaltunterbrechung: Warum Religion Gewalt nicht hervorbringt, sondern bindet. Ein Einspruch* (Gütersloh: Gütersloher Verlagshaus, 2009); *Und erlöse uns von dem Bösen. Die Chance der Seelsorge in Zeiten der Krise* (Gütersloh: Gütersloher Verlagshaus, 2005); *Die tödlichen Spiele der Erwachsenen. Moderne Opfermythen in Religion, Politik und Kultur* (Freiburg i. Br.: Herder, 1995).

Werner Kahl is Associate Professor for New Testament at the University Frankfurt and Head of Studies at the Academy of Mission at the University of Hamburg. Publications: *New Testament Miracle Stories in their Religious-Historical Setting: A Religionsgeschichtliche Comparison from a Structural Perspective*, FRLANT, vol. 163 (Göttingen: Vandenhoeck & Ruprecht, 1994); *Jesus als Lebensretter. Afrikanische Bibelinterpretationen und ihre Relevanz für die neutestamentliche Wissenschaft*, Neutestamentliche Studien zur kontextuellen Exegese, vol. 2 (Frankfurt: Peter Lang, 2007).

Jean-Pierre Karegeye is Assistant Professor at the French and Francophone Studies Department at Macalester College in St. Paul, Minnesota, and co-founder of the Interdisciplinary Genocide Studies Center in Kigali, Rwanda. Publications: editor of *L'Eglise Catholique a l'Epreuve du Genocide* (2000); editor of *Récits du Genocide, Traversée de la Memoire* (2009).

Laura Koch is a student of Protestant Theology in Hamburg particularly interested in Homiletics, Liturgical Studies, and Systematic Theology.

Tinyiko Sam Maluleke is Executive Director of Research at the University of South Africa and Professor of Missiology. Publications: »Of Lions and Rabbits: The Role of the Church in Reconciliation in South Africa.« *International Review of Mission*, 96, no. 380/381 (2007): 41–55; »Black and African Theology After Apartheid and after the Cold War: An Emerging Paradigm.«, in *Exchange*, 29, no. 3 (2000): 193–213; »Half a Century of African Christian Theologies.«, in *Journal of Theology for Southern Africa* 99 (1997): 4–23.

Brigitte Sion earned her Ph. D. in Performance Studies from New York University in 2008. She is the Director of Learning and Engagement at Central Synagogue in New York. Publications: *Absent Bodies, Uncertain Memorials* (forthcoming with Lexington Books). »Conflicting Sites of Memory in Post-Genocide Cambodia.« *Humanity*, vol. 2, no. 1, Spring 2011. Editor of *Staging Violent Death: The Dark Performance of Thanatourism* (forthcoming with Seagull Books).

Phillip Tolliday is Senior Lecturer in Systematic Theology at Charles Sturt University (St Barnabas' College) in Adelaide, Australia. Publications: »Obedience and Subordination in Barth's Trinity.« in Myk Habets and Phillip Tolliday, eds., *Trinitarian Theology After Barth* (Eugene, OR: Wipf and Stock, 2010), 136–158; »Karl Barth: Reason Beyond Autonomy?« in Wayne Cristaudo, ed., *Transformations in Philosophical Theology from the 18th to 20th Cen-*

turies (Washington: University Press of America, forthcoming); »Augustine and Marion: On Reading the World as Icon or Idol.«, in Wayne Cristaudo and Heung-Wah Wong, eds., *Augustine: His Legacy and Relevance* (Adelaide: ATF Press, 2010), 263–285.

Ulrike Link-Wieczorek is Professor of Systematic Theology at the Carl von Ossietzky University Oldenburg. She is a member of the Standing Commission of Faith and Order in the World Council of Churches. Publications: *Reden von Gott in Afrika und Asien* (Göttingen: Vandenhoeck & Ruprecht, 1990); *Inkarnation oder Inspiration* (Göttingen: Vandenhoeck & Ruprecht, 1998); in cooperation with Ralf Miggelbrink, Michael Haspel, Uwe Swarat, Heinrich Bedford-Strohm and Dorothea Sattler, *Nach Gott im Leben fragen: Ökumenische Einführung in das Christentum* (Freiburg: Herder, 2004).

Anne Wehrmann studied Protestant Theology in Bochum, Münster, Hamburg, and Bangalore/India, with a focus on Women's Studies and Pastoral Care and Counseling. She recently graduated from Hamburg University.

Heike Springhart

Aufbrüche zu neuen Ufern

Der Beitrag von Religion und Kirche
für Demokratisierung und Reeducation
im Westen Deutschlands nach 1945

360 Seiten, Paperback
ISBN 978-3-374-02612-8
EUR 38,00 [D]

Auf dem Weg zu einer demokratischen deutschen Gesellschaft nach 1945 wurden Religion und Kirche von den amerikanischen Planern dieses Prozesses als »eines der wichtigsten Instrumente« betrachtet. Erstmals wird in dieser Monographie auf der Basis umfangreichen Quellenmaterials die Rolle von Religion und Kirche für die Reeducation aus der Perspektive der amerikanischen Besatzungsmacht rekonstruiert und analysiert.

So entsteht ein komplexes Bild von der Steuerung des geistigen und gesellschaftlichen Wiederaufbaus in Deutschland durch die amerikanische Besatzungspolitik im Allgemeinen und von der Rolle der Kirche im Besonderen. Produktive Wechselwirkungen zwischen den gesamtgesellschaftlichen Erneuerungs- und Bildungsanliegen der Besatzungsmacht und den innerkirchlichen Bemühungen um Neuorientierung und Neuorganisation des kirchlichen Lebens werden freigelegt.

Die diesem Buch zugrunde liegende Dissertation Heike Springharts wurde mit dem John Templeton Award for Theological Promise 2008 ausgezeichnet.

EVANGELISCHE VERLAGSANSTALT
Leipzig

www.eva-leipzig.de

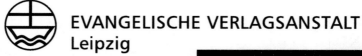